MANAGING PERFORMANCE IMPROVEMENT PROJECTS

MANAGING PERFORMANCE IMPROVEMENT PROJECTS

Preparing, Planning, and Implementing

Jim Fuller

Pfeiffer

An Imprint of Jossey-Bass Inc., Publishers

Copyright © 1997 by International Society for Performance Improvement.

ISBN: 0-7879-0959-9

Library of Congress Catalog Card Number 97-755

Library of Congress Cataloging-in-Publication Data

Fuller, Jim.
    Managing performance improvement projects: preparing, planning, and implementing /
Jim Fuller.
       p. cm.
    Includes bibliographical references and index.
    ISBN 0-7879-0959-9
    1. Industrial productivity—Management. 2. Performance. I. Title.
HD56.F829   1997
658.3'14—dc21   97-755

Printed in the United States of America

Published by

An Imprint of Jossey-Bass Inc., Publishers
350 Sansome Street, 5th Floor
San Francisco, California 94104-1342
(415) 433-1740; Fax (415) 433-1342
(800) 274-4434; Fax (800) 569-0443

Pfeiffer

Visit our website at: http://www.pfeiffer.com

Outside of the United States, Pfeiffer products can be purchased from the following Simon & Schuster International Offices:

Prentice Hall Canada
PTR Division
1870 Birchmount Road
Scarborough, Ontario MIP 2J7
Canada
(800) 567-3800; Fax (800) 263-7733

Prentice Hall
Campus 400
Maylands Avenue
Hemel Hempstead
Hertfordshire HP2 7EZ
United Kingdom
44(0) 1442 881891; Fax 44(0) 1142 882288

Prentice Hall/Pfeiffer
P.O. Box 1636
Randburg 2125
South Africa
27 11 781 0780; Fax 27 11 781 0781

Simon & Schuster (Asia) Pte Ltd
317 Alexandra Road
#04-01 IKEA Building
Singapore 159965
Asia
65 476 4688; Fax 65 378 0370

Prentice Hall Professional
Locked Bag 531
Frenchs Forest PO NSW 2068
Australia
61 2 9907 5693; Fax 61 2 9905 7934

Printing 10 9 8 7 6 5 4 3 2 1

CONTENTS

PART THREE: IMPLEMENTING THE PLAN 177

THE AUTHOR

Jim Fuller is director of learning and performance technology at the Hewlett-Packard Company. His organization represents HP's research and development (R&D) efforts in the area of learning and performance, with specific responsibility for performance improvement processes, instructional design methods, education evaluation systems, and the application of technology to accelerate learning.

Jim has worked at Hewlett-Packard for seventeen years and has held management positions in R&D, manufacturing, marketing, sales, support, and education. He holds a master's degree of science in instructional and performance technology from Boise State University, where he taught graduate-level project management for performance technologists. He is currently pursuing an education doctorate in performance technology from the University of Southern California. Jim has been appointed to the faculty at USC, where he is leading efforts to develop a new graduate program in human performance technology.

He is a frequent speaker at conferences such as those of the International Society for Performance Improvement, where he is an advocate representative, the American Society for Training and Development, and Lakewood's Training. He has spoken on implementation of performance technology, evaluation strategies, use of technology in training delivery, metacognition in learning, and gender-based communications in the workplace.

ACKNOWLEDGMENTS

A work of this magnitude is never accomplished alone. Countless people contributed to this book by lending their expertise as well as helping to refine the thinking that went into it. My many thanks to all of them. The contributions of some require special recognition:

Mark Eisley and David Cox at Boise State University, who provided me with the opportunity to pilot this text in a graduate-level human performance technology project management course.

The students of my project management course, who excelled throughout the pilot and all that accompanied it.

Linda Pfeifer, whose research in accelerated development was instrumental in the development of Chapter Two.

And special recognition to Jeanne Farrington, whose expert editorial efforts transformed the more complex chapters into something that a person might actually want to read.

A CALL FOR PROJECT MANAGEMENT

The field of human performance technology is young and vibrant. It appears to grow and mature each day that professionals such as yourselves explore richer and deeper application. However, the field is still very much in development. We continue to define and perfect aspects of it, and other professions (such as management) are still watching and learning to appreciate the impact that human performance technology can make.

The purpose of this book is to help you develop skills in the area of project management—in making human performance technology happen. If we impress management or a client with insightful, data-driven performance analysis, then fail to deliver the performance improvement interventions in a reliable manner, we do little to further the human performance technology profession (and no, it doesn't do you much good as a professional either).

One evolving aspect of the field is the increasing complexity of performance improvement solutions. As we deal more systematically with performance problems, we find that solutions are becoming more holistic and complex. More complete solutions usually require a greater number of participants or experts to implement them, which usually means putting together a performance improvement project team. The team's efforts will need to be managed and coordinated through solid and reliable project management methods.

If you are new to the human performance technology profession, you might want to do some supplemental reading. This book is written on the premise that you understand processes such as performance analysis, gap analysis, and performance improvement interventions. An excellent overview can be found in the *Handbook of Human Performance Technology*, edited by Stolovitch and Keeps.

Definition of Project Management

Consider the word *project*. What does it make you think of? Developing or creating a quantifiable service or product? An abundance or lack of time or resources (people, equipment, money)? Complexity? Authority and influence (or the lack of it) over others? Issues related to staying within budget?

Projects involve a development effort that has a definite beginning and a definite end. These efforts are undertaken to create an end product or a specific deliverable. A human performance technology project produces an intervention designed to improve performance, one that increases the worth of human accomplishments. When a decision is made to engage in a human performance technology project, metrics (measurements for results) are set for determining the success of the project. These projects are completed within specified project parameters, including fixed time, cost, human resources, and asset limits (Grey, 1981). The goal of this book is to help you become more systematic and organized as you manage projects in this emerging field.

Project management refers to taking an active role in planning, monitoring, tracking, and managing the various aspects of working on a project. This discipline will help you to manage the human elements, the schedule, the finances, and the quality of work as you begin, execute, and finish your projects (Randolf, 1988). You will find two major benefits to using project management techniques:

1. *Communication.* You will be able to create the technical and business documentation necessary to clarify the project plan and the status of progress.
2. *Managerial skills.* You will develop these to better facilitate the work of people and their projects.

Project management provides a proactive approach to getting work done. Its use fosters good communication, problem-solving techniques, and skills for analysis. In addition, it builds in evaluation of the project's performance against the original objectives. One of the important outcomes of good project management is the application of high standards of quality to project work.

Without project management, the complicated set of tasks, deadlines, resource availability, and quality concerns of a complex project would seem like a large pile of disorganized puzzle pieces. With project management, we learn to deal with both the human and the technical aspects of this essential discipline. We need a definition of project management we can use throughout this book.

PROJECT MANAGEMENT IS A SET OF PRINCIPLES, METHODS, TOOLS, AND TECHNIQUES FOR THE EFFECTIVE MANAGEMENT OF ACHIEVING OBJECTIVE-ORIENTED WORK.

The project management process encompasses these tasks:

- Creating a clear definition for the end result of the project
- Obtaining and utilizing sponsorship for the project
- Defining and managing the environment in which the project will run
- Planning the project
- Managing the inevitable changes and problems that occur during the project
- Controlling the undertaking so that it is completed on schedule and within budget
- Keeping the client or the management team informed (Note: We will use *client* throughout the book to refer to anyone receiving services, whether it is a department inside your organization or an outside customer.)
- Concluding and evaluating the project

Project management as a discipline provides support for both the goal of producing an end product and for the enabling processes of planning, change management, control, and preventive and corrective action. When the decision is made to devote resources to accomplishing a specific goal, project management begins. It ends when the desired result is obtained.

It is important to note what project management is *not*. It is not the discipline to employ when working to make the non-project-oriented, day-to-day activities within an organization run smoothly. Day-to-day planning, operations, control, and facilitation of staff members involve standard management methods and remain the province of functional (rather than project) managers. Functional managers also have the responsibility to direct the technical aspects of their employees' work. Functional business managers should support performance improvement project managers rather than becoming engaged in the details of project management (Kezsbaum, 1989).

The Technology and the Art of Project Management

Project management has technological and artistic aspects. The technology side of project management is systematic and involves an analytical approach, as illustrated by the use of charts and graphs that require mathematical calculations and the use of technical tools. This side of project management requires "hard" skills. The side that requires "soft" skills is where the art comes in. Projects can be influenced by the human side of getting things done: interpersonal, political, and organizational factors. Facilitating, compromising, communicating, and resolving conflicts are just a few of the many soft skills used in the art of project management (Thomsett, 1993).

As you explore each topic in this book, you will learn about both the hard and the soft skills needed to manage projects efficiently and effectively. You will also learn about the technical tools of project management and the more artistic techniques related to working with and managing the human side of making a project successful.

The Critical Attributes of Project Management

The word *project* has gained a certain popularity. Often it is used to describe activities that are not projects.

Many people refer to almost any task they have decided to do as a project. My administrative assistant refers to sending out a large stack of catalogs to learning centers around the world as a project; teachers refer to cleaning up their classrooms as a project. For some, painting the house is a project. These and similar tasks, however, do not possess the characteristics that would require applying the discipline of project management. Project management is helpful (sometimes essential) with work that has three major characteristics (Baker and Baker, 1992):

1. *An objective that is both specific and measurable.* There should be a clear definition of the end product or service that will result from a project; otherwise planning becomes extremely difficult. Even if some vague type of planning may be possible, without a clear objective one is not doing project planning. When an objective is not clear, the project should be divided into several smaller projects, the first being creation of a specific and measurable end product for the main project. The project manager should make sure that the end product can be objectively evaluated to determine whether it provides the desired results and quality specified by the organization for which the project is undertaken. If subjective criteria are to be used in evaluating the end product, planning and managing the project will be much harder.

2. *A deadline.* Determining the date for project completion can be done before the project plan is created, or decided between the project manager and the client after the plan has been outlined. The performance improvement project team

will then work toward a particular deadline, with rewards or consequences tied to on-time completion or delay.

3. *A budget.* Usually we mean project dollars when we refer to a project's budget. However, it can also specify the staffing resources required for a project. Again, this can be determined before the project plan is written, or negotiated between the project manager and the client once the plan has been created.

In addition to having a measurable objective, a deadline, and a budget, the project must be divisible into small steps or tasks that can be completed and measured as the project is carried out. As the project manager or other team members who have the necessary knowledge and experience divide the work into discrete segments, a list of tasks is created. Often the tasks will be interdependent and hierarchical and have a logical structure. When this is the case, the task list is referred to as the work breakdown structure.

The project manager should establish a particular sequence for completing the tasks of the project. If this does not seem necessary because the tasks can be completed in a random sequence, the project can still be planned but much of the discipline of project management will not be relevant (Martin, 1976).

The project manager should also make an estimate of the effort required to complete each component or segment of the project. If large chunks of the project defy estimation, then the methodology of project management will not work particularly well.

The effort expended on project management should be proportional to the length and complexity of the project itself. Clearly, spending a week planning a weeklong project would be overkill. That kind of attention to detail might lessen your chances of being given another project to manage. However, it could be perfectly reasonable to spend a week planning a project destined to take six months.

Project Managers and Project Implementers: What's the Difference?

Most people in the workplace become involved in projects at one time or another. Sometimes people are referred to as "project managers" who are engaged in fairly standard practices but who are not actually practicing project management. Projects are often implemented, but too seldom actually managed. Specific differences exist between project managers and project implementers, as pointed out by the following descriptions of what project managers do.

- *They carry out beginning-to-end planning rather than figuring it out one step at a time.* Some people feel constrained by having things planned ahead of time. When taking a vacation, these folks pile everything in the car, point it toward some destination, and take off without having in mind an exact route, what time they will arrive, or whether there will be a place to stay once they get there. When I travel, I like to know where I am going and have a plan for getting there. I once traveled with a person who preferred making plans as he went along. Our approach was certainly carefree, but the four-hour wait in the airport with an additional six-hour layover did not impress me; never mind the cost of an airline ticket purchased four hours before the flight. It is the same with project management; if you have no plan, you tend to have long periods of downtime waiting for people or assets. The last-minute costs are higher than planned ones. People working with you will experience high frustration with "figuring as you go." It is simply not the stuff promotions and raises are made of.

- *They learn from the past and from other projects.* The project manager is always looking for information about how past projects have gone in the organization. Valuable information is always to be found in both the projects that went well and those that didn't. What causes of a successful project can you incorporate into your plans? What were the causes of failure that you can avoid? This requires management and planning.

- *They have the ability to manage or coordinate the participation of others.* Project implementers—well, they implement. They personally do most of the work; they pull in the assistance and participation of others. Very rarely is the project manager the best person to do every task associated with a project. The ability to identify tasks, identify the appropriate owners, and coordinate their participation in the project will have tremendous impact on project results.

- *They focus on the goal, not the activity.* Project managers ensure that the goal (the end result) receives constant attention and remains the focus of the project. I have witnessed a number of projects where all the planned activities were completed but did not add up to the desired result. Project implementers lack this goal-oriented approach to project planning and implementation.

- *They manage decisions based upon priorities.* Very few plans remain intact throughout the implementation of a project; events occur that force changes. The difference between a manager and an implementer is most visible at such times. The project manager will have agreed-upon priorities for managing the project and deciding how to adapt to the new requirements. The implementer will waste time figuring this out while emotions run high and the project clock is ticking.

- *They obtain, manage, and utilize managerial sponsorship.* The management team (or the client, depending on the circumstance) is an important member of the project team that the project manager is responsible for. They hold authority over people resources, finances, and assets. Most likely, they also evaluate your efforts in managing the project. Project managers enlist a visible managerial sponsor for the project; project implementers usually just complain that they could do so much better if they had resources.

- *They adapt to changing conditions instead of being victimized by them.* As mentioned earlier, changes are going to happen. Project managers plan for them and work out contingency plans. When changes are proposed by the management team or the client, they are prepared to say yes but also to ask for offsetting resources. The project implementer is usually not so prepared.

- *They steer and control management involvement to further the project.* Performance improvement projects using human performance technology usually have much at stake. The potential for increasing performance can get clients and managers quite excited, and they will want to help. Project managers anticipate this, steering these stakeholders' involvement toward areas where they can actually do some good and away from areas where they would cause tension, distraction, or delays. But most project implementers have no such strategy; the typical result is multiple project managers, changing priorities, mass confusion, failed results, and focused blame (guess where!).

Benefits of Good Project Management

The benefits of professional project management should now be evident. As a professional human performance technologist, your ability to create reliable results through solid project management will develop your overall credibility. Applying a professional project management approach (Baker and Baker, 1992) accomplishes the following:

- Structures and controls resources (time, money, people).
- Estimates and manages time for creating and implementing human performance technology projects. This increases the probability of meeting deadlines by measuring progress throughout the project.
- Identifies tasks to be completed so that items or issues are not overlooked.
- Identifies what personnel are necessary and when—critical for scarce resources.
- Identifies what resources (machinery, tools, equipment, facilities) are needed, and when, to avoid delays in the project.

- Identifies the cost of activities to ensure the project remains within budget.
- Provides a vehicle for reviewing the activities in light of established priorities.
- Keeps the client or management team informed. Consider Fuller's First Law of Communication: if they don't know what you are doing, they suspect you are doing nothing.

Why Learn Project Management Now?

Your current ability to take on the project manager role may be very limited. You may already have a project manager and thus be a project participant. So why bother learning project management now?

To put it simply, waiting until you start your first project is a bad time to begin learning. Consider some contingency planning for a moment. What happens if the current project manager takes another job, leaves the company, or becomes disabled for a time? Who will move into the position? If it is you, learning how to manage while you are doing it is a difficult task at best, a nightmare at worst.

Almost all instructional design and human performance technology activities include the participation of others—coworkers, subject matter experts, intervention deliverers, vendors, and reviewers. You can start to use some project management skills and approaches now, without usurping authority from existing project managers.

Learning project management now increases your potential for taking on larger, more important projects. If you can demonstrate your ability on smaller projects and tasks, you are more likely to be invited to take on the larger projects.

It can also be used on simple projects to increase reliability and to optimize environment and results. Again, there is no reason to wait for the one-year project to begin to apply the contents of this book. The practices are scalable to almost any project.

Overview

In this book, we will focus on several key project management processes and a specific approach that works well for most human performance technology performance improvement projects. The processes have been grouped into three major areas:

FIGURE I.1.

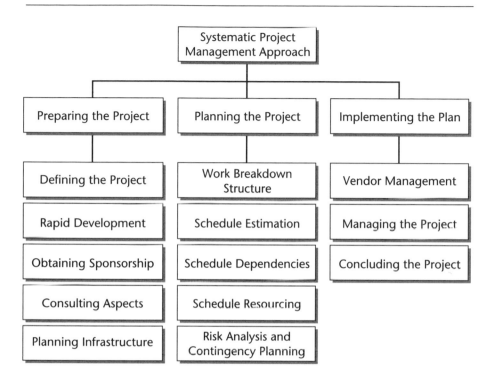

- Preparing the project (ensuring that the project planning phase is successful).
- Planning the project (creating the plan for managing the project)
- Managing the project (implementing the plan)

The model is arranged hierarchically, so that you can keep track of where you are in the project management approach.

Chapter One thoroughly discusses the key questions that project managers must answer in order to initiate and define a project. A clear definition keeps the project on track and ensures that the end product will achieve the desired results.

Some projects have the schedule as their number one priority, as performance improvement interventions need to be put in place quickly. Chapter Two covers considerations and practices for expediting the project.

Because human performance technology uses more than training to achieve the desired performance of people, it is usually wise to identify and work with a managerial sponsor for the project. Chapter Three deals with selecting and assessing sponsorship for the project before you begin.

Many, perhaps most, human performance technologists operate on a consultative basis. They are either external resources that have been called in, or floating resources within an organization. Chapter Four addresses the dual role of consultant and project manager.

Human performance technology is built upon the premise that human performance exists within a system. The project exists within a performance system as well. Chapter Five helps define system infrastructure for projects to ensure that environmental issues are aligned with and not against them.

The foundation of all projects is the plan. Chapters Six, Seven, and Eight provide extensive coverage of project planning. Chapter Six addresses work breakdown structure, defining what needs to be done to achieve the goal of the project. Chapter Seven looks at determining how long each task will require. Chapter Eight focuses on determining dependencies—when the activities need to occur.

Determining what resources will be required to complete the project is an important issue that is covered in Chapter Nine. Additionally, it examines how to align the resources to achieve the project priorities selected by the management team or clients.

The project management environment is dynamic and constantly in flux. Chapter Ten analyzes the typical changes that take place in project baseline schedules, resource allocations, and budgets. This will allow solid risk analysis and contingency planning that will make you look like a hero when all hell breaks loose.

Many human performance technology projects require the participation of outside vendors. Managing outside resources in a project plan requires special thought and effort. Chapter Eleven looks at methods to manage vendors and accurately specify their deliverables.

Once the project is underway, keeping it under control is an exciting challenge. In Chapter Twelve we look at methods and practices for day-to-day management of the project, and how best to keep the management team or client informed and involved.

We would be poor human performance technologists if we did not take a systems approach to our project management practices. Chapter Thirteen looks at concluding and evaluating the project. The project team members, sponsors, and the organization should learn from what did and did not go well, and incorporate that learning into future efforts.

The Saga of Bill and Karen

There are a couple of people you need to meet. You will encounter them several times as you read through this book. Through their experiences, you will have the opportunity to see human performance technologists work through the issues of managing human performance technology projects.

NewIdea is a very young company of about 7,000 employees. Its business is manufacturing new products in small quantities for evaluation purposes. This allows innovators and small companies to create working models to demonstrate to financial backers. People are more willing to fund projects that can be seen (they're funny that way).

This has been a very lucrative business for NewIdea, as product innovation is definitely on the rise. Unfortunately, others have noticed the profitability of the business and have become competitors. Lately, NewIdea has been losing jobs to lower-bidding, faster-turnaround competitors. The president of the company has not been pleased with this turn of events. "They're eating our lunch," she has said, "and I am *not* happy about it! We need to fix our cost and speed performance *now*."

Bill has been at NewIdea for almost three years. He joined the East Coast operation where mechanical products are created. He was hired into the training department as a training developer, but began to transform the approach of the organization the day he arrived. Bill had earned a master's degree in performance technology and was applying what he had learned. He has established a reputation for delivering reliable business results with his performance solutions. Up to this point, his performance solutions have been fairly simple, but well designed and effective.

Karen also works for NewIdea, but on the West Coast where electronic products are produced. Karen is much like Bill. She has a master's degree in performance technology and has put it to work in the West Coast training department. Like Bill, Karen has established a reputation for achieving business objectives through her performance solutions. In almost all respects, Bill and Karen are the same.

There is one important difference between Karen and Bill. His project management approach is built from his limited experience on small performance improvement projects. Karen has studied and understands more advanced project management strategies and practices. As she has with her performance technology skills, she is ready to put her project management approach to work.

PART ONE

PREPARING THE PROJECT

Before you can plan a project, you must answer many questions, select alternatives, establish relationships, determine responsibilities, and determine and clarify priorities.

Many inexperienced performance improvement project managers jump right into the planning stage and skip the preparatory work. The problem with this approach is that the preparatory work still needs to be done. The questions about alternatives, roles, responsibilities, and priorities still need to be answered. Skipping the preparation simply pushes the work into the midst of the planning or implementation, where time is short and emotions run high.

Investing time in preparation usually pays off with interest, and it increases your reputation as a professional human performance technologist who achieves reliable, efficient, and effective results.

FIGURE P1.1.

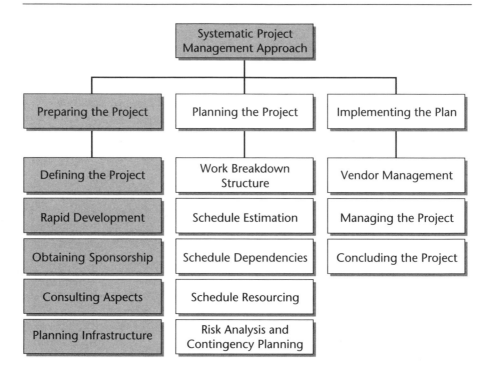

CHAPTER ONE

DEFINING THE PROJECT

To keep a performance improvement project on track, all participants in the project need to know what they are attempting to achieve. If they do not, the result will be project confusion.

Bill's Story

Bill was having one of those days. Unfortunately, every day for the last four weeks had been "one of those days." He had a pile of phone messages stacked on his desk, and a line of people in front of it seeking his attention. It didn't look good. He started to wonder where he could get a number dispenser and a sign reading, "For Better Service, Please Take a Number."

Life had become a whirlwind for Bill four weeks earlier, when he accepted responsibility for implementing a large and complex performance improvement project at his company, NewIdea, where he works in the East Coast training department. Bill began the project with two other people. The three of them had conducted a well-designed performance analysis. They clearly defined the performance that was required of the product producers. They conducted a thorough gap analysis to determine where the performance discrepancies were. They carried out a data-driven root cause analysis to determine exactly why the performance gaps existed. They chose performance improvement solutions that would effectively and efficiently close the performance gaps and allow NewIdea to achieve lower costs and faster performance.

The performance improvement solution was holistic in nature, addressing the true root causes of the performance issues. However, the solution required significantly more participants than usual. The following problems were identified:

- The product specification process was slow and inaccurate, creating long delays and expensive errors in production. It had to be reengineered.
- The product producers were using outdated tools. New computer-controlled milling machines would increase speed and accuracy; they were expensive, but the time and material savings would pay for them in seven months. Who could argue with an investment like that?
- If a product was late, the product producers were allowed to work overtime to catch up; in effect, the company was handing out bonuses for working on late projects, which were increasing in number as a result of the opportunity to earn overtime pay. Thus, the reward and compensation system had to be fixed.
- The product producers did not know how to use the product specification process. Training was part of the solution; through careful instructional analysis, Bill determined that a videotape delivery would support the learning objectives and the training method. This would allow the product producers to receive training at a convenient time and also reduce the training costs as compared to a classroom delivery.

But now, it seemed like everybody involved with the project was at Bill's desk. They were all arguing. Phil thought the videotape should explain how to use specifications, but Barb thought it should cover how to write them. Brian wanted to wait until all the solution components were completed before any were implemented; Kelly wanted to implement them as soon as they were available. Dwight thought they were creating a bonus system, but Pam insisted that a complete restructuring of the pay system was in order. From the six people around Bill's desk, there were at least twelve opinions regarding what the project was and was not. Yet it was all so clear to Bill. What was wrong with these people?

The phone rang. Bill was grateful for the interruption until he found out who was calling. His manager wanted to see him pronto, and she did not sound very happy.

As Bill sat down at her desk, Linda hung up her phone. "Do you know who that was?" she asked. "That was the personnel manager. He wants to know why the training organization is messing with the compensation system. I couldn't tell him. I have no idea why you are messing with compensation. I've heard from almost every functional manager today about the project. I don't know what you're doing, but make sure you don't interfere with the charter of other departments.

"There are a couple of other things," Linda continued. "I need to pull Dwight from the project team and have him cover the delivery of the new health care training."

Bill knew he couldn't revise the pay system on time without Dwight. "How can I finish the project?" he asked Linda.

"I'll let you work on that, Bill. You are the project manager. While we're on the subject, my manager is concerned about other training projects slipping while we're working on this project. I know the president is hot to fix the problem, but what would be the effect of slipping project completion by one or two quarters?"

Bill was at a complete loss. "I don't know," he responded. "I thought getting the problem fixed fast was all-important."

Bill felt as though he were in quicksand and sinking fast. Team members were in disagreement about what they were doing. His manager didn't know what they were doing. But Bill knew; why didn't the others?

The Purpose of Project Definition

To keep a performance improvement project on track, all participants in the project need to know what they are attempting to achieve. Without a clearly written definition to guide the team members, project management becomes rather like attempting to herd cats—each will run in a separate direction. Bill was suffering just such project confusion.

As Jackson and Addison (1992, p. 67) say, "Why is project management important, and how is it related to human performance technology? HPT is a set of methods and processes for solving problems or realizing opportunities related to people's performance. Project management involves seeing that those methods and processes are applied with economy and care."

They continue: "Project management errors can be fully as detrimental to a project's purpose as technological errors can. Most of us have seen technologically sound projects that were rejected or misused. The error often lies in the failure, early in the project, to gather all the information needed for managing the process."

Project Definition for the Human Performance Technologist

Human performance technologists become involved in projects at two different stages. The first may be the initiation of the performance improvement project. By then the business need or objective has been identified (such as to lower costs, improve product quality, or improve customer satisfaction), but the organization has not been through the performance analysis to determine what needs to be done to achieve the objective. The second stage occurs at the conclusion of the analysis, when the solutions to the performance gaps have been identified.

Human performance technologists are frequently asked for solutions to performance problems before having an opportunity to conduct a performance analysis, but they must define the problem through analysis before attempting to provide solutions. They may also be asked before the performance analysis to define how long the entire project will take. This question cannot and should not be answered at such a point either; if you do not know what the solution is, you certainly do not know how long it will take or how much it will cost.

The human performance technologist should take a two-phase approach to performance improvement project management (Barkley and Saylor, 1994). The first phase is performance analysis, and the second is development and implementation of the performance improvement solutions. Unless you have strong clairvoyant powers or are planning to change jobs very soon, do not attempt to do both at the same time! Both phases will require a project definition to ensure that there is clarity of purpose among the participants, clients, partners, and managers.

At first, it may seem that time spent defining the project is a low-productivity activity. However, remember the problems Bill encountered without clear project definition. Additionally, some research on the value of detailed project planning (Stallworthy, 1983) has examined the time allocations of projects in detail. The projects were divided into two groups: those that invested heavily in planning and those that did so only minimally. The results are depicted in Figure 1.1.

You can see in Figure 1.1 the difference between the groups in time spent on project planning. Also, notice the difference in time spent dealing with development setbacks and, more significantly, in time spent fixing the end product of the project. The time spent planning is more than recovered later in the project.

FIGURE 1.1. TIME REQUIREMENT CONTRASTS.

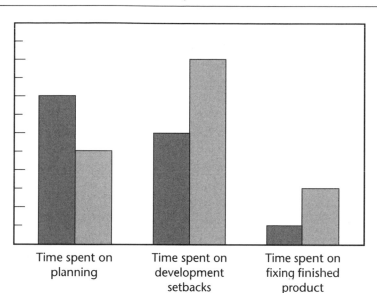

Time spent on planning

Time spent on development setbacks

Time spent on fixing finished product

The Process of Project Definition

It should come as no surprise that a book on project management for human performance technologists takes a process approach to defining the project. The process of creating project definition results in the following:

- Identifying intended project outcomes
- Clearly defining the project scope and the deliverables
- Validating the project and securing approval to proceed

There are many potential approaches to defining projects, but major authors on the subject (Gilbreath, 1986; Grey, 1981; Martin, 1976; Stallworthy, 1983) agree on a five-step approach:

1. Identify the project.
2. Create a written definition document.
3. Create a project objective statement.

4. Validate the definition.
5. Create a project priority matrix.

The following sections detail each of the steps in the process and look at the implications for performance improvement projects.

Step 1: Identify the Project

The first step is to identify the project. What rationale is driving the organization to consider initiating a project that will consume time and resources? Having this clearly defined and well understood will allow you to proceed through the project definition process in an informed manner. To create the project definition without understanding the organizational needs is to risk producing a definition that is not aligned with the objectives and desires of the organization (Gilbreath, 1986). This would most likely result in the need to completely redo the entire project definition process, as the assumptions on which the definition is built would be faulty. And it would not have a positive effect on your career, nor on the human performance technology profession.

There are several areas to consider in the identification of the project. Do not skip any of them, regardless of the nature of your intended performance improvement project; they tend to be areas that managers and clients are concerned about and will most likely want to discuss before agreeing to proceed with the project. Thus, carry out each of the following.

Define Why Something Must Be Done. What current situation in the organization is causing it to consider initiating a project? How extensive (in both intensity and pervasiveness) is the dissatisfaction with the current situation? Is this characterized as a "nice to do" performance improvement project, or is the organization's future survival at stake? What motivation does the manager or client have to proceed?

Define What Would Be Done and the Intended Outcomes. What is the current recommendation for solving the situation? As a human performance technologist, you will probably be recommending one of two approaches. If there has been no data-driven analysis of the performance problem, your recommendation should be to initiate one to determine the cause of the performance gaps; the outcome of the project then would be identification of the performance improvement solutions necessary to close the performance gaps. If the performance analysis has been completed, your recommendation will probably be the design, development, and implementation of the performance improvement solutions, and the intended outcome would be closure of the performance gaps.

Create a Preliminary Cost-Benefit Analysis. It is important to assess if the cost of closing the performance gap is greater than the cost of allowing the gap to continue. Human performance technologists are concerned with engineering "worthy performance," where the value of the performance is greater than its cost (Gilbert, 1978). Additionally, most managers and clients will want to know this from a business management perspective.

An effective model for portraying the cost benefit analysis is borrowed from the world of product engineering project management (creating products for revenue, such as automobiles or computers). The model is called break even time (BET) and is intended to illustrate whether the value from the project will ever equal or exceed the costs of the project (Obradovitch and Stephanou, 1990). An example of a BET model is illustrated in Figure 1.2.

Most BET models are not precise and are certainly not exacting financial analyses. Rather, they are a representation of general costs and benefits over time. The vertical axis indicates financial costs (below the zero point) and benefits (above the zero point). The horizontal axis illustrates the activity over time.

Time is a very important feature of the BET model. Most human performance technologists and managers overlook the issue of performance improvement durability. Performance improvements do not last forever; they have a limited life. If the created value is due to competitive advantage, it is an accepted fact that the competition will eventually catch up. If the value is created by improved

FIGURE 1.2. THE BET MODEL.

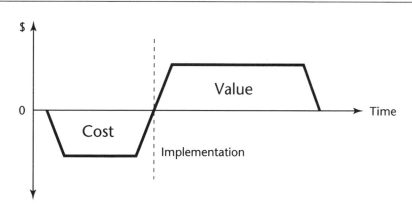

performance on a specific job, the requirements of that job will eventually change due to changes in business or technology.

As the project begins, so do the costs associated with analysis, design, and development of the project deliverables. As the development ends, the costs ramp to zero. The line that shows financial costs over time defines an area on the model labeled *Cost*, which represents the total costs of the project.

When the performance improvement solutions are introduced, benefits from the improved performance begin. These continue until the performance improvement is rendered ineffective by changing conditions. The line that shows the financial benefits over time defines an area on the model labeled *Value*.

Now for the analysis determination. Is the total value area larger than the total cost area? If it is, you may proceed with identifying the project. If not, show the BET model to the manager or client, who may want to stop now.

The BET model appears again later in this chapter when the potential economic impacts of a poorly defined project are described.

Analyze the Risk. This is different than the typical project management risk analysis that looks for risky assumptions about time estimates in the plan that could cause slips. Chapter Ten describes risk analysis and contingency planning. Risk analysis at this stage is a determination of what negative consequences will occur if the performance improvement project is or is not implemented (Hertz and Howard, 1983). This information will most likely exist within the organization targeted for the performance improvement. The manager or client will have insights and an opinion. However, there is probably additional and potentially revealing information to be discovered from the targets themselves.

Define the Project's Relationship to Other Performance Improvement Projects. This is really an assessment of some performance improvement political issues that must be identified now because discovering them later is unpleasant. Check the alignment of this project with other performance improvement efforts. What are their priority, and how does the priority of this project stack up? Can the results of this project be leveraged to others or vice versa? Will this project conflict with other performance improvement projects for resources or attention? Is there overlap with other performance improvement projects, thereby giving the perception of duplication of effort?

Evaluate Future Opportunities. Determine what other performance improvements this will lead to. Is this a single and isolated performance improvement project, or will it give rise to additional projects?

Assess Organizational Readiness. This is probably the most important yet most frequently overlooked issue in performance improvement work (Kissler, 1991). In some instances, well-designed performance improvement solutions have been introduced to organizations that patently rejected them. The reasons can be highly varied. Perhaps this is the sixth major performance improvement solution launched at the targeted performers in nine months. Perhaps the management team has no credibility in reinforcing or sponsoring the performance improvement changes. It can be difficult to tell. To assist you with this task, see the organizational readiness assessment tool in Exhibit 1.1 at the end of this chapter.

Once the assessment of your performance improvement project is complete, it is beneficial to make copies and hand them to several people in the target organization. Average their assessments and compare them with yours. Use the guidelines at the end of the assessment to determine the risk level and how (or whether) to proceed.

Step 2: Create a Written Definition Document

The second step is to develop a complete written definition of the project and a project objective statement. Bill probably spent some time on step 1, but it is evident from the actions of others that he failed to communicate it well. Getting it in writing is a key activity. It ensures consistent communication with others and also facilitates step 3, validation of the definition. So what should be included in the project definition document?

According to Barkley and Saylor (1994), the project definition should include the following information:

- Description of the project (what we are doing)
- Purpose (why we are doing it)
- Completion criteria (project end, acceptance criteria)
- Project start date
- Target population
- What the project will and will not include
- Dependencies (both internal and external)
- Staffing (in terms of skills and balance of experience)
- Risk of doing the project versus not doing it
- Cost
- Technology required
- Hardware and software required

The definition document should answer the typical questions that a project participant, client, or manager would have about the project. See if your definition answers these questions:

- Is there a specific time by which the project must be completed? What circumstances mandate this time frame?
- What implementation constraints are there (if any)?
- How will we know that the project is complete?
- How will we know if it is successful?
- Are the requirements defined in quantifiable terms?
- Who are the decision makers?
- Who should we provide with published decisions?
- What are the most important project performance criteria by which the project will be measured, such as time, costs, or quality?
- Why should this project be done? Why now?
- What are the risks (controllable versus noncontrollable)?
- What impact will the project have, both internally and externally?
- What assumptions are we making? For example, are we assuming that a certain technology will be available?
- Are there any imposed time or resource constraints? What are they? Why?
- What are the risks identified in the organizational readiness analysis? What are the recommendations for minimizing the risks?

The project definition document will require several pages to cover the necessary information and will serve as a reference to the performance improvement project team as it works through the project. Unfortunately, most team members will not memorize the document or carry it around with them. So what's a project manager to do?

Step 3: Create a Project Objective Statement

Management consultants typically recommend that organizations have a mission statement to help the organization keep focused on its intended results (Kouzes and Posner, 1987). NASA had a great one in the 1960s that was provided by President Kennedy: "Send a man to the moon, and return him safely back to earth, before the end of the decade." It kept everyone on the project focused and on track.

Your performance improvement project will also benefit from a project objective statement (mission statement). The criteria for a good project objective statement (Kezsbaum, 1989) are the following:

- It clearly states what you are going to do (scope), by when (date needed), and for how much (resources allocated).
- It is stated in no more than twenty-five words.
- It uses ordinary English, not technical jargon, buzzwords, or expertise-specific phrases.

The task of creating a simple project objective statement is not easy; an unclear statement of 1,300 words loaded with jargon is much easier to create. Get some help creating the project objective statement. If you involve the project team, you will not only improve the quality of the statement, but through its creation you will ensure that all the team members really understand the project definition.

Step 4: Validate the Definition

Once you have created the project definition document and project objective statement, it is time to ensure that you have it right. Get project team members, client, and managers to review and correct the definition now, before you begin the project. Changing the definition in the midst of the project is quite unpleasant.

It is important that all parties involved participate in and approve the project definition (Barkley and Saylor, 1994). You might even want to have them sign the document indicating agreement. Do not be surprised if you find that there are errors in the definition—perhaps big ones. It is important to flush out all the errors now, while they are easy to fix. Be sure to thank the people who point out the errors in the definition document. They are saving you from future time loss and frustration.

Document all the assumptions you are making, even if they seem obvious (Lewis, 1993a). Consider this example: a performance improvement project manager assumed that the team would be working on the project full-time but found out later that management expected half-time work on the project and half-time work on other responsibilities. Unfortunately, this was not discovered until a delivery date had been set.

Step 5: Create a Project Priority Matrix

Managing the priorities of the project can be tricky business. Which is more important, the completion date or project costs? How do you know? The project priority matrix is a tool for determining and managing the project priorities. It can help you to explain and avoid impossible situations in which there is no chance for project success.

There are three major components to any project (Kerzner, 1989): time (how long you have to complete the project), scope (what you will accomplish), and resources (funds, equipment, and people to achieve the project objective). Projects cannot be successful without having all three to some degree. Rarely will a project be allowed an infinite quantity of time, scope, and resources; there will be some limitations.

The project priority matrix allows you to organize the priority of these three project aspects. However, the project manager does not get to fill out the matrix. Sorry. That responsibility falls to the manager or client who has asked for or is funding the project. That person gets to choose, and you get to explain the implications of the choices.

An example of a project priority matrix is shown in Figure 1.3. Do not let its simple appearance fool you. Like the hammer or screwdriver, it is a simple tool that can produce significant results if used properly.

As mentioned, few projects are allowed infinite amounts of all three project aspects. As the project manager, you must determine trade-offs between time, scope, and resources. The project priority matrix allows for three different priority levels:

- *Constrain.* The constrained aspect must be met; it is the highest priority. The other two aspects are considered less important.
- *Optimize.* The optimized aspect is either maximized (if scope) or minimized (if time or resources) within project objectives. The project team will do its best on this aspect but will not compromise the constrained aspect to achieve it.
- *Accept.* This means that management is willing to accept the project team's best performance on this aspect but understands that the constrained and optimized aspects take priority.

The sample project priority matrix in Figure 1.3 has only one aspect in each of the three priority levels. It is not permissible to constrain all three aspects. To

FIGURE 1.3. SAMPLE PROJECT PRIORITY MATRIX.

	Time	Scope	Resources
Constrain	X		X
Optimize			
Accept		X	

do so will create project failure (Lewis, 1993a), as quality will be compromised in the following ways: scope (deliverables will not be complete), time (the schedule will slip), or resources (the project will go over budget and people will burn out). This has always been an interesting issue within project management, because no rational person would attempt to constrain the aspect of any personal project. Imagine walking onto a car lot and informing the salesperson that you would like a Rolls Royce (scope), you want it today (time), and you want to pay $50 (resources). It cannot be done, and neither can constraining all three aspects of any other project.

Use the project priority matrix after the scope is defined and before any work begins on the project. This allows for prioritization while everybody concerned is calm and rational. Attempting this exercise in the midst of a project problem is not advisable and rarely successful.

Using the definitions for the priority levels, ask (in this case) management to select the aspect that they would like constrained. What has to be managed without compromise? As the selection is made, mark the aspect that is constrained. In the example in Figure 1.3, management chose to constrain time (the project had to be completed on a specific date).

Next, ask the manager which aspect should be maximized or minimized. In the sample, the manager chose resources. The project costs and people investments had to be kept as low as possible. Mark resources as Optimize. Mark scope as Accept, as that is the only priority left for it.

To ensure that management really knows what it is signing up for, describe a potential scenario and how the project priority matrix would be used to make decisions. Here are some scenarios for the sample case.

If the manager of another department suggests adding to the performance improvement solution, should you do it? No, because it would require more time, which has been constrained.

What if you were forced to include the additional material? Then scope would be optimized, meaning that resources would move down in priority to Accept and that whatever resources (personnel, finances) were needed to include the additions would have to be accepted.

What if you had to remove a resource from the project? As resources are being optimized, this would be okay; but understand that this will result in a reduced deliverable. Because scope is prioritized as being accepted, there should be no problem scaling down the project to optimize the resource requirements.

If management disagrees with the scenario outcomes, do not take it personally. It simply indicates that they did not get the priorities right on the first pass. Allow them to move aspects up and down in priority until they are satisfied. Once they have finished selecting the priorities for the project, you have an effective management tool.

Priorities are not guaranteed to remain constant through the project; indeed, they rarely do. But if it can be changed at will, what is the value of the project priority matrix? The matrix acts as a decision tool and allows you to ensure that you do not end up with a project in which all three aspects are constrained. Management should be allowed to change the priorities as necessary. As the project manager you should provide them with that flexibility; however, you should not allow more than one aspect to be given any single priority. One aspect should always be constrained, one optimized, and one accepted; otherwise the project will fail (Lewis, 1993a).

Economic Consequences of Poor Project Definition

Poor project definition clearly results in frustration; the performance improvement project team members do not understand the objectives, the management team may not support the end result, and chaos seems to be the order of the day. And there are additional consequences that the BET model can help illustrate.

The BET model illustrated in Figure 1.2 is repeated in Figure 1.4 to demonstrate that there is substantial value to be gained by the project beyond the cost of creating it. In short, the project makes economic sense.

FIGURE 1.4. THE ORIGINAL BET MODEL.

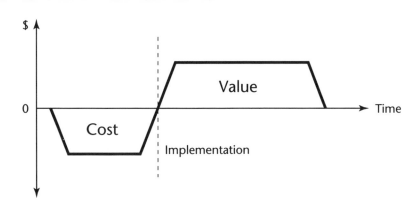

With poor project definition, it is likely that confusion will cause a slip in the implementation date (Hertz and Howard, 1983). The definition will be corrected in real time as the project proceeds and new activities or project requirements are discovered that result in rework. This will result in the project team working longer to complete the project than anticipated. The BET model in Figure 1.5 shows that the slip increases the cost and decreases the value (remember, the life of the project result is limited, fixing the endpoint). Suddenly, this project no longer looks like a good investment.

If the human performance technologist has not adequately assessed organizational readiness and prepared the organization for the performance improvement solutions, a readiness gap may occur (Stewart, 1991). The solution may be finished on schedule, but without the organization being ready (for whatever reason) to implement it. Until the barriers to implementation are resolved, the solution sits idle. Figure 1.6 illustrates the effect of this on the BET model. Costs do not increase in this scenario, but the idle time cuts into the value, decreasing the economic gain from the performance improvement project.

If the organization readiness issue is not serious, the implementation may occur on schedule but with reduced acceptance from parts of the organization. They may wait until the solution is mandated by the management chain and still resist implementation. Figure 1.7 illustrates this effect on the BET model. Slow acceptance reduces the potential value in the early stages of the implementation. The slow acceptance can be moderate (as shown here) or substantial, reaching all the way to the obsolescence point. The value of the performance improvement project is greatly reduced.

FIGURE 1.5. BET WITH A PROJECT SLIP.

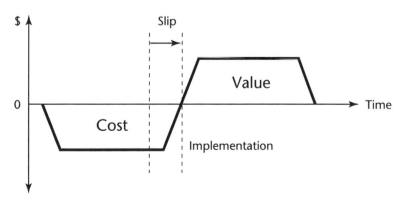

FIGURE 1.6. BET WITH A READINESS GAP.

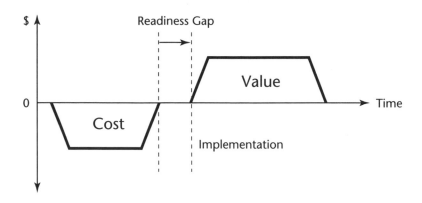

FIGURE 1.7. BET WITH SLOW ACCEPTANCE.

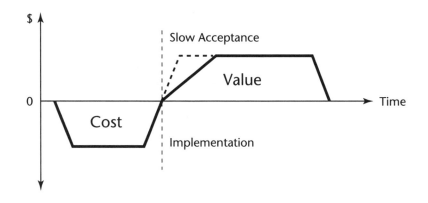

Karen's Story

Among the other organizational problems at NewIdea, communications were not working well. Both the East Coast operation, where Bill is located, and the West Coast operation knew about the president's edict to fix the performance problem, but neither were aware that the other was working on it.

Karen is Bill's counterpart at NewIdea's West Coast operations. She applied the same rigorous, data-driven performance analysis process to the problem that

Bill had. There were great similarities on both coasts in the tasks that product producers were asked to do and in the performance barriers. It should be no surprise that Karen's team selected the same performance improvement solutions that Bill's team did. However, things were going differently for Karen.

All members of the team had copies of the project definition posted in their cubicles. They could all explain exactly what the project team was out to achieve. Each subproject also had a clear definition. Every project team member knew exactly what the team was to produce. Not that it was easy getting agreement; there had been some disagreements and misunderstandings, but they were resolved early as the team created the definition statements.

Karen received a call from her manager. He wanted to discuss the project with her. As she sat down at his desk, Jim hung up his phone. "That was the personnel manager," he said. "He's still nervous about the training organization messing with the compensation system. I'm glad you identified that as a potential issue and involved his people to lower resistance. That organization readiness survey seems to have paid off. The other function managers are dealing with the three issues you identified.

"My manager dropped by this morning to discuss what we were doing about the president's edict. Fortunately, I was able to pull out the project and subproject definitions and describe the projects. But," Jim continued, "I do have some bad news. I need to pull Kathleen from the project team and have her cover delivery of the new health care training."

"Okay," replied Karen. "We can do that. But let's pull out the project priority matrix that we agreed to and determine the impact on the project. We said that the schedule was constrained, because the competition is forcing us to improve quickly. We also said that the scope was to be optimized, because the performance improvement had to work effectively. That means we accepted whatever resources are necessary to maintain the scope and schedule."

"Yep, that's correct," said Jim.

"So," Karen continued, "by pulling Kathleen from the project, we are constraining resources. Because only one item can be constrained, we need to move the schedule's priority down. Now, I need your managerial guidance here, Jim. We can optimize the scope and accept the schedule. That means pushing out the schedule and waiting for Kathleen to become available. The other alternative is to optimize the schedule and accept the scope. This would mean cutting the compensation portion of the project and implementing an incomplete solution."

"I don't particularly like either alternative," said Jim. "Can't you keep the schedule and produce all the solution components without Kathleen?"

"No, I can't," replied Karen. "As we discussed, we can't constrain all three."

"Okay," Jim said, "but my manager is concerned about other projects slipping while we work on this one. What happens if we take longer to develop the solutions?"

Karen thought for a second, then pulled out her BET analysis. "Look at this, Jim. We know our competitors are working on improving their performance, so our solution has a fixed duration. We know that at some fixed point in time the competitive advantage we receive from this performance improvement project will disappear. If the end point is fixed, moving the start point further out will significantly decrease the benefit NewIdea gets from its investment."

Jim looked at the model. Karen was right. "Sounds like slipping the schedule is a bad solution, Karen. Well, we agreed to accept the resources required to accomplish the project. We'll have to find somebody else to do the health care training unless we want to change our priorities."

EXHIBIT 1.1. A TOOL FOR ASSESSING ORGANIZATIONAL READINESS.

1. Decisions about making change in this organization have required approval at too many managerial levels.

1	2	3	4	5	6	7	8	9	10

Rarely the case   Usually the case

2. This organization has a poor history in identifying and resolving problems when implementing changes or performance improvement interventions.

1	2	3	4	5	6	7	8	9	10

Rarely the case   Usually the case

3. Risk taking has been discouraged and creative ideas have been ignored due to an emphasis on finding and punishing errors.

1	2	3	4	5	6	7	8	9	10

Rarely the case   Usually the case

4. This organization fails to stay on track when implementing performance improvement projects because it is not clear who has the responsibility and authority to implement the changes.

1	2	3	4	5	6	7	8	9	10

Rarely the case   Usually the case

5. Failure in involving supervisors and middle managers in planning and implementing performance improvement has resulted in their indifference or resistance to the intervention.

1	2	3	4	5	6	7	8	9	10

Rarely the case   Usually the case

6. The organization has usually not allowed sufficient time for the implementation of performance improvements or change.

1	2	3	4	5	6	7	8	9	10

Rarely the case   Usually the case

7. There are usually no negative consequences associated with failing to implement a performance improvement project.

1	2	3	4	5	6	7	8	9	10

Rarely the case   Usually the case

8. The management of the organization has a history of not being sufficiently disciplined to get day-to-day tasks done when implementing change or performance improvements.

1	2	3	4	5	6	7	8	9	10

Rarely the case   Usually the case

9. Past change or performance improvement projects have received very little attention.

1	2	3	4	5	6	7	8	9	10

Rarely the case   Usually the case

10. There have been poor incentives for finishing projects on time and within budget.

1	2	3	4	5	6	7	8	9	10

Rarely the case   Usually the case

11. Past performance improvement efforts have not been communicated effectively down through the organization, resulting in people being confused about how the changes affect them, what their responsibilities are, or what they should do differently.

1	2	3	4	5	6	7	8	9	10

Rarely the case   Usually the case

12. The managers in the organization have shown little or no interest in encouraging people to communicate their opinions about how performance improvement efforts affect them.

1	2	3	4	5	6	7	8	9	10

Rarely the case   Usually the case

13. Rigid policies, rules, and procedures have made it difficult to implement changes in the way work is done in the organization.

1	2	3	4	5	6	7	8	9	10

Rarely the case   Usually the case

14. During past performance improvement efforts, cooperation and support between departments or work teams have been weak or nonexistent.

1	2	3	4	5	6	7	8	9	10

Rarely the case   Usually the case

15. The management of the organization has a history of losing its focus on important projects when other problems or issues compete for attention or resources.

1	2	3	4	5	6	7	8	9	10

Rarely the case   Usually the case

16. People have been forced to comply with performance improvement efforts rather than encouraged to become involved and committed.

1	2	3	4	5	6	7	8	9	10

Rarely the case   Usually the case

17. When deciding whether or not to support performance improvement efforts, people have done what they believed would gain visibility rather than what was best for the organization.

1	2	3	4	5	6	7	8	9	10

Rarely the case   Usually the case

18. People have expected performance improvement changes affecting part of the organization to have little or no effect on other areas.

1	2	3	4	5	6	7	8	9	10

Rarely the case   Usually the case

19. Managers and supervisors in this organization have often felt pressured to implement performance improvement changes that they did not fully understand or support themselves.

1	2	3	4	5	6	7	8	9	10

Rarely the case   Usually the case

20. In the past, when managers said that they supported performance improvement change, their behavior often suggested the opposite.

1	2	3	4	5	6	7	8	9	10

Rarely the case   Usually the case

21. People expect little to happen when new performance improvement efforts are announced because of the organization's poor track record of completing changes.

1	2	3	4	5	6	7	8	9	10

Rarely the case   Usually the case

22. People have rarely understood how specific performance improvement efforts supported the organization's overall goals and objectives.

1	2	3	4	5	6	7	8	9	10

Rarely the case   Usually the case

23. Management-created committees and task forces in this organization have not been effective for keeping changes or performance improvement projects on track.

1	2	3	4	5	6	7	8	9	10

Rarely the case   Usually the case

24. During past performance improvement efforts, managers were more focused on making themselves and their departments look good rather than on how to best accomplish the goals of the change.

1	2	3	4	5	6	7	8	9	10

Rarely the case   Usually the case

25. Within this organization, it is more important to appear to support performance improvement efforts than to express doubt or disagreement.

1	2	3	4	5	6	7	8	9	10

Rarely the case   Usually the case

Scoring the Organization Assessment

Step 1: Total the responses to all 25 items.

Step 2: Divide the total by 25 to determine the average score.

Step 3: Review the items with the highest scores and list the four that you believe will contribute most significantly to implementation problems.

Issue 1:

Issue 2:

Issue 3:

Issue 4:

Interpreting the Results of the Organization Assessment

High-Risk Situation: Be Aware of Organizational Dangers (6.6 and above)

A score of 3.3 and above indicates that there have been significant problems in implementing performance improvement projects in the past. A history of previous problems frequently causes people to respond negatively to new initiatives. Because of this history, with its probable morale problems and the fact that past problems are usually repeated in the future, new performance improvement projects will require substantial project management efforts. Major investments of time and other resources will be needed to secure the participation of the organization and achieve the intended performance improvement goals.

Moderate-Risk Situation: Exercise Caution (3.5–6.5)

A score between 3.5 and 6.5 is sufficiently high that it should be considered a significant issue in the success or failure of any new performance improvement project. Be aware of the areas that pose the most significant issues and ensure that their effects (additional time requirements, people and resource availability, and management support) are adequately reflected in the planning of the project.

Low-Risk Situation: High-Opportunity Organization (1.0–3.4)

A score between 1.0 and 3.4 is sufficiently low that it should not be considered a substantial issue when planning the performance improvement project. However, be alert to changing conditions within the organization during the project. Additionally, any item with a score of 3 or greater should not be ignored. These items require some special attention to ensure that they do not *become* a problem during the project.

CHAPTER TWO

ACCELERATING PROJECT DEVELOPMENT

Welcome to the late 1990s. This decade has seen an unprecedented increase in competitiveness. More organizations than ever before want to earn business; this competitiveness has caused them to focus on being trim, efficient, and effective.

Bill's Story

Bill was nervous as he sat in the blue chair by Linda's desk. It was a clear case of classical conditioning; every time he sat in this chair he got bad news. Now all he has to do is see the chair and his stomach begins to hurt.

Linda cleared her throat. "Bill, I have some bad news. We just found out that the Inventor's Convention is going to be held early this year. As you know, all the inventors will want their working products finished in time to display at the show. Unless we can guarantee that their products will be ready, they'll take their business to our competitors. The only way we can have all the products ready is by implementing the performance improvement solutions earlier than we planned."

Bill really didn't want to know, but he asked anyway. "How much earlier?"

"Well," replied Linda, "I'm afraid that we need to be done three months sooner than we first thought."

"What?" yelled Bill. "Are you kidding me? Please tell me you're not serious!"

"I'm afraid I'm very serious," said Linda. "Why don't you go back to your desk and find a way to do it. Come back when you're ready."

Bill left the office and gathered his thoughts quickly. He carefully considered the objectives of the project and the resources he had available to him. He even talked to the project team to get its inputs. But he could see no way to make it happen. He returned to Linda's office, ready to present his argument. There was that blue chair again. Darn.

"You obviously don't understand the challenges we face," Bill began. "I don't see any way to trim three months off the project. I'm not even sure we can make the original date. Let me tell you what I'm up against.

"Barb is a new hire. She's really bright and energetic, but she has almost no experience. She can't possibly get her part of the video project done that quickly. She can hardly tell one end of the camera from the other.

"We put this project team together from all over the organization. As a result, we're spread out all over the place. Communications are a real problem. We spend more time walking than talking. And the management team is driving us nuts. They've come downstairs three times during the last week to change various requirements for the project. We can't possibly hit a constantly moving target.

"And finally," continued Bill, "the people just won't do it. I did some quick calculations and figured it would require sixty- to seventy-hour weeks to cut three months out of the schedule. They aren't willing to do that. I'm sorry, Linda, but it just can't be done."

The Issue of Rapid Development

There is at least one truism about today's increased competitive environment: being the first to provide a product or service is important—*very* important (Smith and Reinertson, 1991).

Why? If you are the first, it is usually for only a brief time. There is a term for being the only provider: monopoly. When you have a monopoly, you can charge whatever the market will bear. Large profits can be made while the monopoly lasts; the problem is that competitors eventually arrive with similar products and services. This usually results in decreasing prices as the competitors struggle for market share (Smith and Reinertson, 1991).

Human performance technologists help companies gain a competitive edge by improving employees' performance. This usually results in lower costs, improved quality, or the ability to produce a service or product that the competition cannot.

This allows companies to lower prices, offer better quality, or hold a short-term monopoly. Organizations want improved performance, and they want it now. The number of performance improvement projects with a rapid development focus will probably continue to increase.

Identifying Rapid Development Projects

So how do you tell when one of these hot potatoes has fallen into your lap? Some distinct characteristics allow you to diagnose a rapid development situation (Stalk, 1990).

First, the definition of a rapid development project is that the combination of desired objective and schedule is not reasonable. It may even be classified as ridiculous. If the objective can be reasonably achieved within the desired schedule, then the performance improvement project is not a candidate for rapid development. Manage it as a normal project.

Second, the project priority matrix must indicate that resource has the priority of Accept. Time and scope must be the top two priorities as indicated by management, and there must be an urgent need for some specific performance improvement. If the manager indicates significant concern regarding resources, then rapid development cannot be too important. Use the project priority matrix as a decision-making tool and manage the performance improvement project as described in Chapter One.

Third, the client or manager indicates that this is a do-or-die project. The results of your project identification should indicate the importance of the performance improvement project. Is it critical? The methods for rapid development are costly in terms of resource and effort.

Practices for Rapid Development

Do you know what to do when you encounter a project with a rapid development focus? Or when rapid development is imposed on an existing project? Some tested practices and approaches can help you manage a rapid development performance improvement project (Lewis, 1993b). It is best to use them while you are defining the project and people are more rational. However, they can be used to transform a project to rapid development while it is in progress. Here they are:

- Project objective statement with rapid development delivery date
- Simultaneous development
- Leverage and reuse

- The right people
- The right resources
- Senior management support
- Co-location
- Frozen design documentation
- Dogmatic milestone tracking
- Visible recognition

The following sections examine each practice and explain the potential impact it has for moving a project to rapid development.

Project Objective Statement with Rapid Development Delivery Date

Chapter One explained the issue of creating a project objective statement during the process of defining the project. The project objective statement helps keep the project team focused and on track. This becomes all the more important during a rapid development project (Smith and Reinertson, 1991). Time is crucial and should not be wasted on rework due to confusion over the project objective.

In general, people will perform to expectation if the performance system is appropriately managed. One of the critical elements of the performance system is information input to the performers. If you tell them what they need to do, frequently they will attempt to successfully do it. Therefore, it is reasonable to expect that performers will change their participation on the project team if they are informed that it is a rapid development project with a mission-critical completion date (Mager, 1992).

Incorporating rapid development into the project objective statement is one of the easiest means to ensure that the project team internalizes the project's time element. There are additional benefits to incorporating rapid development into the statement. Because management or the client must validate the project objective statement, they also validate the rapid development element. Also, wide distribution of the written objective ensures consistent communication to all participants in the project.

Some specific recommendations should be considered when using this approach to facilitate rapid development. Members of a project team may of necessity be geographically dispersed. If so, you may not be able to convene the team prior to beginning the project. But team support of the rapid development approach is critical, and because resources are prioritized as Accept in rapid development projects, the human resources must understand and support what they are going to be asked to do. Write a draft project objective statement, distribute it, then let the project team revise it to get team participation and support.

Be certain to give everyone (project team, management team, and support personnel) copies of the project objective to post in their cubicles. This will serve as a reminder of the critical nature of the performance improvement project and the importance that time plays in its successful implementation.

Review the project statement at each project review or staff meeting. This will ensure that the focus of the meeting remains on track and again reinforces the time element as a major consideration.

Evaluate all project decisions to ascertain if they support the objective statement. Over time, most projects suffer from an interesting condition (Hertz and Thomas, 1983): it has many names, but the most descriptive is "creeping elegance." As time goes on and innovative minds continue to work, new features or components continue to be added to the performance improvement solution. This is not necessarily because they must, but because they can. These enhancements will almost always require additional time or resources or both. Creeping elegance is a serious threat to rapid development. Review all decisions relative to the objective; is the enhancement absolutely necessary to achieve the performance objective? Can you still achieve the rapid development goal? In asking these questions, many enhancements will move to a "wait" status. A second performance improvement project may be created in which the postponed solutions can be used.

Simultaneous Development

The purpose of simultaneous development is to break the paradigm of sequential development by finding opportunities for parallel development. Who says that Chapter Two cannot be written at the same time as Chapter One? Certainly, sequential development of performance improvement solutions is the simplest to manage, but it is also the slowest method available.

To implement simultaneous development, search for development and implementation tasks that can be done at the same time to shorten total project cycle time. You will need to secure parallel resources to work on the simultaneous tasks; asking people to do two tasks at once at the same speed as they would have done one will usually not work.

Be sure you create a clear and compelling design that will keep parallel development teams on track and able to understand how their pieces fit into the whole. Otherwise, you could lose the time you gain by having to rework pieces so that they work together.

Assess risks and lay out contingency plans to stay on track. The opportunity for things to go wrong while in simultaneous development is greater than in sequential development, and there is a greater chance of simultaneous need for scarce resources or equipment. The risk of schedule slippage is also higher should items be left off the schedule or if estimates of task duration are too optimistic.

It is important that you not attempt to create a simultaneous development scenario by yourself. Look to development team members for creative methods or opportunities for simultaneous development activities. This will also increase their ownership of the plan and their desire to make it successful.

Leverage and Reuse

If time is of the essence, then project teams should always be willing to look for opportunities to accelerate the process. One of the best means for creating rapid development is the practice of leverage or reuse (Gilbreath, 1986).

Most instructional design models include an analysis of whether existing materials can be used rather than creating new ones. This is usually classified as reuse, as you are using some materials again on a different population. It is important to consider reuse in the area of noninstructional performance improvement solutions as well.

In some cases, a solution is available but not acceptable in its current form. Only parts of the existing solution may be useful or applicable. Taking those parts and building upon them is classified as leveraging (Gilbreath, 1986). It does not accelerate the process as quickly as reuse, but it is better than creating the performance improvement solution from scratch.

A significant organizational barrier usually stands in the way of reuse and leverage. You will need to address this fully before the performance improvement project team will embrace leverage and reuse as a tactic. The barrier is that many organizations reward behavior rather than accomplishment (Gilbert, 1978). The reward and recognition system will typically reward people who work hard and produce something. An employee who finds a product that can be reused (saving extensive time from the project schedule) is usually not recognized as positively as the employee who creates something from scratch.

It is difficult to ask employees to use a development approach that will lower their evaluated performance and reduce their pay-increase potential. To overcome this, work with the management team to ensure that the recognition and reward criteria are linked to leveraging existing materials and solutions, not creating everything. Do not underestimate the enormity of this task. The practice of rewarding behavior rather than accomplishment is usually ingrained in the culture and resistant to change.

The Right People

Having the right people working on the performance improvement project can mean the difference between achieving rapid development or not (Lewis, 1993b). If you were the project manager on a rapid development project, would you prefer a staff composed of new college hires who cannot even operate the phone system yet? Of course not. You would want individuals with experience across several projects who are masters of their profession. Rapid development requires that tasks are completed in the shortest possible time.

You will probably need to work with the management team or client to secure the resources. They may hesitate; if so, pull out the project objective statement and the project priority matrix. Remind them of the rapid development objective and the fact that resources are prioritized as accepted on this project. If they are still hesitant, it may indicate that the project is not as critical as once thought. Offer them the opportunity to change the priorities by moving either scope or time down in priority relative to resource. This will either cause them to formally change the priorities or revalidate their accuracy. If the priorities have changed, you will not need the specific resources. If the priorities have not changed, the resources must be made available.

Following are several approaches to consider in securing the right people to participate on the performance improvement project (Lewis, 1993b):

•   Examine previous projects similar to yours and determine who worked on them. Talk to the participants to assess the skills and competencies that were required for the projects' success. Take a learning organization or historical approach to identifying necessary competencies, skills, knowledge, and abilities.

•   Recruit the people with the appropriate and necessary competencies to meet your project goals, especially the goal of rapid development. Once you have a profile of the participants you need, begin the recruitment and selection process. Have a clear project definition, and implement some of the other rapid development issues such as senior management support and visible recognition. Top performers will normally accept the opportunity to work on a critical performance improvement project that is well managed and offers appropriate recognition.

•   Identify the participants you want, then work creatively to secure their participation. Though top performers will normally accept the chance to participate in well-run critical projects, they can be difficult to acquire because others do not want to let them go. Rather than attempting to use power to extract them from their current assignment, find out what is needed to secure their participation. Consider the example of a project manager who traded two new hires and a high-speed computer to another manager for a top performer. Both managers saw it as a win-win solution and were successful with their projects.

•   If needed competencies are lacking (they may not exist in the organization), establish a plan to acquire additional resources to compensate for team deficiencies. These resources do not need to be engaged with the project full time or for the entire duration of the project. As you create the detailed schedule for the project, determine exactly when they will be needed and secure their participation to fulfill the need.

• Inform the senior-level management team about who you need to achieve the rapid development time. In many cases, you will need this team's support or permission to achieve the necessary project staffing changes. Whenever you can, involve the management team in supporting the project. Their visible support plays an important role that will be discussed in the next chapter.

• Look at personalities early and continue to monitor their status through the project. Take steps to keep personality conflicts and politics to a minimum. Putting a group of top performers on a project can have drawbacks; they may be accustomed to being project stars and may seek excessive control, visibility, or recognition. The effect on the project could be detrimental. Watch for dysfunctional relationships, and seek to build teamwork and collaboration whenever possible. Ensure that there is sufficient visibility and recognition to go around. If there is a personnel or human resources department within the organization, you may want to solicit its support in analyzing and solving personality and communication problems.

The Right Resources

Having the right resources available can be almost as important as having the right people. As people work within a performance system, barriers to performance can arise even for top performers. Frequently, the performance barriers are resources that would maximize individual and team performance (Stalk, 1990).

The resources can take many different forms. They can be as varied as a new computer resource to speed production, secretary time, money for contractors or to purchase materials for leverage and reuse, space in which to operate, or various equipment.

But what are the right resources to maximize project success? You might possess some insight into this as the project manager, but the project team will frequently have a richer, more detailed understanding of the resources they will need to achieve rapid development. Be certain that you ask them, and indicate your willingness to consider resource requests during the performance improvement project as well.

Consider the example of a performance technologist who was working on a hot project and looking for methods to speed the performance analysis process. She informed her project manager that she could cut the performer interview time in half if the interviews were recorded and sent out for transcription. Her project manager looked at the cost and determined that it had a return on investment of about a hundred to one—a good investment in any case, but particularly for the rapid development emphasis. Her project manager would not have thought of the solution, but she did. As a human performance technologist, you may want to consider implementing a performance analysis on the project team to determine the barriers (resource and otherwise) to the desired performance of rapid development.

As when obtaining the right people, you will most likely need to secure the approval of the management team or client to secure the necessary resources. And as with the people resources, you may encounter hesitancy; to counter it, use the same method as for clarifying the project priorities.

Senior Management Support

As previously mentioned, a rapid development project requires substantial resources and support to be successful. Some of the resource requests may be more substantial than the authority level of the manager or client who initiated the project. If so, you will need senior manager support for the project. In any case, you will want senior manager sponsorship to speed decisions and reinforce the critical nature of the performance improvement project. Following are some specific practices for aligning management support with the rapid development project:

- Have an upper-level manager as an active sponsor of your project for achieving rapid development time. Achieving this sponsorship is covered in detail in the next chapter.
- Ensure that one or more key upper-level managers are included as part of your project team to continually emphasize support for rapid development.
- Involve upper management in the validation process for the project objectives and the business fit for rapid development.
- Advocate and expect a rapid response by upper-level management to needs (resources, recognition, and removing barriers) that support rapid development.
- As project manager, have project participants list the barriers to completing the next project milestone. Senior management needs to support the project manager in removing these barriers.
- Ensure that the capacity of the project team is not being drained by activities or requirements that do not contribute to the project or rapid development. Use the project activity list (Figure 2.1) as a tool for identifying and removing distracting activities.

FIGURE 2.1. SAMPLE PROJECT ACTIVITY LIST.

Project Activity List

Directions: List all of the activities that you are currently involved in each week. Circle those activities that do not contribute to the rapid development project that you are working on. Return this list to your manager.

_____

_____

_____

_____

_____

_____

_____

The project activity list is a simple method for identifying distracting activities that do not advance the performance improvement project. Have project participants list how they spend their time and indicate which activities do not contribute to rapid development. As the project manager, you will need to work with management to relieve participants of tasks that do not add value to the rapid development project. Be cautious; some organizations hold status reports and staff meetings as culturally sacred. You may need to help the organization deal with the necessary changes.

Co-location

To enhance rapid development, project members should be co-located—that is, work in proximity to one another (Lewis, 1993b). Communication between project members is important as tasks and project components are passed from one project team member to another. Some project components may be developed jointly, in which case communications are even more crucial to productivity. Having project members spread across buildings, sites, states, and countries does not enhance the rapid development of the project.

In some cases co-location may not be practicable. If start-to-finish co-location is not possible, key members should co-locate during strategic periods of the project and then return to their normal locations. Alternate communication methods should be explored to increase communication productivity when members are not co-located.

FIGURE 2.2. EFFECT OF DISTANCE ON COMMUNICATION FREQUENCY.

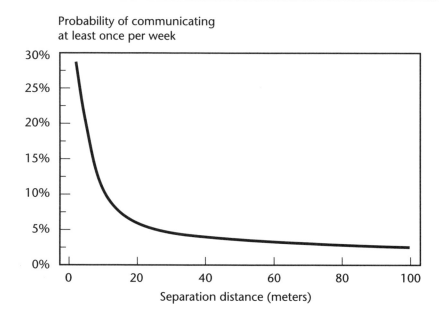

Experts on rapid development agree that project team members should sit together (co-locate). Figure 2.2 reflects the results of a study on co-location by Thomas Allen of the Massachusetts Institute of Technology. Allen measured the frequency of communication of 512 individuals in seven organizations over six months and developed an analytic relationship between communication and distance. As the results indicate, team members must be located close together (definitely closer than ten meters) to communicate effectively (Smith and Reinertson, 1991). This is particularly important if simultaneous development is being employed in the project and communication to keep the project components aligned is of great importance.

Frozen Design Documentation

Few people can hit a moving target, particularly if the motion is erratic. The same holds true for a performance improvement project team. If the project design changes, it creates rework of previously completed tasks and stalls progress as the changes are assessed and incorporated into the project plans (Lewis, 1993b). Neither of these enhance a rapid development approach.

The management team or the client needs a frozen design mentality. If it is perceived that the design is open to change or enhancement at any time, changes will occur frequently. The design should be considered set and open to change only when it can be demonstrated as absolutely necessary to project success, and even then only when approval can be gained from the top sponsoring manager (who should understand the time consequences of the change).

Why do changes to the project definition occur after the project has begun? What is the root cause of the behavior? It stems from the old myth that making changes to a project is permissible, costs nothing, and is a management prerogative. As the project manager, you must challenge myth with fact. The fact is that changes become exorbitantly costlier the later in a project that they are made (Kerzner, 1989).

Consider the example of change occurring during the creation of a new car. How much does a change cost while in computer design? Very little. How much once the models are created? Significantly more. After prototypes are built and tested? Substantially more. Few things are as important to a project's success as up-front planning to conceive the product correctly, validate its accuracy, and prevent later changes.

The following are key points to consider in freezing the performance improvement design:

- Rapid development requires freezing the definition before beginning the project. Only minimal changes can happen if you are to accomplish a rapid development goal.
- Project documentation must be complete for the project team to use it to guide quick decision making and rapid design efforts.
- Some suggestions for change cannot be dismissed. Ensure that the management team or client has a full appreciation of the change impact on project time.
- Create a stringent change management process to ensure that changes do not work their way into the project without specific consideration and approval.

Dogmatic Milestone Tracking

As transportation methods have changed over the years, appreciation for the term *milestone* has been lost. In the days when horse or foot were the only transportation, maps were generally not available. Road builders erected stone markers that indicated a mile of progress along the route. This allowed travelers to adjust their pace to achieve their destinations on time.

Project managers still use milestones, with a new definition, in the same manner. By this definition, milestones are events that mark a unit of progress on the overall schedule. They may be events such as "unit one completed," "manual sent to printers," or "final sign-off." These milestones indicate progress along the project route so that participants can judge if they will complete the journey on time.

For a rapid development project, the progress on milestone completion must be tracked and met with precision (Stalk, 1990). If the development team is moving slower than necessary, it is important to know that early, while corrective action can still be taken to meet the rapid development goal.

Specific practices in tracking and managing milestones include the following:

- Make the first milestone very visible to participants and sponsors. Ensure that everybody concerned recognizes the importance of meeting the milestone if the project is to be completed with its rapid development objective.
- Make milestones no more than two weeks apart. If you wait longer to assess progress, you may be too late to take effective corrective action. If you need to create milestones to assess progress more frequently, do so. Milestones do not cost anything and can help prevent serious delivery slippage.
- Assign each milestone a deliverable with metrics. Whenever possible, make the milestone tangible and measurable. This will ensure that the milestone has actually been accomplished and can be demonstrated as such. It is too difficult and risky to judge the progress of a rapid development project on intangible milestones.
- Collect status frequently on all critical-path project tasks, including soft data as well as task completion information. You need to know as soon as possible if the schedule is slipping. You will want to keep all project reporting data current and visible to the project team; it may make the necessary corrections without managerial intervention.
- Highlight all significant schedule variances and publish plans to address their root causes. As a human performance technologist, you will be expected to take a systems approach to resolving schedule problems. Look for the real cause of the slippage and resolve it. Fixing schedule variance symptoms will only allow the problem to resurface later, when there is less time available to correct it.
- Be able to tell the management team who is the critical member working on the next milestone at any time. This allows the managers to lend encouragement, support, and recognition to the important task within the organization.

Visible Recognition

Why would anybody want to work on a performance improvement project with a rapid development focus? It certainly does not sound very appealing. There is the potential for long work days; pressure to stay on schedule is significant; progress and deliverables are scrutinized by the management team. This does not sound like a fun adventure. The participants in a rapid development project will require additional recognition and appreciation to remain personally motivated through the rapid development project (Lewis, 1993b).

Recognition can take many forms, but on a rapid development project it should always be visible. You want to create a feeling of prestige among those working on the project. Recognition need not be elaborate or expensive, but it does need to be valued by the team members, visible to the organization, and sincere. It will generally be ineffective if it does not meet all three criteria (Kouzes and Posner, 1988).

Consider this example of how the manager of a hot project with a rapid (almost unrealistic) development focus provided recognition to the team. The manager arranged for the general manager of the business unit to drop by weekly with a six-pack of soda. This manager, four levels higher in the organization than the project team members, dropped by for fifteen minutes to check the team's progress. It was a short time of conversation and encouragement during a break, it cost next to nothing (even including the time spent by the general manager, who appreciated the opportunity to fulfill the role), and the project team thrived on the attention and recognition.

Use your creativity to generate easy and effective recognition. Ask other project managers what they have done, and begin to develop a list of ideas that work consistently with your style and approach. Remember: the recognition must be sincere. If it is contrived it will not be effective. Here is a short list to give your creativity a kick start:

- Have a large sign made that states the project name and hang it over the project group.
- Have special T-shirts or polo shirts made that feature the project team's logo, motto, or other form of identity.
- If there is an internal organization publication, get the team's photo on the cover and a story inside.
- Place signs around areas where the project is being carried out, such as: "Do not disturb: critical project in progress."
- Plan high-ranking manager drop-ins (these need to be carefully managed).
- Arrange special parking places to be designated for team members.
- Plan lunch meetings (for which the organization supplies the meal) for the team.

Karen's Story

Karen was nervous as she sat in the chair by Jim's desk. It seemed that every time she sat in this chair she got bad news. She was sure Jim was going to give her another tough challenge; he had that look about him.

Jim fumbled with some papers. "Karen, I have some bad news. We just found out that the Inventor's Convention is going to be held early this year. As you know, all the inventors will want their working products finished in time to display at the show. Unless we can guarantee that their products will be ready, they'll take their business to our competitors. The only way we can make that guarantee is by implementing the performance improvement solutions earlier than we planned."

Karen asked, "How much earlier?"

"Well . . . three months."

"What? Please tell me you're not serious!"

"Very serious, I'm afraid," said Jim. "Take some time to think about it and come back with a new plan when you're ready."

Karen discussed the situation with the project team. Together they devised a new plan and Karen went back to Jim's office to present it. "You asked for a plan to remove three months from the project," she said. "The project team and I worked out a solution we believe will work."

"I'm all ears," Jim said. "What have you got?"

"To begin with, we believe we can save substantial time by employing some simultaneous development. Right now, activities are laid out sequentially on the schedule. But we could do several at the same time and still maintain schedule integrity. It will require adding a second development team of three people to the project for six weeks."

Jim jumped right in. "Karen, you know we don't have any available resources in the company right now. I even checked with the East Coast operation. They're tied up in some hot project too."

Karen was ready. "Unless the priorities have changed, we agreed that whatever resources were needed would be accepted. We need the people if we're going to meet the schedule. There's one alternative. We can put all the simple work on the second team and hire some instructional design consultants. All it takes is money."

Jim thought for a minute. "Well, I stand a much better chance of getting money than people. I'll work it out with my boss. What else do you have?"

"Well, Jim, while we're talking money . . . we need more. We were planning on creating the training for the new milling machines. The existing training course doesn't fully meet our needs, but if we buy it and leverage from it, we think we can save three weeks on the schedule."

"That's not a bad idea," said Jim. "If I remember correctly, the course isn't that expensive, it just doesn't cover all the areas. But we can deal with that. What else do you have up your sleeve?"

"Another resource request," Karen said. "I want to trade project members with another group in your organization. Kevin is very new. If we are to achieve this rapid development, I really need somebody who can turn out the video project quickly. I'd like to trade him for Bob. He's the right person for a critical, time-sensitive job."

"Ouch," replied Jim. "That's not going to go over very well. But you're right. Kevin would never survive the productivity expectations. We'd probably be setting him up for failure. Anything more?"

"Quite a few more things, Jim, and all of them require your support. We're going to be asking these folks to put in some extra time and effort. They need to feel supported and recognized. I thought carefully about this, and I know the company is under heavy cost pressure, so I ruled out expensive alternatives. What I want for the team costs very little. It would be valuable to have some strong senior management support for this project. I'd like to see the team receive a short visit from your boss once a week and from the operations manager once a month. We could keep them up to date, and the team would sense the importance of the performance improvement project. The team also said it would like to celebrate the completion of each two-week milestone. Nothing elaborate—just pizza and a little bit of your time."

Jim thought about it and said, "I suppose I could do that. I like not appearing to throw money around on recognition. But you mentioned having other issues."

"Just one more, but it's vital. We need to freeze the project description. I know this project is very important and very visible, but we can't make rapid progress if the objective keeps changing. We need to get agreement from the entire management team and freeze the description. If we don't, I guarantee we'll miss our objective and miss the Inventor's Convention."

Jim said, "Karen, I have to tell you. This is a tough set of recommendations. We're really asking for a lot from the organization. But the organization is asking a lot from us. We agreed to accept the resources necessary to pull this off. I'll start selling this up the management chain. You start putting the wheels in motion."

CHAPTER THREE

OBTAINING PROJECT SPONSORSHIP

The outcomes of human performance technology (HPT) projects are different from those of other projects that need to be managed. In a research and development lab, for example, the typical project results in a new product that increases the company's ability to earn money; most employees would be positively influenced by the new product introduction. In a civil engineering project, the result might be the installation of a new bridge to provide a more convenient transportation system. But in HPT, the result is people changing their work performance. Quite often, people resist and even dislike having to change.

Bill's Story

It was Friday afternoon, the time when Bill took a few minutes to review the events of the week and plan his course of action for Monday. Unfortunately, it looked like he was going to spend some time during the weekend attempting to fix some of the problems that had come up during the week—problems he had never expected to occur. Each was different, yet somehow they seemed to be related.

The first problem was really a surprise. Bill was informed that the East Coast operations manager supported the performance improvement project, but business was business. It was not clear that the project was going to have the funds and people necessary for successful implementation. This was so confusing. How could the operations manager be so enthusiastic one week and so conservative the next? Would support erode even further next week?

Then there was the little incident down in the engineering group. Bill had called a meeting to discuss reengineering the specification process. Like any good human performance technologist, he wanted the target performers involved in the design process to ensure that the new process met their needs. Bill gathered the top performers in the specification group to lay out the new process design for input and modification. Bill was more than surprised when the product producers said they didn't want the specification process changed. The top performers were especially vocal. Bill was politely asked, "Who are you to tell us how to do our job?"

Engineering was not the only source of rebellious discontent. The production manager had announced that the milling function would be changing to computer-controlled milling machines, but the first-level supervisors and the millers seemed to have different ideas. They were doing everything possible to prevent progress. Bill was stumped. The production manager was three levels up in the organization; how could they disobey her?

Matters had become worse on Thursday afternoon. The personnel manager came storming into Bill's work area. He was clearly not a happy camper. He had just seen the recommendation for the new reward and compensation system design. Although the design was technically excellent, it had one minor problem: it would never be accepted at NewIdea. The company had a certain way of doing things, commonly referred to as the "NewIdea Way." The recommended system violated several widely held company values. The personnel manager vowed to block the recommendation and see it killed.

It was not a great week. Bill was frustrated. Why had things fallen apart?

The Purpose of Sponsorship in HPT Projects

People prefer constancy, permanence, and tradition (Stewart, 1991), but the human performance technologist suggests new ways to do things. Often, resistance is the first reaction to proposed changes. Because of it, performance improvement projects may fail during implementation. The employee who refuses to adopt the new performance required to make an intervention successful may have the attitude, "I don't have to do this new thing, and you can't make me."

In addition to not being able to force people to change their performance, most human performance technologists do not have the authority to make large financial expenditures or to change people's work or job assignments to accomplish project goals. However, it may be impossible to successfully implement a particular project without spending fairly large sums of money or moving people around.

If you are a human performance technologist responsible for managing a performance improvement project, you need support in the form of resources as your project is progressing. You will also need support for the consequences of implementation. Sponsorship is all about providing resources and consequence support for a project.

Roles in Performance Improvement Projects

When assigning roles to the people who work on a performance improvement project, you will find that they generally do not follow a straight line up or down an organization chart. As people work together on a project, their interactions and relationships may have many complex or even convoluted twists and turns, with some people taking on more than one role and others shifting roles as the project progresses (Kissler, 1991).

To satisfy their client's goals, human performance technologists must understand and carefully make use of the key roles that are played in performance improvement projects. Adapting to the various possible configurations of these roles and orchestrating role assignments is necessary for implementing a project successfully.

Four distinct roles are essential: sponsors, human performance technologists, performance improvement targets, and advocates (Kissler, 1991).

Sponsors

A sponsor is an individual or a group with the power to decide whether the project is undertaken or not. During the life of the project, they can also decide when or whether to terminate it. In deciding whether a project will be launched, good sponsors make decisions based on the potential for improvement to come from the project, the possible dangers of change, and the opportunities that might be lost if the project is not undertaken. Sponsors are responsible for determining which goals will be targeted, supporting changes that will enable the accomplishment of those goals, communicating changes and priorities to the organization, and providing the proper support and rewards to enable success. Without the sponsor's support, the environment will not be supportive enough for the changes required by the project to be made on time and within budget.

Human Performance Technologists

A human performance technologist is responsible for actually making the performance change occur. The human performance technologist's success depends on the ability to diagnose potential implementation problems, develop a plan to deal with them, and implement the project effectively. The participation of human performance technologists who possess these skills is a crucial factor in the success of any performance improvement project.

Performance Improvement Targets

Targets are those people who, during the course of the project, will actually change their performance. The term *target* was chosen because these people are the focus of the performance improvement effort. Because they are the ones whose performance will change, they are crucial to the short- and long-term success of the project. During the course of the project, targets should have the opportunity to learn what changes are expected from them and they should also be involved, as appropriate, in the implementation process.

Advocates

Advocates are individuals or groups who do not have the power themselves to initiate or sustain a performance change, but who do recommend that the change occur. When ideas for saving time or money or increasing productivity are championed by strong advocates, they may be able to win support for performance change projects. Without strong advocates who have the skills to win support for projects, even great recommendations for change may never achieve approval or sponsorship.

Relationships of the Roles

The relationships of roles in an organization take one of two basic forms: triangular or square. Either, depending on how they are managed, can add to or detract from the success of an organization (Kline and Saunders, 1993).

The triangular relationship can be complicated and may sometimes be less than effective. In the example illustrated in Figure 3.1, the human performance technologist and the performance improvement target both report to the sponsor.

FIGURE 3.1. THE TRIANGULAR RELATIONSHIP.

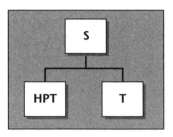

Often, sponsors are senior managers or executives, targets are line managers and their employees, and human performance technologists work in a staff organization (such as human resources or training and development). Many other kinds of triangles exist in organizations in addition to the line-staff relationships, but these are often the kinds of organizations where the performance technologist works.

According to research findings, many organizations with triangular relationships have found them to be less effective than they should be about 80 percent of the time (Kissler, 1991). The cause of this poor performance is from well-meaning but misguided attempts at delegation. If sponsors try to delegate their power for approving changes directly to the human performance technologist, the targets may not accept their implementation—the human performance technologist may not have sufficient influence with the targets for the desired changes to be initiated.

When human performance technologists attempt to tell performance improvement targets who don't report to them what to do, their efforts almost always fail (Stewart, 1991). In the case of small adjustments to performance, there may be some success with this approach; however, it almost never works for major changes. When performance improvement staff members try to initiate major changes that must be carried out by the line organization, it usually appears inappropriate to line managers, so they ignore it. This generates much of the conflict we often see between line and staff functions today.

This conflict is not because the human performance technologist has done something wrong, but because the dynamics of the situation make it inevitable. When sponsors expect their performance improvement managers or technologists to tell their peers how to run their business, problems naturally occur. For example, they may expect the human performance technologist to tell other managers to use a new compensation system or a new selection procedure for hiring employees. In effect, the sponsor wants the human performance technologist to exert influence over people who report to someone else. This is tantamount to saying, "Your job is to tell your peers what to do." And when the line managers resist, the human performance technologist appears to not be getting the job done.

Triangular structures by themselves are not the cause of the difficulty. These relationships naturally occur in many organizations and are not necessarily dysfunctional, but they become a problem when people do not realize how to optimize the dynamics present in them. For the sponsor and technologist roles in the relationship, following certain guidelines will help to ensure successful undertakings. What follows is some advice for people engaging in each of those roles:

- *Sponsor.* You must make it clear before the project begins that you support the change. This means that the targets must receive the endorsement directly from you, not relayed through from the human performance technologist. Your employees will be more liable to commit their efforts and do their part to make change happen when they realize you are behind it.
- *Human performance technologist.* If you are asked to tell people who do not report to you what to do, you must persuade the sponsor to deliver a request for cooperation and convey support for the project before you begin to help facilitate the change. Then you will be assisting the targets to carry out their manager's wishes, instead of telling them what to do.

Square structures are illustrated in Figure 3.2. In this example, the human performance technologists report to one sponsor and the performance improvement targets to another.

As is the case with triangular relationships, square relationships are also dysfunctional in most organizations (Kissler, 1991). This dysfunctionality often occurs when the human performance technologist's manager (Sponsor One) expects

FIGURE 3.2. THE SQUARE RELATIONSHIP.

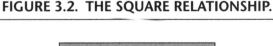

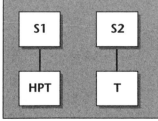

her to tell the targets, who report to someone else entirely (Sponsor Two), what to do. Typically, people asked to make a major change by someone in another organization will not comply unless the directive also comes from their own manager, who is usually primarily responsible for their assignments—and their rewards.

In this formation, neither Sponsor One nor the human performance technologist are in a position to tell the targets what to do. Instead, they fill the role of advocates. Trying to influence the targets directly will usually fail because the targets will not see their sponsor as supportive of the change. If, for example, the director of learning and development asks one of his human performance technologists to go to the firm's customer service manager and insist on a new procedure for implementing feedback in the organization, this will probably result in incomplete compliance at best, if not outright refusal to change the status quo. A much more likely formula for success would be for the director of learning and development to persuade the director of sales and customer service that the new feedback system would meet their department's goals and then let her request her employees to make the change.

The Important Role of Sponsorship

Each of the four roles described for performance improvement projects are required for success, but the sponsor's role is crucial. Without the sponsor's demonstrated commitment, large-scale changes in performance will not succeed (Kline and Saunders, 1993). Sometimes people confuse advocating change with sponsoring change. They are not the same thing. Just because someone is emphatic about the need for a particular performance improvement to occur does not mean that he has any authority or power with the target population. An advocate can be anyone who convincingly suggests and communicates the need for a particular change. But a sponsor needs more than the right words. The sponsor must also have the authority and the desire to provide the appropriate direction, support, and rewards to ensure that the project will be completed successfully.

If an advocate for a change is faced with a sponsor who does not support a project, there are essentially three choices: convince the sponsor that the change is important, find a way to change sponsors, or be resigned to participating in a performance-improvement project that will fail (Kissler, 1991). The importance of the sponsor's role cannot be overemphasized. When in a situation without adequate sponsorship, the advocate must get the sponsor to provide the necessary support, replace the sponsor, or give up on the success of the project.

A sponsor must provide sufficient energy and resources to a major performance improvement project or it will not progress much beyond being a good idea. Commitment from a sponsor includes attention and action where required. If the performance improvement project is perceived by the sponsor as being truly needed by the business, a serious commitment to its success is much more likely. To sustain that commitment, the sponsor must expect and support the changes that will occur in the organization, both during the project's implementation and over the long term. In addition, the sponsor should be able to understand how the targets will feel during and after the change.

During its implementation, a performance improvement project requires time, money, expertise, and other resources. A sponsor must be aware of what these resources are and champion their use publicly to the target population. In private, with key stakeholders and influential people within the organization, the sponsor must communicate resolve to ensure that the change succeeds. In addition to communicating support, the sponsor must provide rewards for those members of the target population who support the change and establish consequences for those who do not.

Besides the stated support and direction for the performance improvement project, a sponsor shows seriousness about the success of the effort by staying informed of the progress the project is making. This could be in the form of a visible tracking system that shows the status of the project. A savvy sponsor should also know that changes have personal, political, and organizational costs, and should anticipate and be willing to pay them. The sponsor's commitment to the project must also mean not abandoning or suboptimizing it for the sake of another good idea that comes along in the meantime. If, during implementation of the project, other changes come to the sponsor's attention that seem like good opportunities, they should not be attempted if they will cause the current project not to meet its goals. Finally, a sponsor must engage in follow-up activities to ensure the success of the project.

The following list outlines the qualities to look for in good sponsors:

- They feel the need for change; they have a dissatisfaction with the status quo that makes the effort to change the situation more attractive than business as usual.
- They have vision—a clear, compelling, and well-articulated picture of the desired performance.
- They have a perspective on the future—a clear and complete realization of the effect the performance changes will have on the organization.
- They are capable of making a realistic appraisal of resources; they have a complete understanding of the time, money, and people required to make and sustain the performance change as well as the ability and willingness to commit them to the effort.

- They have empathy—the capacity to anticipate, respect, and be sensitive to the thoughts and feelings raised in the target population by the change as it progresses.
- They possess sensitivity to scope, realizing how broadly the effects of the change will be felt in the organization and having a sense of who will be affected by the performance change.
- They have power within the organization—the authority and influence to initiate and sustain the performance change with the target population.
- They are publicly supportive—willing to provide visible, strong organizational commitment to the performance improvement project.
- They are privately supportive—willing to make opportunities, as necessary, to express strong support for the performance improvement project in private meetings with key stakeholders.
- They can manage consequences. They are ready to support those who assist in the change effort with rewards and to provide negative consequences for those who do not.
- They follow the progress of programs and will direct the installation of monitoring procedures to track it and identify problem areas that need to be addressed.
- They are willing to pay the price. They realize there will be costs associated with the performance improvement, but are willing to stay committed to the project and make the necessary sacrifices.
- They are consistent, demonstrating persistent support for the project and rejecting short-term actions that do not further the long-term performance improvement goals.

Obviously, the demands of being a successful sponsor mean that no one can sponsor more than a few major performance improvement projects at a time. Ineffective sponsors often engage in far too many performance improvement initiatives, draining their time and energy to the point of being unable to adequately perform their sponsorship duties.

Sustaining the Performance Improvement Effort

There are two ways to approach performance improvement efforts: simply initiate the change and watch to see what happens, or engage in a process that will require persistence. Getting started, just initiating a performance change, takes very little commitment. Every day, managers who do not realize what is required to sustain a performance improvement project send messages, talk about changes, or make pronouncements about changes they would like to see occur. But this is an ineffective way to accomplish real improvements. Maintaining a performance change effort over time presents a challenge and requires a good deal of invested effort. A critical attribute of those who are successful at implementing performance improvements is their persistence. Building commitment for a performance improvement project requires a systematic, step-by-step process. Without this kind of attention, you can have the best ideas for improving performance but they will almost never be carried out.

A prerequisite for committing to performance change is the recognition that the cost of current performance is significantly higher than the cost of change (Lewis, 1993b; Gilbert, 1978). The easiest part of the entire process usually is convincing the organization that an improvement should be made. Getting started on the improvement is also relatively easy. The difficulty comes when the project hits a snag, becomes costly, inhibits some long-cherished way of doing things, or in some other way causes problems. This is when real skill comes into play.

Initiating sponsors are people with the power and influence to authorize major effort. Often, they are quite high in the organization's hierarchy and are typically not the direct managers of the target population. Once a performance improvement project has been initiated, a sustaining sponsor is required. The sustaining sponsor is generally lower in the management hierarchy and close enough to the targets to help provide focus on and motivation to achieve the performance improvement goals.

Once a change initiative is launched, if the initiating sponsor assumes that it will develop a momentum of its own and proceed to completion without his or her continual guidance, the change effort is doomed. To ensure success, the initiating sponsor must identify and recruit sustaining sponsors to support and monitor the change at the correct levels in the organization.

It may seem surprising or unlikely that an executive could launch a performance change directive and then have it be ignored. Actually, this occurs with great regularity in most organizations.

For example, let's say the initiating sponsor of a performance change is a corporate CEO. He has a videotape made for employees in which he announces the firm's new focus on customer service and outlines the changes in the performance he desires from them. Once the video is shown, local managers say something like, "Oh, never mind, he can't be that serious about this, and we don't have time for it anyway." Even the best idea or the best-designed intervention cannot be implemented in a climate where the target's managers do not support the change.

Great-sounding changes, no matter how strategically apt or how good the rhetoric, cannot compete with local consequences. Employees will be more attuned to what they are rewarded for than to great ideas from on high. When senior management touts great ideas to employees in speeches but fails to align them with positive and negative impacts from their own managers, then the ideas fall into a kind of never-never land.

Black Holes in the Organization

In his landmark book *Managing at the Speed of Change,* Daryl Conner (1992) identified this never-never land phenomenon as a "black hole." In astrophysics the term describes an area in space where the gravity is so strong that it pulls even light into it. It is instructive to realize that black holes can exist, at least metaphorically, in the corporate world. When management pronouncements about performance improvement initiatives are released into the organization and then exert no visible influence, you might say that they have vanished into a corporate black hole.

Part of this effect occurs when managers at different levels in the hierarchy release only part of the information required to allow a change to occur, or distort some aspect of the performance improvement initiative. This keeps the information from getting to the target population in a form that will enable action. Somehow the life of the initiative has succumbed to the gravity in the corporate black hole. When the right information does not get to the people who need it, then of course the performance improvement implementation will not succeed.

To implement a performance improvement project successfully, all the roles are important, but especially the sponsor's (Hertz and Howard, 1983). The role the sponsor plays must be clear, not confused. Sponsor support and follow-through are essential elements of a successful change effort.

Many costs are associated with the failure of a performance improvement project. One of the most devastating is what happens when management initiatives are repeatedly disregarded: erosion of employee confidence in leadership. When executives or managers make announcements about changes that do not happen, employees will come to think of management's strategic ideas as empty words resulting in no real action. If this happens often enough, sponsors wanting to initiate performance improvement projects will have no credibility within the organization, and the reputation of human performance technology to achieve results will be irreparably damaged. This will doom further attempts to implement performance improvement projects within the organization.

Black holes are born when managers who should be acting as supporting sponsors do not do the job well—when they should, but do not, make sure their employees are implementing the new performance improvements. There are a number of reasons why sponsorship is not forthcoming: confusion about what to do or say, outright (but usually secretive) sabotage, or lack of rewards or pressures tied directly to the new performance. The supporting sponsor role must be filled with someone who demonstrates a strong commitment to the change; otherwise very little if anything will be done by the targets to implement the change.

For example, suppose a company's director of customer service launches an initiative requiring customer service representatives to provide a comprehensive solution when customers call in with a problem. Of course, this will lengthen their contact with customers, which may result in more customer satisfaction, but it will also mean that the customer service representative's daily call rate will go down. If the daily call rate remains a measurement of success, the targets will not be inclined to implement the change.

The director of customer service, the initiating sponsor in this case, is not close enough to the targets to reinforce with them the necessity for making the change; she is removed from their day-to-day instructions, tasks, feedback, and rewards. If she does not ensure that the direct managers of the customer service representatives are supporting the effort with clear, sustained messages and tangible incentives, the change in performance will never occur. Whenever the target's incentives are not aligned with the initiating sponsor's strategic direction and requests for changes, the strategy will not be sustained.

When enough performance improvement initiatives fall into corporate black holes, employees begin to think of new suggestions as the "flavor of the month." If the sponsor does not ensure follow-through on their projects, their credibility will be questioned; employees will begin to wonder if they should pay attention to new initiatives when they are announced. If they truly begin to think of them as transient ideas that will blow over soon, they will automatically, after a while, disregard new directives for performance improvement projects. They will think, "Ah, they're not serious, anyway. I won't bother with this."

When managers and employees develop this kind of attitude, an organization's ability to make changes—to implement performance improvements—will be drastically reduced. Disregarding management directives will elongate the time an organization requires to respond to major performance changes. Communication will be incomplete or faulty and the desired performance improvements, if made, are likely to be later, less effective, and costlier than necessary. Without the ability to change swiftly, many organizations will find themselves too slow to be competitive.

When lack of follow-through becomes the order of the day, employees will continue with the status quo even when a major change is announced. They will consider the track record of change at their company and shrug off the new directives: "Ha! Last month was the Think Bold Campaign and before that the Dream Big vision thing. If we just pretend they never mentioned it, they'll forget this one, too."

Creating Sponsorship That Flows

There is a cure for the black-hole phenomenon. It requires creating sponsorship that flows, beginning with the initiating sponsor of the performance improvement and ending with the performance improvement target. To achieve a performance change, the initiating sponsor must ensure a flow of sustaining sponsorship from his office down through all levels of management to the people who must actually implement the changes. This network of sponsors must continually underscore its support for the change and its importance to the organization (Stewart, 1991). To make sure a performance improvement project will succeed, an initiating sponsor must begin by ensuring that the managers below him are committed to the project. They, in turn, must work with the managers below them. This process must continue to flow down through the organization until it reaches the target population.

When support for the project flows throughout an organization, the rewards and consequences for successful completion can be applied in a way that ensures achievement of the project's goals. Gaps in commitment between layers of the hierarchy in an organization can create logistical, budgetary, or political difficulties for the project. When there is alignment between the initiator's expressed support for a change effort and the intervening managers' actual support of the project, the black hole will disappear.

Here is an example of how human performance technology can help make sponsorship flow. To improve organizational performance in building error-free machines, the inspection process at one company needed to be modified to catch more defects. The vice president of manufacturing announced that the way all manufacturing employees interact with parts and assemblies would be improved. Because she was the initiating sponsor, the vice president met with her manufacturing directors to explain the new procedure. In this meeting, she considered them to be initial targets, realizing that their performance would be affected by the change; workers on the factory floor were the ultimate targets. She worked to counter any resistance the directors expressed. In the process, she explained their new roles and the new expectations of their organizations, as well as the new performance expected of each layer of the organization, including the target population. In the process, she gained their commitment, explaining how this change would align with their other responsibilities and how it related to the overall corporation's goals and vision. Last but not least, she detailed the rewards the directors would receive for implementing the change.

The manufacturing directors then initiated similar meetings with their own direct reports, who were managers of the various departments in their organization. As their vice president had done, the directors considered their managers to be targets of the performance improvement project, addressing their issues and then laying out their responsibilities as sustaining sponsors. These managers were then responsible for directing and supporting their supervisors or employees to make the required changes. In doing so, it was important for them to link the new performance to new incentives. Using this flow from initiating sponsor to sustaining sponsors to targets, performance improvement initiatives can move down through the organization with support and appropriate rewards at every level. This will go a long way toward ensuring that the project is fully implemented and sustained. For initiating as well as sustaining sponsors, a high level of commitment is required to achieve success.

Guidelines for Fulfilling the Roles

Black holes can exist between any two levels in the hierarchy of an organization; to eliminate them, each manager in the chain must demonstrate a commitment to the project.

Sponsors

Be sure not to take on more performance improvement efforts than you or those who report to you can sponsor. Failure to follow this edict probably will result in the desired changes not taking place. Also, you will suffer a loss of credibility and your employees will be less likely to take your leadership seriously in the future.

Human Performance Technologists

Learn to say no to projects that are doomed. Failure will result when those who should sponsor a project do not or cannot provide the authority or commitment to see the project through to completion. Although a doomed project (one without the appropriate sponsorship) may start off on a promising note, it will fail; it is just a question of when. When it does, it will be you, not the sponsor, who takes the blame.

If you take on a project and then discover that the sponsor has turned to other priorities and is not fulfilling her role, do not try to fill in the gap yourself. Trying to shore up her lack of sponsorship by your own activity may be tempting, but it will not work. When you contract with your sponsor to take on the performance improvement project in the first place, let her know what will be required of her for the project to succeed. If, during the course of the project, she does not take a direct role in sustaining the appropriate level of sponsorship, it may be that the project is not important enough to complete. Should you find yourself in this position, communicate with your sponsor to see if she will execute a stronger level of commitment. If she cannot adjust her priorities and provide sufficient sponsorship, delay or cancel the project.

Performance Improvement Targets

Before jumping to change your performance, make sure it is clear what is expected of you. You should also know how any reward systems that affect you have been adjusted to support the change. In addition, you should know who is sponsoring the change and whether they are committed to the performance improvement project.

Advocates

Remember that no matter how strongly you support the performance improvement effort, your support is not necessarily correlated with the project's ultimate success. A major performance improvement project will only be successful if it has appropriate and adequate sponsorship.

Key Skills in Managing Project Sponsorship

In order to excel at performance improvement project management, you should strive to master some specific abilities:

1. Understand and recognize the key roles in a change project.
2. Be familiar with the effective operation of triangular and square relationship configurations.
3. Understand the general requirements associated with strong sponsorship.
4. Recognize that a performance improvement project must be clearly and strongly sanctioned by those in the position of initiating and sustaining sponsorship.
5. Ensure that the rhetoric of change is consistent with meaningful consequences.

Organization Culture and Performance Improvement

An organization's culture must support the performance improvement you are recommending or your project will be extremely difficult, if not impossible, to implement. But there may be little similarity between the existing beliefs, behaviors, and assumptions of your organization and those required for your performance improvement project (Caisse and Posner, 1988).

When there is a wide discrepancy between your organization's current culture and the performance improvement you want to make, the changes you are working toward will probably not occur. But the more the current culture has in common with the beliefs, behaviors, and assumptions required by the new performance initiative, the more likely the project is to be successful.

If your performance improvement project does not clash with the current organizational culture, there will be little resistance to implementation from that front. However, if the change goes against the cultural grain, your project will be more difficult. Corporate cultures are extremely resistant to change. Making changes in a corporate culture requires major sustained and coordinated effort. When the culture of an organization does not support the desired change, you have three choices:

- Change the performance improvement solution so that it more closely matches the existing beliefs, behaviors, and assumptions of the culture.
- Launch an extremely well-supported cultural change effort, involving high levels of well-communicated and thoroughly sanctioned sponsorship. It will take a major effort to modify the beliefs, behaviors, and assumptions of the current culture.
- Expect your performance improvement project to fail.

The wider the gap between the culture and the requirements of the performance improvement project, the more sponsorship you will need. You must assess this gap between the culture and the new performance and determine, with your sponsors' input, whether they will be able to provide the level of support needed by the project. If not, it should be modified or abandoned. Otherwise, the change you are working toward will probably not happen.

Principles of Project Sponsorship Summarized

Without sponsorship, your performance improvement project will fail. For major performance improvements to occur, the appropriate sponsors must demonstrate what appears to the target population to be significant commitment with appropriate consequences.

Furthermore, the sponsorship must be strong for the project to succeed. If you find yourself with weak sponsors, they must learn to take the reins, secure resources, and fill their sponsorship role. In cases where they cannot or will not do this, they must be replaced if possible. If education does not help and replacement is impossible, you will not be able to successfully complete the project.

Human performance technologists cannot be sponsors. Only those who have the legitimate authority and influence to secure major changes can be sponsors. Human performance technologists can be responsible for designing and implementing performance improvement projects, but they do not have sufficient authority to act as sponsors.

Initiating and sustaining sponsorship are not interchangeable. To initiate a performance improvement process, the sponsor must have broad organizational power. To function in a sustaining role, the sponsor must have direct influence over the logistics, economics, and political climate of the target population.

Sponsorship must flow from the initiating sponsor through the sustaining sponsor or sponsors to the target population. There must be no gaps in sponsorship between the initiating sponsor and the target population. Each intervening layer in the organization must do its part to sponsor and support the performance improvement project or the initiative will fail.

Karen's Story

It was Friday afternoon, the time when Karen took a few minutes to review the events of the week and plan her course of action for Monday. The plan she had created last Friday was a demanding one, but well worth it. She had spent time this week securing and improving sponsorship for the performance improvement project.

First, she had sat down and assessed the level of sponsorship she was receiving from the sustaining sponsor. Given the cross-departmental nature of the project, this sponsor had to be the West Coast operations manager; he was the only one with the authority to endorse and require the performance changes. Karen noted a couple of areas of specific weakness: his public support for the performance improvement project wasn't very strong, and there was the issue of the resources necessary to implement the project during the busy season. Karen made an appointment to meet with him to discuss his sponsorship role. She laid out the needs and her specific recommendations. He felt that they were all reasonable requests and agreed to them.

On Tuesday, she had met with the engineering manager to secure support for reengineering the specification process. They discussed how to introduce the project to the group. He agreed to call the meeting and kick it off. He discussed the strategic importance to NewIdea, and the fact that he would be assessing performance based on helping implement the new process as well as on their typical responsibilities. It seemed to capture their attention; the meeting went well, and several really good recommendations were made by the engineering team.

The production manager was another story. She fully supported changing to computer-controlled milling machines, but she was three levels up from the supervisors in the organization. A black hole was sure to occur. Karen talked to her about a plan to create cascading sponsorship to build support down through the organization. The production manager wasn't sure about this flowing sponsorship stuff, but she agreed to proceed if Karen would help coach the process.

On Wednesday, Karen had met with the personnel manager to discuss the recommendation for the new reward and compensation system design. Karen wanted his inputs and needed to build his sponsorship for implementation. She presented the recommendation and asked for feedback. The design was technically excellent, but violated several widely held company values. The personnel manager pulled out his pencil and helped Karen make some adjustments that would bring it into alignment with the NewIdea way.

It was a hard week, but Karen was happy with the results. Next week would be tougher. She had to deal with a small additional project that was being requested by another part of the organization.

Sponsorship Tools for Human Performance Technology Projects

The following tools are provided to assist you with managing the sponsorship requirements of your performance improvement project.

Exhibit 3.1, Desired Performance of Sponsors, details the approach that should be utilized by the sponsors of performance improvement projects. This document can be used as a template should sponsors need to be educated on their role or reminded of their function.

Exhibit 3.2, Performance Improvement Sponsorship Assessment, is a tool that allows the human performance technologist to assess the quality and functionality of the sponsorship in place for the performance improvement project. This assessment can be used by the technologist alone, or it can be used as a survey to collect and quantify information from either the organization or project participants.

EXHIBIT 3.1. DESIRED PERFORMANCE OF SPONSORS.

1. Prioritize the major performance improvement changes facing the organization in relation to the commitment for results and the assessment of business or organizational dangers and opportunities.
2. Communicate these performance improvement change priorities to the organization.
3. Ensure that a synergistic environment exists so that performance improvements can be effectively implemented.
4. Apply the appropriate amount of logistical, economic, and political resources to the performance improvement project to demonstrate the level of commitment that should be conveyed.
5. Create a flow of sustaining sponsorship between the initiating sponsor and the final target population.
6. Use the sponsor evaluation form as a means for self-assessment and as a refresher to remind yourself of the key elements of good sponsorship. It also provides a method for discussing your role in the change process with other key players and the assessment of sustaining sponsors below you.

EXHIBIT 3.2. PERFORMANCE IMPROVEMENT SPONSORSHIP ASSESSMENT.

1. Dissatisfaction with the present performance level
   The sponsor is . . .

Very satisfied with the present performance				Somewhat dissatisfied with the present performance				Satisfied with the current performance level	
1	2	3	4	5	6	7	8	9	10

2. Objectives of the performance improvement objectives
   The sponsor has . . .

A clear understanding of what is to be accomplished				A vague sense of what is to be accomplished				No idea of what is to be accomplished	
1	2	3	4	5	6	7	8	9	10

3. Need for performance improvement
   The sponsor . . .

Demonstrates a strong belief that performance must improve				Believes that improvement would be good				Does not believe that improvement is necessary	
1	2	3	4	5	6	7	8	9	10

4. Performance improvement impact on the organization
   The sponsor . . .

Has a complete, in-depth understanding of the impact				Understands the implications at a superficial level				Does not really understand the impact on the organization	
1	2	3	4	5	6	7	8	9	10

5. The effect on people of the performance improvement project
   The sponsor . . .

Can empathize and appreciate the effect on people				Has only general, intellectual understanding of the effect				Does not really understand what people will need to do	
1	2	3	4	5	6	7	8	9	10

6. The scope of the improvement project
    The sponsor . . .

Has a thorough understanding of the number of people affected				Has a vague, general sense of the number of people affected				Has an clearly incorrect sense of the number of people affected	
1	2	3	4	5	6	7	8	9	10

7. Resources necessary for performance improvement project
    The sponsor . . .

Has a thorough understanding of the resources necessary				Is supportive, but lacks detailed understanding of the requirements				Has very little appreciation of the resources necessary for success	
1	2	3	4	5	6	7	8	9	10

8. The resource commitment necessary for performance improvement
    The sponsor . . .

Is willing and able to commit the resources that are needed				Is reluctant to commit the resources that are needed				Does not perceive the improvement is worth the cost	
1	2	3	4	5	6	7	8	9	10

9. The sponsor's visible role in the performance improvement project
    The sponsor . . .

Is able and willing to demonstrate visible support of the project				Will approve the project, but does not want to demonstrate support publicly				Is not able or willing to have any visible association with the project	
1	2	3	4	5	6	7	8	9	10

10. The sponsor's political role in the performance improvement project
   The sponsor . . .

Is willing to meet with key groups and individual to convey strong support				Is willing to discuss project but not to take a strong personal stand on it				Is unwilling or unable to convey importance to others	
1	2	3	4	5	6	7	8	9	10

11. Consequence management
   The sponsor . . .

Is able and willing to reward those who assist the performance improvement, and express disapproval to those that impede progress				Expresses desire that people support the performance improvement, but will not use incentives and pressures				Is unable or unwilling to use any means of positive or negative consequences to support the performance improvement	
1	2	3	4	5	6	7	8	9	10

12. Evaluation support
   The sponsor . . .

Will insure that monitoring of progress and problems occurs during implementation				Is willing to ask for reports, but is reluctant to establish specific evaluation methods				Refuses to ask for formal or informal reports regarding implementation progress	
1	2	3	4	5	6	7	8	9	10

13. Awareness of organizational sacrifice required for implementation
    The sponsor . . .

Is fully aware of potential short-term losses and consequences caused by implementation				Is only somewhat aware of the potential sacrifices during implementation				Does not understand that there could be any sacrifice required at all	
1	2	3	4	5	6	7	8	9	10

14. The commitment to sacrifice
    The sponsor . . .

Is willing and able to agree to the organization costs, even if high				Will be hesitant to support the improvement if the costs are too high				Is unable or unwilling to commit to the sacrifice	
1	2	3	4	5	6	7	8	9	10

15. Sustained support
    The sponsor . . .

Is willing and able to provide support to the implementation over time				Is inconsistent in providing support over time and is easily distracted by other activities				Is unwilling or unable to provide support over time	
1	2	3	4	5	6	7	8	9	10

Scoring the Sponsorship Assessment
Step 1: Total the responses to all 15 items.
Step 2: Divide the total by 15 to determine the average score.

Step 3:   Review the highest item scores and list the four that you believe will contribute most significantly to sponsorship problems.

    Issue 1:

    Issue 2:

    Issue 3:

    Issue 4:

Interpreting the Results of the Sponsorship Assessment

High-Risk Situation: Be Aware of Danger (6.6 and Above)

Most performance improvement projects with a sponsor assessment score in this range fail to achieve full implementation. The only exception is when the sponsor does not consider the change to be a significant alteration of the current situation—that is, the change is minor. However, performance improvement projects that are significantly disruptive or potentially threatening must always have sponsorship much greater than indicated by an assessment score in this range. The three options you have with sponsor assessment scores in this range are the following:

- *Strengthen sponsorship.* Use this assessment as a tool to help the sponsors better understand and value the critical nature of their role in supporting the performance improvement project.

- *Identify alternate sponsorship.* If it is not possible to strengthen the existing sponsorship support, identify some other person or group with the power to legitimize the performance improvement project and secure their agreement to serve as the project sponsor.

- *Prepare for project failure.* Without strengthened sponsorship or new sponsorship, the probability of successful performance improvement implementation is low. Faced with these circumstances, the human performance technologist should consider aborting the performance improvement project or significantly altering the objectives so that new perspectives on the issue can develop. If, for political reasons, there is pressure to continue the project without these changes, contingency plans should be made to deal with the problems that will arise when the project fails to produce intended results.

Moderate-Risk Situation: Exercise Caution (3.5–6.5)

Partial or tentative support from sponsors does not always result in project implementation failure, but it does increase the chances of failure. It certainly means implementation of the project is more complicated. A sponsor assessment score in this range should alert you to the following possibilities:

- The sponsor may have a shallow or intellectual commitment to the performance improvement project, but fails to understand the full meaning of what is necessary for successful project implementation.
- The sponsor support for the performance improvement project could deteriorate rapidly and with little or no warning.
- A significant amount of time and effort will need to be invested in sponsor education and maintenance.

Low-Risk Situation: Strong Project Sponsorship in Place (1.0–3.4)

Sponsorship should never be taken for granted, but assessment scores in this range usually indicate that the project sponsor commitment is at the level necessary for successful performance improvement implementation. Although the overall score is promising, any item with a score of 3 or more should not be ignored.

CHAPTER FOUR

ACTING AS A CONSULTANT

In Chapter Three, role relationships were presented in the context of securing and managing sponsorship. The relationships that were presented assumed a simple working environment. But such is not always the case.

Bill's Story

It was bad enough that his major "do or die" performance improvement project was going poorly. But now Bill's manager was on his case about other projects he was responsible for managing. He knew the discussion was not going to be an encouraging one.

"Oh, hi, Bill. Come on in and have a seat." Linda motioned him into her blue chair. "I wanted to discuss the performance improvement project you're managing in the finance group. I have some concerns."

Bill had some concerns of his own. "What do you want to know?"

Linda opened her projects folder. "I'm really concerned that the project is taking too much of the department's time. It feels like resources are being pulled away from the performance improvement project that needs to be completed before the Inventor's Fair. I can't let that happen."

Bill shifted in the chair. "Well, Linda, I think we're kind of stuck with the finance project. The written agreement allows them to extend the project work if needed. Carl and I had a very difficult time getting the project started. Neither of us were there when you put together the agreement with the finance manager. We spent an entire week just trying to figure out what we were trying to do and who's responsible for which activities."

Linda made some notes in her folder. "Bill, we have to get the resources back on the other project. It's our top priority. I want you to go talk with the finance folks and help them understand that the project needs to be concluded quickly. While we're on the topic, I'm concerned that this project doesn't have a training component in the solution. I think we'd all feel more comfortable if there were some training available. Please sell the finance organization on eliminating some of the noninstructional activities and replacing them with training. Any questions?"

Bill knew that there wasn't much sense arguing the point. Linda was his manager, and she called the shots. The client would just have to live with the conflicting needs of the training organization. "No, I guess not. I'll talk to finance today."

Linda stood and walked him to the door. "Thanks, Bill. I appreciate your dedication to doing the right thing." As Bill headed back to his desk, he wrestled with the question of whether he really was doing the right thing. But one thing he knew: Linda *is* the boss.

The Consultant Role

In the last chapter, the initiating sponsor, the manager, and the human performance technology (HPT) consultant were in the same organization. If this is the case for you, then you can manage performance improvement projects that are requested higher in the organization and the relationship issues remain fairly simple.

But what if the request for a performance improvement project comes from a different group in the company? A trend in HPT is the creation of a centralized service that is available to the wider organization. Many of these HPT departments act as internal consulting firms. That is, they contract with a client within the organization and charge internal funds for the services they provide. In these cases, clarifying and managing the relationship with the client is critical to the successful management of a performance improvement project (Lippitt, 1986).

Another possibility is that you have decided to strike out on your own and establish an HPT firm. If this is the case, you will benefit from this chapter, but your needs are broader than are discussed here. This chapter seeks to increase your awareness of internal consultant issues and how to effectively manage them;

it is not written to serve as a detailed guide to consulting. Many fine books exist for that purpose.

Differences Between Internal and External Consulting

When you are an internal consultant, you have to work within the hierarchical structure and the current politics of your organization. You must thus take into account and satisfy a number of differing goals to varying degrees. Even those of your manager and your own department may have internal variations. Other parts of the organization will have their own business and performance focus, which may be quite different from yours.

Having differing managerial and departmental objectives affects the way an internal HPT consultant works and contracts with internal clients (Weiss, 1992):

1. You may want or need to follow processes and procedures that conflict with the client's own philosophy and style. This can make it impossible to respond exclusively to your client's wants and needs.
2. Your department's system for conducting performance improvement projects may be part of the evaluation criteria for you or your manager. For example, you may be evaluated on how many performance improvements are made using a specific approach. This will create an overwhelming pressure to sell that particular approach, regardless of your client's preferences.
3. As an internal HPT consultant, you may need to work with people in the larger organization who have rejected your department's services for years. In fact, you may be expected to convince people who have had an adversarial relationship with your department to become clients who pay for your services.
4. If one or more key managers become dissatisfied with your work, it can be a disaster. Word of their dissatisfaction can travel quickly and the demand for your services can disappear. This could mean that you have a service to offer, but no takers.
5. Although not always the case, there can be some difficulty in being a "prophet in your own land." In addition, line managers may see you as being detached or isolated from their organization's real issues and conditions. After all, you are from some performance improvement organization, maybe from corporate. Because your connections to the bottom-line concerns of the business seem remote, they may resist your efforts to help. They may be slow to trust you and to recognize that you have the ability to effectively manage and implement performance improvement projects.

External HPT consultants must face many of the same issues, but being outside the organization, they experience them with less intensity. They are generally not dependent on one organization for their client base and their market is potentially much wider. As long as they have satisfied clients and business continues to roll in, they do not have to be so concerned with individual clients who may have issues about consultants' philosophy, style, or methodology.

Because of their dependence on one organization for clients, internal HPT consultants' positions are more tentative. They may find themselves in the delicate position of needing to point out sensitive issues—for example, that management practices are the root cause of the problem they were asked to investigate. Because their jobs may be vulnerable if they upset the wrong people, they must constantly evaluate the level of risk they are willing to take in getting to the heart of performance problems. If they constrain themselves to overly cautious behavior, they may purposely ignore some performance gap causes and end up confined to implementing relatively low-level performance improvement tasks. But if they do not engage in constrained (savvy) behavior, they may be dismissed as immature, disloyal, or "unaware of how we do things here."

Relationships in Managing HPT Projects as a Consultant

Whenever you are providing HPT project management services for another part of the organization, you will want to create a written agreement, or contract, to ensure that you and the client have a clear and mutual understanding of the relationship and project details (Lippitt, 1986). In addition to the contract, it is also important to be sure you have a clear contract with your own manager. Having an understanding with one of these parties and not the other means that the contracting process is still incomplete, which may cause problems before the project is over.

Your internal project will always have at least two major objectives: that of your HPT organization (such as the number of interventions or performance improvement projects for the year) and that of your client (reaching their performance improvement goals and objectives). These major objectives may or may not be in perfect alignment. Therefore, internal HPT consultants must frequently find a way to serve the client's needs while implementing their own department's priorities. This is why a contract with each is required. Of course, this results in a triangular relationship with the internal consultant in the middle, which requires a delicate balancing of the two contracts. Figure 4.1 shows the minimum relationship an internal HPT consultant should retain with clients.

FIGURE 4.1. THE MINIMAL RELATIONSHIP FOR AN INTERNAL HPT CONSULTANT.

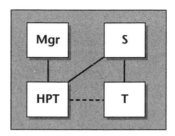

When managing a performance improvement project as an internal HPT consultant, it is essential to map out the relationships and ensure that you are effectively managing them all (Lippitt, 1986). Given just the minimal relationship, if you meet the needs of your client at the expense of your manager's objectives, you will fail; you will be equally unsuccessful in the long run if you meet your manager's objectives at the cost of the client's. More complex relationships may require even more finely tuned juggling of objectives.

The Relationship to Avoid

Avoid the relationship that occurs when your manager contracts with the performance improvement initiating sponsor directly and without your involvement (Weiss, 1992). Setting up the relationship that way creates a difficult situation for you and for the sustaining sponsor, as neither of you are involved in the contracting process. This generally makes it difficult to create a reliable win-win project management scenario. Such a situation is illustrated in Figure 4.2.

In this scenario, a commitment to begin the project has already been made. Then you, the HPT consultant, arrive to work on a performance improvement project where neither you nor the client were involved in specifying what should be done. Often the result is a series of miscommunications, with several starts and stops occurring in the midst of trying to clarify misunderstandings. To make matters even more difficult, strong emotions and opinions may make this situation a breeding ground for conflict.

To avoid this, you should be involved in creating the initial contracting agreement. This will help you develop a clear view of the project as it begins and lay a firm foundation of understanding so that confusion can be avoided in the

FIGURE 4.2. A POOR CONSULTING RELATIONSHIP.

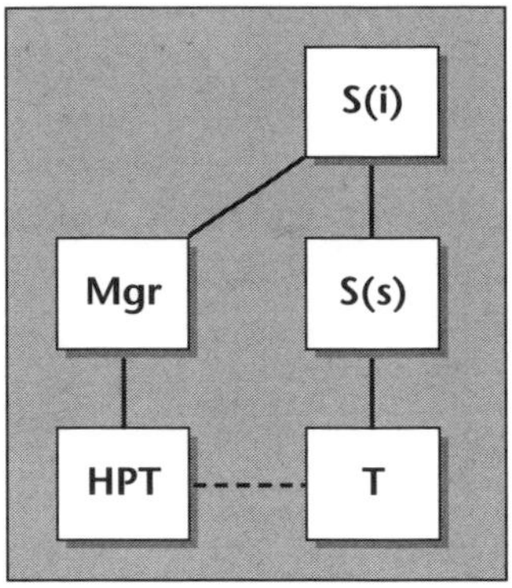

future. If your manager needs to be involved or even to conduct the initial nego-tiations and contract definition, you should still suggest that you be present while the talks and negotiations occur. If you can encourage the parties involved to also invite the sustaining sponsor to attend the initial contracting sessions, that would also assist in setting the project on a firm footing.

Dealing with Your Manager

During the contracting process, many problems that exist between internal HPT consultants and their clients turn out to have roots in problems between the consultants and their own managers (Lippitt, 1986). Some managers have expec-tations of their consultants that cannot be fulfilled. For example, you may feel that you can never say no to requests for your services, even if you are sure it is a lose-lose situation.

In any internal consulting business, norms develop about how to conduct busi-ness. These can be the result of implicit and explicit expectations of managers and coworkers in the department. When asked what their department asked of them, a group of consultants responded with the following set of sometimes contradictory expectations:

- Always get the job done, even if it seems impossible.
- Keep your contracts extremely flexible.
- When you have a recommendation, make sure the client takes it.
- Convince the client to use your department's methodology.
- Loyalty to your own department takes precedence.

- If you are good at what you do, your client will be convinced you are right.
- Important technical issues outweigh client concerns.
- Avoid conflict or other upset with the client.
- Don't promise that you will do work for the client later on.
- If you make a mistake, do not admit it.
- Resist the temptation to make negative comments about anyone.
- Be cool, calm, and collected. Do not show any emotion.
- Always appear dignified, tactful, and confident.

Although the expectations listed here are not taken from any one manager, they do illustrate the kind of unrealistic and contradictory norms that can be generated or assumed. The creation of expectations like these can result from unclear contracting between the manager and the internal HPT consultant, who can end up feeling burdened by impossible demands. To avoid this quandary, the internal consultant and the manager need to set up a clear and explicit contract.

To do so, first decide what you need for a successful project. The following list of criteria for success was provided by a group of internal consultants. They suggested that having these commitments from their managers would help them to be successful and to know how to react to the pressures they are under:

- A clear definition of the project before it begins
- Ability to get information, input, decisions, and the like from the manager as needed
- Support for political issues and for the nontechnical aspects of the project
- Assistance with environmental factors that may interfere, such as commitments to other projects
- Openness to the internal consultant's recommendations for how the project should be conducted

When the same group of consultants were asked what they need for success that their clients could provide, they listed the following items. Note the similarities between the two lists.

- A clear definition of the project
- Ability to interact with a person who can make decisions for the client organization
- Access to data required to complete the project
- Opportunities to cooperate, as required, to complete decisions or solve problems
- Commitment of the time and resources required to complete the project
- Starting with an open mind about the outcome

- Providing the physical needs required to complete the job
- Clear communication and thorough review through all stages of the project

The clarity of understanding and agreement with your manager greatly affects your ability to respond appropriately to your clients (Weiss, 1992). If you do not have the firm foundation that a clear contract with your manager would provide, you may still embark on contracts with clients but you may have difficulty delivering difficult messages, holding firm on your recommendations when you know you are right, or keeping rein on the scope of the project. You may also find yourself taking on projects even though you are convinced that they have little chance of turning out successfully.

You and your manager can work together to create an effective agreement about how you will work together. First, make a list of your key requirements. What do you need from your manager? Ask your manager to make a list of what she needs from you. What does she need to make the department successful? Second, arrange a meeting, exchange lists, and see what areas you can both agree on that will further your mutual success. You may need to discover together a balance between what you need to remain focused on your client's requirements while doing an excellent job managing the project, and what your manager feels the department must have for success in the wider organization.

Karen's Story

Things were pretty busy with the big performance improvement project. Karen wished she didn't have the distraction of other projects to worry about, but other parts of the business had performance improvement needs as well. Now her manager had asked her to drop by his office.

"Oh, hi, Karen. I've been expecting you. Have a seat." Jim motioned her into his visitor chair. "I wanted to discuss the performance improvement project you're managing in the marketing group."

"Sure, Jim. What do you want to know?"

Jim shuffled the stacks of memos and notes on his desk. "I'm really concerned that the project is taking too much of the department's time. It feels like resources are being pulled away from the performance improvement project that needs to be completed before the Inventor's Fair. I can't let that happen."

Karen leaned forward. "Jim, we were all there in the meeting where we created the agreement. We identified exactly what the goals for the project were, and the training department agreed to supply the necessary resources to complete the job. I realize the training department is probably under substantial pressure to role out the big performance improvement project. But if we break our agreement with the marketing group, we probably won't have too many new opportunities lining up at our door. We may find ourselves without credibility in our own organization. The agreement was clear. I don't see how we can change it."

Jim shifted in his chair. He was obviously uncomfortable with the situation. "Hmm. You may be right. But this is a real problem. What would you recommend we do to solve this?"

Karen thought for a moment. "We could authorize overtime, or we could offload some low-level tasks to a few of the interns. Either might give us the resources to complete both projects."

Jim made some notes. "I'll see what can be done. I really dislike these kinds of problems. By the way, I was looking at the results of the analysis on the marketing project. I liked the recommended interventions for improving performance. But I think that folks would be more comfortable if there were some training included in the solution. After all, we *are* the training department."

Karen flipped open her project folder that she takes to every meeting with Jim. (You never quite know where he will be coming from, and it helps to be prepared.) "Jim, do you remember the agreement we worked out six months ago? We wanted to get really clear on balancing my relationship with you and with our clients."

He nodded. "I remember very clearly. I thought it was a great approach. I know exactly what I can depend on you to do."

Karen pulled the agreement out of her folder. "We stated that you would not impose a performance solution on a client. We agreed that the analysis would dictate what solutions were necessary to achieve the performance goals. I need to have that support to maintain my credibility and ethical relationship with the customer."

Jim looked at the agreement and smiled. "Can I retract my statement about the training?"

Karen smiled back. "Thanks for your support, Jim. You're a great boss."

CHAPTER FIVE

PLANNING THE INFRASTRUCTURE

For most systems and activities, an infrastructure must be in place to allow them to achieve their ends effectively and efficiently. This is true for manufacturing, accounting—or, for that matter, sewer systems.

Bill's Story

Monday morning found Bill in his office early, as was becoming the norm for him as the project continued. It seemed that his meetings with project team members were constant, primarily to discuss how to proceed or how to resolve different interpretations of what was previously agreed to. This seemed rather unproductive to Bill, but he didn't know how to fix the situation; he was the one who knew all the information, so he had to fix the problems.

Today, Bill was looking for the latest update reports on the project status. He had to run around to all the project members to get the information. He thought they had all agreed to send him a report every other week, but he was the only one who seemed to remember the discussion. Stacks of paper cluttered Bill's work area; his meeting with Linda was in only fifteen minutes and he still could not find the status reports. He wished he had taken the advice to create a project notebook where everything is stored and anybody can look up information. It was too late now, of course; even if he had the time to create it, he certainly did not have enough to reorganize all the information that now existed in the midst of the project.

Bill located the latest status and dashed off to Linda's office. Darn, there's that blue chair again. "Come in," said Linda, "and have a seat.

"Bill, we seem to have a couple of problems with the management of this strategically important performance improvement project. As you know, its effectiveness will have a big impact on the company's success. So I'm rather disappointed with the frequency of project updates I'm getting from you. I really don't think waiting three weeks for an update is appropriate."

Bill was stunned. "Well, how often do you want an update?"

Linda thought for a moment. "I suppose I'd like to review progress toward all the major milestones every week. By the way, what *is* our status?"

Bill shifted uncomfortably in the blue chair. "Well, I didn't think you'd want that level of detail. I only brought information on the current activities. I'll have a complete update to you by tomorrow."

Now it was Linda's turn to shift uncomfortably. "Okay, Bill. But it really needs to be on my desk by 7 A.M. I have one more issue to discuss. I've heard rumors that video production has started without the legal folks checking the script."

"What would legal want with an internal-use video script?" asked Bill, confused. "Besides, we're halfway through shooting. It's too late to change anything now."

Linda leaned forward. "Two years ago we were sued by one of our investors when an internal tape got into their hands. Since then, all video scripts must go through legal. Didn't you talk to them about the issues surrounding this project?"

Need for Infrastructure

If you look behind most systems or activities, you will find infrastructures that allow their main purposes to be achieved effectively and efficiently (Kerzner, 1989). The infrastructure for a city is rather complex. There is a water system to distribute safe water conveniently, and a power system to provide electricity. People are also within the infrastructure—they may plan roads, or make or enforce laws, among many other roles. All these systems and activities are important to the functioning of the city; however, none is the purpose or main activity of the city.

If all citizens had to tote their daily water from a well three miles away, the potential achievements of the society would be significantly reduced. If there were no preestablished laws, the city would be thrown into chaos. The infrastructure keeps the system running smoothly so that the main purpose can be achieved. Similarly, performance improvement projects require infrastructure to keep the project management system running smoothly so that it can achieve its main objective.

Create and define the infrastructure before the project begins (Grey, 1981). Attempting to do so in the midst of the project is seldom a pleasant experience. Defining the infrastructure allows you to do the following:

- Make decisions that will facilitate planning, tracking, and communicating about the project and gain agreement from project participants about the decisions.
- Clarify the expectations of project participants with regard to the management of the project.
- Determine the environment and processes for project planning and management.
- Decide where and how to plan and manage the project, who will do so, and why.

Significant work has been done and experience gained by other project managers on the topic of infrastructure (Kerzner, 1989; Lewis, 1993; Randolf, 1988; Stallworthy, 1983). Attempting to identify all the potential infrastructure issues from scratch is difficult and time-consuming. A sample checklist in Exhibit 5.1 at the end of this chapter is for your use in planning the infrastructure. The checklist includes the following broad categories:

- Planning decisions—centered around schedule preparation
- Tracking decisions—centered around status reports and status meetings
- Practices decisions—focused on procedures and processes such as continuous improvement
- Relationship decisions—having to do with ownership by the project team members

The Process of Defining the Infrastructure

Because of the complexity of the project infrastructure, it is best to move through the definition in an organized, methodical manner. Here is the recommended process for achieving an effective project infrastructure:

Step 1: Review the Infrastructure Checklist

The sample infrastructure checklist at the end of this chapter is only a guideline. It does not include every potential infrastructure issue that you will need to consider. Likewise, there may be many listed items that have no significance to the specific performance improvement project you are working on. In reviewing the checklist, you will be creating a custom infrastructure list for your project. Although creating it is time-consuming, the second time you make one up will usually be faster, because much of the agreed-upon infrastructure will remain the same. In reviewing the checklist you should do the following:

Review All Checklist Categories. You may be tempted to skip over sections that seem unimportant at first, but give each major category attention in considering what might be needed to successfully support your performance improvement project.

Add or Delete Checklist Items. Do this as needed. Consider the specific infrastructure needed by your project, organization, environment, and client. Remember that each project will have different needs.

Develop a Draft Checklist for Your Project. Once you have your project-specific infrastructure list, create a draft for further development, review, and validation.

Prepare Draft Answers. Look over the project-specific draft that you have created. Some items will be immediately answerable. Mandatory operating procedures within the organization may dictate some of the answers; some items may require a specific answer to ensure successful project completion or implementation. In these cases, providing the known answer will help create a shorter review and validation process.

Consider Other Sources of Information. Now that you have done your best thinking on the infrastructure necessary for a successful project, it is time to expand your sources of information in considering the answers. There are several potential sources of additional information. Look at historical data. Was a past project manager fired for not keeping the manager or client informed regularly? This might have a bearing on the infrastructure you create for today's project. Are there postmortems or other reports from previous projects? Reviewing them might help you avoid problems discovered by others. If other project managers are in the organization, they might provide additional considerations or information as well.

Solicit Input from Team Members. Asking the project team members for input will help build the infrastructure from their past project and organization experiences. As they participate in its creation, you will also be obtaining their buy-in on the infrastructure decisions.

Several different methods exist for obtaining project team input, including the following:

Look at the "Big Picture." As the project manager, you must look at the overall matters that may be overlooked by others. In some cases, different sources of information will present conflicting recommendations. It is important to keep the entire project system in mind to make decisions on key points. Document the reasons for the decisions so you can refer to them later; the manager or client may ask why you chose certain solutions.

Write Down All Assumptions Made. You will need this information as the project proceeds, as infrastructure decisions may be challenged later in the project. If you know the reason for the decision, you can weigh the reason against the current circumstance and make an informed decision.

Resolve Open Issues. Write down all the unresolved issues and ensure that each one has an owner and a due date for resolution. Open issues have a way of slipping through the cracks if they are not carefully managed. Infrastructure issues that are unresolved due to disagreement are future project land mines if they are left that way.

Step 2: Meet to Reach Agreement

It is best to convene a meeting with all the project participants to come to an agreement on all the checklist items. Making decisions about project infrastructure without the inputs of the project participants can be hazardous. Most likely, at least one participant will have experiences or insights that you do not (Lewis, 1993b). At the least, it is probable that they will see at least one issue that you have overlooked.

Involving the other participants helps to build their agreement to infrastructure answers and decisions. Attempting to enforce a change in management policy that has not been agreed upon is difficult in the midst of project development or implementation.

To gain the insights and support of the project team members or participants, consider doing the following:

Discuss Each Infrastructure Checklist Item. You may be tempted to skip over some items that appear to be simple and fairly straightforward. But future disagreement on just one point in the project infrastructure will probably take more time to resolve than reviewing the entire list.

Encourage Discussion of Alternative Processes. You should expect that the project participants will have some alternate recommendations from the ones you created. Getting the ideas out for group discussion will help ensure that the participants' inputs are considered and the best project infrastructure selected. Remember, the project participants are the ones who will have to live within the infrastructure they create.

Build a Sense of Team Accountability. Ensure that the project participants feel accountable to the project infrastructure decisions that are made. It should be clear to all that the infrastructure will be the operational expectations for the project, and that raising disagreement later will not help in the successful completion of the performance improvement project.

Step 3: Document and Distribute the Decisions and Assumptions

Project managers are frequently surprised at how quickly people can forget or distort decisions and information. Unfortunately, these instances rarely occur during convenient times in the project. Now that you have some level of agreement on the project infrastructure decisions, you must ensure consistent understanding among the participants in the project as well as the manager or client of the project.

Following are some recommendations for documenting the project infrastructure (Grey, 1981).

File It in the Project Notebook. Keep a master copy of the project infrastructure in the project notebook for reference and as a control document for potential future changes. This will also assist performance improvement project managers who follow you and want to refer to the notebook for historical information.

Give Each Participant a Copy. Having a copy of the project infrastructure allows project members to check their activities and decisions against the agreed-upon infrastructure decisions. Allowing them to regulate their own activities is much easier than attempting to impose the regulation of the infrastructure (Thomsett, 1993).

Manage Unresolved Issues. As the project manager, you need to ensure that unresolved issues are included in the infrastructure documentation along with their owners and due dates for resolution. Otherwise, issues may soon fade from memory until they arise in the midst of the project.

Manage Changes Carefully. If modifications are requested, be certain to secure agreement from the manager or client and the participants of the performance improvement project. After agreement is reached, update the documents and reissue them so that all concerned have an accurate copy of the operating infrastructure.

Karen's Story

Monday mornings were busy for Karen. She reviewed the status reports every project team member turned in on Friday before going home. That allowed her enough time to prepare for her meeting with Jim.

Kathleen peered around the corner. "Can I take a look at the project notebook? We can't seem to remember what we agreed to regarding the change process."

Karen gathered up the latest status reports. "Sure. Just let me put these reports in the status update section so they don't get misplaced."

She then headed off to her meeting with Jim. "Hiya, boss. Ready for our weekly update meeting?"

Jim set down the memo he was reading. "Sure, Karen. Come in and have a seat. What's the status on the project?"

Karen sat down and handed Jim her report. "Here is the top-level schedule we agreed to review each week. As you can see, all the major milestones are on schedule except one. Legal found some problems in the video script, and we lost two days reworking it. But Kathleen has a plan to catch us up within the next two weeks."

Jim was confused. "Why is legal reviewing an internal-use video script? It sounds like a waste of time to me."

"It turns out we were sued two years ago by one of our investors when an internal tape got into their hands. Since then, all video scripts must go through legal. I wouldn't have thought about it, but when we reviewed the infrastructure plan for the project, one of the team members brought it up and said we should include legal in our planning process. I'm glad we did. I can't imagine how painful it would be if we found out in the middle of the shooting."

Jim smiled brightly. "Nice catch, Karen. I'm certainly glad we're not repeating a mistake. I'll make certain to mention it when I see the team."

EXHIBIT 5.1. THE INFRASTRUCTURE CHECKLIST.

Planning Decisions

Development

How will the project plan be developed?

Will meetings be scheduled to define the project plan? When and where will these meetings be held?

Which product life cycle will the plan follow?

Is there a lexicon of project management terms that all team members agree on? If not, will one be developed?

How will we use experience information and reviews of other projects?

How do we plan to continually improve our management of the project?

Which tools will we use to support the project?

Will we use a project management software tool? If so, which one?

Who will enter planning information into the tool?

Who will enter tracking information into the tool?

Who needs training to be able to use the software effectively?

Who do we call when we have questions about the software?

What additional software (such as for a spreadsheet or database) do we need to support the project management tool?

What equipment do we need to use the project management tool and any additional software?

Involvement

Who will be involved in the overall project?

Who in addition to the project manager will be involved in planning the project?

What are the specific roles and responsibilities of all participants?

Who needs to be informed of decisions made? How will they be kept informed?

What does my manager expect in the project plan? My manager's manager?

What expectations do others have?

Deliverables

What are the deliverables of the project planning process?

Which formats are most appropriate for each deliverable?

How detailed should the deliverables be?

How will we know that each deliverable step has been completed?

How will we assess the quality of each deliverable?

Who will approve and sign off at the completion of each deliverable?
Who receives each deliverable?

Tracking Decisions

Tracking

    How will we assess progress?

    At what level of detail will we track the project?

    How will we get data from project team members and others about the progress of each activity?

    How often will we get this data?

    Who will assess the impact of each variance?

Reporting

    Who will generate and distribute reports?

    Who needs to be kept informed about project progress, and how will we inform them?

    What content is appropriate for each audience?

    How frequently will each audience receive a status report?

    How detailed should status reports be for each audience?

    Which formats (tabular, narrative, or graphic) communicate best to *each* audience?

    What criteria will we use to define an exception for exception reporting? Note: Exceptions may be defined differently depending on the roles and levels of people with whom we communicate.

    Who will receive and analyze exception reports?

Meetings

    What types of meetings will we hold?

    Who should be included in each type of meeting?

    Where will meetings be held?

    Who will define the strategy and method for managing meetings effectively?

    Who will run these meetings?

    Who will produce an agenda for each meeting?

    Who will be the meeting scribe, prepare the minutes, and distribute them after the meeting? Who (besides the attendees) should be on the distribution list for minutes?

    Review meetings:

        How often will we hold review meetings?

        Where will they be held? How?

        Who will be included?

Who will plan the agenda?

In what format should team members report progress at the meeting?

Practices Decisions

Managing Change

Who will define the change control process we will use?

When will the plan baseline be frozen? Who will make the decision to freeze the plan? What will the decision to freeze it be based on?

What criteria will we use to define change (such as design and baseline changes)?

What type of log will we use to track proposed changes?

Who will have change approval authority?

Who will set adaptive actions?

How will we track the effectiveness of these adaptive actions?

How will we assess the impact of changes?

How will we document approved plan changes?

Who will decide how to make changes to the project plan?

How will we decide whether to update the plan within the original time and resource commitments or to reschedule the project, thus estimating time and resource requirements again?

How much deviation from the plan are we willing to accept before doing a total reschedule?

How will we link revisions to the change control process?

The Project Notebook

Who will create the notebook?

What information will be included?

Who will maintain it?

How often will updates be made?

Who will have access to the notebook (for information only)?

Who will have authority to make changes to the notebook?

Where will it be stored (online or in the library)?

For how long will it be kept after project completion?

Who will keep it after project completion?

How will it be used after the project?

Continuous Improvement and Project Review

Will a project review meeting be held?

Who should attend?

What subjects will be addressed?

How often during the project life will a postmortem be done?

How will you document the project review so that others can learn from your experience?

What information should we keep to provide a historical basis for continuing improvement?

Relationship Decisions

Ownership

Which departments or organizations will we need to interact with during the project?

What are the roles and responsibilities of each organization (such as reviewer, approver, or creator)?

Communication

How will we keep all involved parties informed of deliverables, schedule dates, expectations, and other vital project information?

How do we (the project team) communicate among ourselves?

How do we communicate with nonteam members?

How frequently do we need to communicate?

Are there specific communication dates or intervals?

What information will and will not be exchanged?

What form will communication take?

PART TWO

PLANNING THE PROJECT

With the project adequately prepared, the next major activity is to create a schedule to successfully achieve it. Without a plan, it is nearly impossible to determine what needs to be accomplished and when. Projects without a plan are random, uncoordinated activities.

In creating a plan, forgotten tasks are minimized; realistic time, resource, and cost estimates are created; interdependencies of the tasks are defined; responsibilities for tasks are assigned; and risk is removed from the project plan.

Part Two presents a systematic approach to creating an accurate and effective schedule that will facilitate professional management of performance improvement projects. Time and effort invested in scheduling allows the human performance technologist to accurately set expectations with clients and management, and then confidently meet them.

FIGURE P2.1.

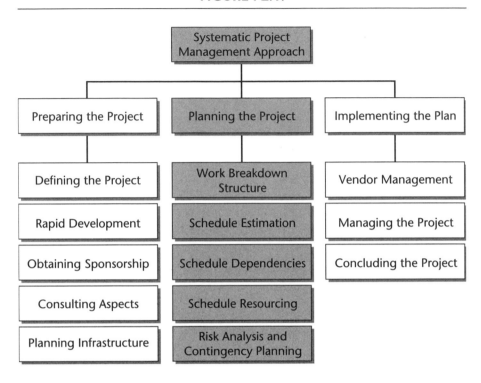

One major company undertook a multiyear study of project problems, analyzing ways to determine the major causes of project failures so they could be eliminated from the project environment. The four boldface items in the list of these major causes in Figure P2.2 are addressed by the scheduling approach described in this part of the book.

FIGURE P2.2.

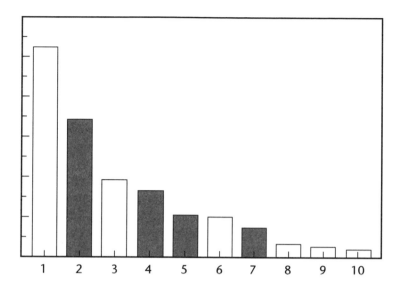

1. Changes in the project definition
2. **Poor estimation of effort required**
3. Other
4. **Unforeseen project tasks**
5. **Resources not available on time**
6. Vendor task slips
7. **Changes in support resources**
8. Financial support changes
9. Lack of technical expertise on project
10. Team too large and communications too complex

CHAPTER SIX

CREATING THE WORK BREAKDOWN STRUCTURE

The first step in creating a schedule for a performance improvement project is determining what tasks or work must be accomplished to achieve the project goal.

Bill's Story

It was 10 P.M., and Bill was the only one in the office. Linda was expecting an update on the progress of the performance improvement project tomorrow, and the schedule was a mess. Things just were not going well. It seemed that the schedule was slipping a week for every week of progress made—like a treadmill, running fast but going nowhere. Bill knew what the problem was: for every task being completed, the team discovered another that had to be done but was not on the schedule.

Bill could not figure out where this additional work was coming from, even though he had spent hours in his office listing all the activities that needed to be completed. He also was having difficulty with his own schedule. Bill had project tasks that he was responsible for completing, but project management activities kept getting in the way. The scheduling and reporting activities were consuming time he had not planned for. He started to wonder if having so many small tasks to track was really such a good idea.

The entire team was complaining that project meetings and meetings with the management team and the target audience were time-consuming and not part of the project schedule. This was causing continual schedule slippage and requiring more resources than planned.

In addition, not every task was being completed perfectly, so yet more time had to be spent assessing the quality of the deliverables and fixing defects. As rework was not in the schedule, this was creating more schedule slippage and more disappointment on the part of the management team.

Perhaps the imperfections were due to all the confusion over the tasks themselves. Phil had a task that produced a deliverable that was to go to Barb so she could start her task. But what Phil produced and what Barb needed seemed to be two different things. They just seemed to interpret the task differently. The task "duplicate" made sense to Bill when he wrote it; why didn't Phil and Barb understand it in its context? Bill didn't even want to think about the time wasted by having two people working on duplicate tasks with different names.

Bill snapped back from his mental meandering. He had to get the entire schedule redone by adding the new tasks that had been discovered today. He wanted to spend as little time in Linda's office and that darn blue chair as possible.

Definition of Work Breakdown Structure

Determining what work must be done, and when, is a crucial step in the planning process, as all further work is built upon the list of work to be done (Dreger, 1992).

Characterizing this work can be done at different levels. If the performance improvement project includes the creation of instruction, the task could describe the work to be accomplished at the highest level: "create instruction." However, accurately scheduling such a large and undefined activity is almost impossible. Breaking down the task to the next level by describing necessary activities such as analysis, design, development, implementation, and evaluation is a more meaningful list of work.

Starting with the project goal and breaking down the work to be done into manageable tasks is referred to as a work breakdown structure (WBS). The WBS is the basic framework for project and cost planning. It identifies and displays all activities that must be conducted to complete the project. The WBS provides a hierarchical tree of major project areas, dividing the project into smaller, more detailed levels of work. The tasks included in the WBS provide a basis for developing the project schedule, estimating the resources required to complete the project, and assigning responsibility for project work (Martin, 1976).

The objective in creating a WBS is to create a top-down logical structuring of project work such that each of the following is true:

- Each level provides greater detail than the previous level.
- Any level can be easily and completely rolled up to the next-higher level.
- All the tasks that must be completed to complete the project are identified.
- Tasks are shown as a hierarchical list or as a diagram.

WBS Contribution to Project Failures

The WBS is the first step in the scheduling process, and all other scheduling work is built upon it. Therefore, if the WBS is done poorly, the quality and effectiveness of the project schedule can suffer greatly. Consider the example of a project that experienced tremendous difficulty because of an inaccurate WBS. In the middle of the project, its manager found that the schedule was slipping a week for every week of progress that was being made; as progress was made, the project team discovered an equal amount of work that needed to be done but was not in the plan. The team had to stop to reschedule the entire project. In redoing the WBS, a total of three months of work was discovered that had not appeared in the original plan. With the new WBS, the team was able to complete the work according to a new schedule.

Refer to the histogram in the Part Two introduction, and note that the WBS has a significant effect on project failures. The fourth greatest cause of failures is unforeseen project tasks, which relates directly to a WBS that lacks sufficient detail. The number two cause is poor estimation of effort required; this is due to poor estimation technique (see Chapter Eight) and the lack of visibility of some tasks involved in completing the work (a WBS issue).

If a WBS fails, one of two major factors is likely responsible (Randolf, 1988). First, the project may lack detail or the plan for it may be underdeveloped—that is, task descriptions at the level of actual physical work may be insufficient. This results in unplanned work appearing suddenly in the schedule and time estimates slipping accordingly.

Consider the example of someone planning a trip who has created a list of tasks that must be completed before departure. Figure 6.1 illustrates the departure task list.

Does the task list look sufficient? Are any major tasks missing from the list that would prevent on-schedule departure? What if the traveler is going to Nairobi? Unplanned but necessary tasks such as securing a passport, visa, and shots are

FIGURE 6.1. TRAVEL TASK LIST.

Tasks

> Choose destination
> Choose dates
> Buy airline ticket
> Buy new clothes
> Pack
> Drive to airport
> Check baggage
> Get on plane

details that would cause the overseas traveler to miss the plane, regardless of how well the other tasks were performed.

Second, the project plan may lack structure. Many projects encounter trouble because critical tasks are overlooked in the planning phase or are not scheduled in the proper sequence. The project plan must be structured so that it is more than just a long list of tasks with no discernible interrelationship.

Consider the travel example again. In this case, the traveler puts passport, airplane ticket, and visa into a group called "paperwork" and attempts to obtain each in the same time frame based upon the necessary lead time. You can get a passport in ten days; a visa requires twenty-five days. Therefore, the traveler plans to apply for the visa twenty-five days before departure and the passport ten days before departure. Unfortunately, the random structure of this WBS leads to failure. In grouping the activities as unrelated paperwork, the fact that one must possess a passport before applying for a visa is overlooked; thus the passport application must be made thirty-five days prior to departure. The schedule should have accounted for task dependencies (see Chapter Eight), but the poor structure of the WBS hid the interrelationships.

Development of the WBS

When creating a WBS, the goal is to identify all major work that must be performed. For a complex performance improvement project, it would most likely include the different interventions that were selected as a result of identifying the root causes of the performance gaps. Major work assignments could include reengineering a work process, installing new equipment to improve performance, changing the reward and recognition system, or creating instruction.

After the major assignments are identified, each is broken down into individual tasks that must be completed to accomplish the assignment. Each task is then broken down into subtasks until each necessary activity is identified and understood. The specific process for accomplishing this task is detailed later in the chapter.

WBS Forms

The format of a WBS can be either a diagram or a hierarchical list. Each has specific advantages. A diagram version of a WBS is illustrated in Figure 6.2, although many tasks have been left off to simplify it.

FIGURE 6.2. DIAGRAM VERSION OF A WBS.

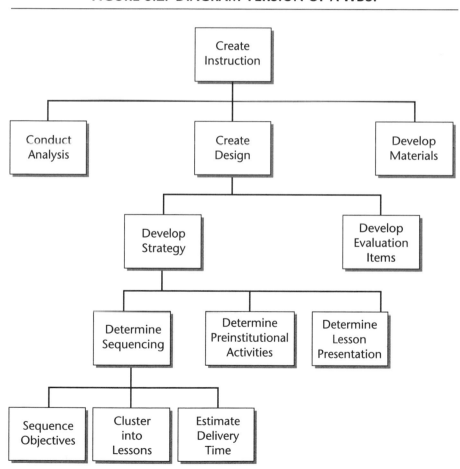

The diagram makes it easy to observe the relationship between the levels of tasks within the WBS. "Create instruction" is the top box on the diagram, and breaks down into three tasks, one of which is "create design." This task breaks down into two tasks. "Develop strategy" breaks down further, as does "determine sequencing." The diagram version is used primarily when developing the WBS. You can imagine how tangled this diagram would be if each box were fully broken down; it would not fit on the page. For this reason, software project scheduling tools use the hierarchical form of the WBS.

The hierarchical form of the WBS is not as graphic and easy to read, but it is much easier to manage. Figure 6.3 shows a hierarchical list version of the same WBS shown in Figure 6.2. Rather than relying upon the structure of the boxes used in the diagram, the hierarchical list uses a numbering system, indentation system, or both to indicate the relationship of the tasks. The major activity "create instruction" has three major tasks labeled 1.0, 2.0, and 3.0. Notice also that they are indented from the major activity. Major task 2.0 is broken down to two tasks indented and labeled 2.1 and 2.2. Task 2.1 is broken down to three tasks indented and labeled 2.1.1, 2.1.2, and 2.1.3. Task 2.1.1 is broken down another level to three additional tasks, which are appropriately indented and numbered.

WBS Durations

Most project managers question how far to break down the tasks. It is possible to get to a level of WBS that becomes ineffective, making the management of the project a larger effort than the project itself (Kerzner, 1989).

FIGURE 6.3. HIERARCHICAL LIST VERSION OF WBS.

Create Instruction

1.0	Conduct Analysis
2.0	Create Design
2.1	Develop Strategy
2.1.1	Determine Sequencing
2.1.1.1	Sequence Objectives
2.1.1.2	Cluster into Lessons
2.1.1.3	Estimate Delivery Time
2.1.2	Determine Preinstructional Activities
2.1.3	Determine Lesson Presentation
2.2	Develop Evaluation Items
3.0	Develop Materials

Again, consider the travel example. The traveler could break down the passport task to the next level: get photographs, fill out application, write check, and mail all. This additional level of WBS may be helpful; it ensures not forgetting to mail a check, and it is an alert to plan sufficient time to have photos taken.

The WBS could go down another level, which would be less helpful. Breaking down "fill out application" into fill in name, fill in address, fill in date of birth, and the rest is unnecessary; at this level of detail the effort of tracking the tasks outweighs that of doing them.

Rough duration estimates typically serve as the measure of whether a task has been sufficiently broken down. This time measure can scale up or down depending on project size and schedule criticality. If a project is expected to take a month, you would be willing to track one-day and half-day activities to ensure that the schedule is met. If it is a three-year project, tracking half-day tasks is less necessary. However, if the schedule is constrained and the project is critical to the organization, you might still consider tracking half-day tasks.

A good rule of thumb for task duration is no shorter than you are willing to track and no longer than two weeks. Any task that takes longer probably has several subtasks that should be identified (Lewis, 1993a).

WBS Effect on Project Schedule

Despite best efforts to create an accurate and sufficiently detailed WBS, some problems typically arise during the WBS creation stage that continue throughout the project (Stallworthy, 1983). Be aware of these and minimize them whenever you are able.

The WBS process typically generates an "if all goes right" schedule. The mental construct of individuals working on a WBS is to think only about the tasks that need to be implemented; rarely does the original WBS allow for contingencies or unexpected problems. Therefore, it is important to update the WBS after the risk assessment and contingency planning is done later in the process.

Even with expert insight, most project managers find that not all necessary tasks are accounted for in the WBS process. Additional necessary tasks will be discovered in the midst of the project. Project managers should have contingency plans in place to deal with such situations when they occur.

In considering task duration, project participants will typically generate optimistic time estimates. If these initial estimates are maintained through the project, it is fairly certain that project completion will come after the scheduled completion date. It is important to reinforce that the initial duration estimates are only a tool for gauging if the WBS has been taken to a sufficient level of detail; more accurate and reliable estimation approaches are implemented later in the process.

The WBS Process

The creation of the WBS should be approached systematically to minimize overlooked tasks that arise later in the project and to ensure that the WBS is sufficiently detailed to facilitate effective project management (Baker and Baker, 1992). Following is such an approach.

Step 1: Break the Project into Major Components

Before getting to the details of determining the work breakdown structure, address the issue of who should determine it. One of the largest errors project managers can make is to attempt to create the WBS completely on their own. They simply do not possess sufficient insight to identify every task in the project. Assume that the triangle in Figure 6.4 represents all the tasks necessary to complete a performance improvement project. The project manager will most probably be aware of the tasks represented by the shaded area. A sizable number of lower-level tasks are not covered.

Conversely, if the project participants were to create a WBS without the input of the project manager, a number of high-level tasks would likely be uncovered, as illustrated in Figure 6.5. These tasks are typically important to the success of the project and could result in ineffective performance improvement solutions if left uncompleted.

FIGURE 6.4. COVERAGE OF PROJECT MANAGEMENT WBS EFFORTS.

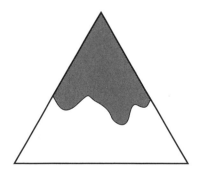

FIGURE 6.5. COVERAGE OF PROJECT PARTICIPANT WBS EFFORTS.

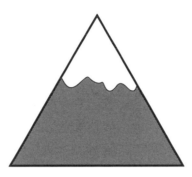

FIGURE 6.6. COMBINED COVERAGE OF WBS EFFORTS.

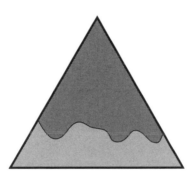

Obviously, then, the project manager and the project participants should be involved in creating the WBS. By combining the insights of both, you attain more complete task coverage, as depicted in Figure 6.6. It may take additional effort to involve others, but the improved accuracy of the schedule and the project management pays for the time spent.

With the inputs of the participants included in the WBS exercise, begin making a list of major activities that must be accomplished. In HPT performance improvement projects, this typically comes from the performance analysis and the list of interventions that must be put in place to improve performance. The major activities should be taken one at a time and broken down into tasks necessary to achieve that activity.

In addition to group brainstorming about the tasks, the team should use continuous-improvement concepts to provide information to structure the project and generate the detailed task list (Kerzner, 1989). Such information can be gathered from other project team members who have worked on similar projects, other project managers who have managed similar projects, project retrospectives, and reviewing project notebooks from other performance improvement projects in your organization. Search for tasks that were overlooked in the initial WBS and discovered later in the project. There is little reason for the organization to repeat such an error.

If a large number of participants are working on the WBS process, hand out pads of sticky notes and have each participant identify as many tasks as possible. As a group, arrange the notes on a wall or large sheet of paper to resemble the WBS diagram in Figure 6.2. As you begin to structure the tasks, additional ones will become evident and should be added.

It is important to realize that not all components break down to the same level of detail. Tasks under one component may break into three or four levels; others may require only one or two. The chart does not have to be visually balanced, so simply structure the tasks to the appropriate level of detail.

When identifying tasks, write each to contain both a verb and noun and make them sufficiently descriptive to avoid confusion or misinterpretation. A task labeled "format" is a disaster waiting to happen. "Format slides" is better, eliminating the question of what is to be formatted. "Format new presentation slides" may be appropriate if there are a number of formatting tasks or if there are various versions or groups of presentation slides.

Continue to break the work down until a task list is developed that meets the following criteria:

- It is possible to assign one (and only one) owner to each of the lowest-level tasks.
- It is possible to define deliverables or output for each lowest-level task.
- Quality can be monitored through performance criteria associated with each deliverable.
- The tasks communicate the work to be accomplished.
- The likelihood that a task is omitted or work flow forgotten is minimal.
- Each task is small enough so that estimates of duration are credible.

Step 2: Add Tasks Specific to Implementation

Those framing the WBS may inadvertently leave off time-consuming project activities. Remember to include tasks for approval cycles; key project review cycles; key project meetings; management or customer interfaces; quality assessments and fixing defects; training on new processes, procedures, systems, or equipment; project management; and retrospectives, phase reviews, and project closing.

Step 3: Ensure That Tasks Meet Duration Criteria

If you believe the WBS is complete, have the project participants make initial estimates as to how long each of the lowest-level tasks will take to complete. Compare the estimates to your criteria for WBS task duration. Remember that the rule of thumb for task duration is no shorter than you are willing to track and no longer than two weeks (or your selected maximum duration). If any tasks last longer than your criteria indicate they should, go back and break them down to the next level.

Fewer levels of detail are generally required for projects that are smaller (that is, have fewer activities and less cost), less risky, similar to past projects, or easier to define (that is, less susceptible to change).

More levels of detail are generally required for projects that are larger, more risky, dissimilar to past projects, or difficult to define (susceptible to change).

Step 4: Convert the Diagram into a List

When you are finally satisfied that you have a complete WBS and that the level of detail is appropriate for your project, convert the WBS diagram into a hierarchical list. This will allow it to be entered into a project scheduling software package for the continued development of the project schedule.

If your project schedule software does not automatically assign coding or numbering to each task, do so to allow for easy reference and to reduce confusion when discussing tasks (especially over the phone).

Step 5: Specify Measurable Deliverables

Every task within a project must have a measurable deliverable or output. Otherwise, it is not really a task; discovering this late in the scheduling process can require redoing the schedule. By defining the deliverables now, you ensure that all tasks are real and you also become prepared for the next phase of project scheduling, in which the relationships between tasks are determined. Being able to match the output of tasks with the necessary input speeds the process. Specifying a measurable delivery could be skipped and completed later, but the advantages of doing it now are significant.

To determine what the output will be, it is best to have the person who will most likely be responsible for the task define the deliverable. These people tend to be more knowledgeable about specifics than the project manager. As the project participants should be gathered to develop the WBS anyway, it will speed the scheduling process to have them work on this.

Tasks need to have clearly and concisely defined deliverables or outputs. There should be no confusion regarding what will be produced by the task. Most people do not want to take on a task with ill-defined expectations. If an output is different than what is needed to begin the next task in the project, the project stops while participants determine how to resolve the problem.

Deliverables must be clearly measurable to provide a basis for determining if the task is really complete. Tasks that result in "understanding" or other intangibles are measurable only by opinion. The problem with opinions is that they are sometimes incorrect. Halting the project to go back and perform a task that was once thought complete causes serious scheduling problems. Look for concrete measures of completion.

Avoid the use of acronyms, technical jargon, and slang in the description of the deliverable. The objective of creating the description is to ensure consistent and reliable communication through the entire project team. Focus on clarity.

Look for missing or redundant deliverables as you review the tasks. If the same deliverable is listed twice, check to ensure that it is really needed twice. If it is, consider changing the wording of the deliverables to distinguish them from one another and prevent future confusion. If they are not needed twice, you may have discovered two different wordings for one task. Remove any duplicate tasks. If a deliverable is needed but missing from the list, check the tasks to see if the deliverable is really there but described differently. For example, producing a book may be described as "document printed" instead of "book produced." If the deliverable is definitely not on the list, a necessary task has been forgotten.

Step 6: Establish Project Milestones

In Chapter Two, the topic of project milestones was introduced: they are events that mark a unit of progress on the overall schedule. A milestone should signal completion of several tasks that represent a significant portion of work or progress within the performance improvement project; it should never be a task itself. Refer to Figure 6.2 to see that "develop strategy" represents a significant number of lower-level tasks. Thus it could be selected as a milestone, contingent upon completion of all the lower-level tasks beneath it.

When establishing milestones, keep the following in mind:

- They should represent the completion of natural groups of tasks. Highly contrived milestones are typically not meaningful to measuring project progress.
- They should correspond with important project decisions.
- They should be limited in number so as to maintain importance. Weekly milestones on a one-year project hardly seem monumental.

- They should be set at useful intervals. A project with all the milestones in the second half of the project could be at risk from little progress being measured in the first half.

A Sample WBS

It might be helpful to go through the creation of a sample WBS. Consider the example of the creation of a cheeseburger with bacon. (Please, no comments about fat or cholesterol.)

Step 1: Break the Project into Components. The project objective: make a cheeseburger with bacon for dinner. A partial list of required tasks: flip hamburger, turn on stove, choose roll, separate bacon strips, grill bun, drain bacon, slice tomato, grill hamburger, slice roll, shape hamburger patty, other.

Organizing the list into a WBS diagram, the major headings look like this:

Bread	**Meat**	**Toppings**
Select	Select	Select
Prepare	Prepare	Prepare
Grill	Grill	

It does not take long to realize that this organization of the tasks will lead to unacceptable final results; a first-time cook might assume that all the bread tasks should be done first, then the meat tasks and finally the toppings tasks. This would result in project failure: a cold burger. Altering the WBS organization for successful results, the major headings now look like this:

Select	**Prepare**	**Cook**	**Assemble**
Bread	Bread	Bread	
Meat	Meat	Meat	
Toppings	Toppings		

Step 2: Add Tasks Specific to Implementation. Reviewing potential issues, for this small project there is only one to be concerned about: quality assessment and fixing defects. This can be added to the list of tasks.

Step 3: Ensure That Tasks Meet Duration Criteria. Because of the critical nature of quality in the project, all identified tasks will be included, regardless of duration.

Step 4: Convert the Diagram into a List. The full hierarchical list based upon the organization looks like this:

1.0	Selection
1.1	Bread
1.1.1	Determine alternatives
1.1.2	Make selection
1.2	Meat
1.2.1	Determine alternatives
1.2.2	Make selection
1.3	Toppings
1.3.1	Determine alternatives
1.3.2	Make selection
2.0	Preparation
2.1	Bread
2.1.1	Slice roll
2.1.2	Apply butter
2.2	Meat
2.2.1	Hamburger
2.2.1.1	Separate portions
2.2.1.2	Shape patty
2.2.1.3	Season
2.2.2	Bacon
2.2.2.1	Separate strips
2.2.2.2	Trim
2.3	Toppings
2.3.1	Slice tomatoes
2.3.2	Lettuce
2.3.2.1	Rinse
2.3.2.2	Separate
2.3.3	Slice pickles
2.3.4	Slice cheese
3.0	Cooking
3.1	Bread
3.1.1	Set grill to medium low
3.1.2	Place bun on grill
3.1.3	Monitor until done
3.1.4	Remove from grill
3.1.5	Assess quality and redo if necessary

3.2	Meat	
3.2.1	Bacon	
3.2.1.1	Set grill to medium high	
3.2.1.2	Place bacon on grill	
3.2.1.3	Turn when ready	
3.2.1.4	Remove when done	
3.2.1.5	Place on napkin to drain	
3.2.1.6	Assess quality and redo if necessary	
3.2.2	Hamburger	
3.2.2.1	Place hamburger on grill	
3.2.2.2	Turn when ready	
3.2.2.3	Remove when done	
3.2.2.4	Place on napkin to drain	
3.2.2.5	Assess quality and redo if necessary	
4.0	Assembly	
4.1	Place hamburger on bun heel	
4.2	Place cheese on hamburger	
4.3	Place bacon on cheese	
4.4	Apply toppings	
4.5	Place bun crown on top	
4.6	Assess quality and redo if necessary	
5.0	Consumption	
5.1	Eat the burger	
5.2	Assess hunger and redo if necessary	

Step 5: Specify Measurable Deliverables. To avoid dragging this out too long, here is but a selection of the measurables:

Item	Task	Deliverable
2.3	Toppings	
2.3.1	Slice tomatoes	Two even slices, cut cleanly
2.3.2	Lettuce	
2.3.2.1	Rinse	Clean
2.3.2.2	Separate	Two large leaves, bun size
2.3.3	Slice pickles	Three thin, even slices
2.3.4	Slice cheese	One large, even slice

Step 6: Establish Project Milestones. Looking at the WBS diagram, we decide on milestones that indicate the completion of "prepare," "cook," and "assemble," as they mark major transitions in the project and serve as an assessment of readiness to move to the next phase.

Karen's Story

It was 10 A.M. and the office was buzzing with activity. Jim was expecting an update on the progress of the performance improvement project, and Karen was finishing a change to its schedule. The project team had come across a necessary task that had not been caught in the WBS session. Karen had expected one or two of these to show up during the project, and this was the first one. She made careful notes in the project notebook to ensure that neither she nor any other project manager left it off any future WBS. Fortunately, it would take only one person-day to complete the task.

At the start of the project, Karen had been concerned about taking an entire afternoon to create a WBS. It seemed like a lot of work, but the team made it through the entire process. Even during the meeting, she began to see the advantage of taking the time and the effort. She had been able to pull the entire project team together for the WBS session; it seemed every participant made a point of being there. And boy, was she glad. They had identified tasks she would not have thought of; the schedule would have been a bust if hers were the only inputs. As a group, they put the project management activities into the WBS, including project meetings, appropriate target-audience meetings, and update meetings with the management team.

They did have some difficulty at first. Attempting to gauge how far to break down the tasks took a few adjustments to avoid making some tasks too short or too long. But in the end, the team had created an appropriate WBS.

Perhaps the most important outcome was the clarity that came from ensuring that there were measurable deliverables for each task. There were clear differences in perception among the team members in the beginning; if they had gone into the project with that initial level of ambiguity, the project would have been brought to a halt. Instead, they spent a little time adjusting task descriptions to ensure that everybody would understand them and their outputs. They even discovered a task that was on the WBS twice with different wording.

Karen had been concerned about the planning time needed to assess quality and make corrections. But the group agreed to create an assessment and rework tasks just before every major milestone. If there was no rework, they would accelerate the schedule; otherwise, the project would still be on schedule.

Karen snapped back from her reminiscing. The latest copy of the schedule had finished printing and she needed to get to Jim's office. She was looking forward to the update and to telling Jim that they were off schedule by only a day.

Dealing with Project Scheduling Software

Project scheduling software has been a blessing and a curse to the project manager. It is clearly a blessing in that it has become the "word processor" for project management activities. The project schedule is the language of project management. In the days before personal computers, project managers created project schedules by hand. Changes were about as welcome as poison ivy. But, just as word processing software allows easy modifications to documents, project scheduling software allows easy changes to schedules. The curse? Most project scheduling software requires a navigator, helmsperson, and science officer to operate. However, the most recent software releases have made significant progress in simplifying operations.

Figure 6.7 is an example of a printout from a project scheduling package. Throughout the rest of Part Two (Chapters Seven through Ten), this schedule will be developed to demonstrate how it is built up in stages.

The printout is a Gantt chart, Gantt being the name of the man who created this kind of chart. It is part of a schedule for producing an instructional intervention. On the left side of the chart is a list of tasks necessary to complete the project; this is the hierarchical list version of the WBS. Notice also that the software has automatically assigned an ID number to each task for easy reference.

This is a time-scaled Gantt chart. Across the top of the schedule is a scale that indicates when tasks will start and end, and how long they will occur. On this scale is a series of boxes next to the tasks, which indicate when the tasks occur. At this early stage in schedule creation, the software assumes that all tasks take one day and occur on the day the tasks are entered. This will change as additional information is entered into the schedule.

Looking at the WBS, note that tasks 1, 17, and 36 are at the highest level in the hierarchy, indicated by the fact that their task names are not indented. Under task 17, tasks 18, 19, 23, 24, 25 are the next level down in the hierarchy, indicated by being indented. Under task 19, tasks 20, 21, 22 are yet another level lower.

You probably have noted that not all tasks have bars on the time scale. Some have brackets. This also corresponds to some of the tasks' bold print. The tasks with bold print and a bracket will not be implemented; they are summary tasks. Look back at task 19, which is a summary task. "Conduct instructional analysis" is broken down into three subtasks (20, 21, and 22). Summary task 19 is never

FIGURE 6.7. SCHEDULE FOR PRODUCING INSTRUCTIONAL INTERVENTION.

ID	Task Name
1	**Front End Analysis**
2	**Conduct Preliminary Planning Activities**
3	Confirm projected timelines for completing each phase of project
4	Draft composition of project advisory team
5	Define specific objectives/activities for first PAT meeting
6	Determine who will produce final instructional materials
7	Hold Project Advisory Team Meeting(s)
8	**Gather/Analyze Competency Assessment Data**
9	Describe current situation (what is)
10	Describe desired situation (what should be)
11	Give general description of the change strategy
12	Describe expected organizational impact
13	Determine outcome levels that should be Evaluated
14	Identify Important Characteristics of the Target Audience
15	Develop Initial Diffusion Strategies
16	Develop Initial Dissemination Plans
17	**Instructional Design**
18	Write Overall Training Goal
19	**Construct Instructional Analysis**
20	Conduct goal analysis
21	Conduct subordinate skills analysis

FIGURE 6.7. SCHEDULE FOR PRODUCING INSTRUCTIONAL INTERVENTION (CONTINUED).

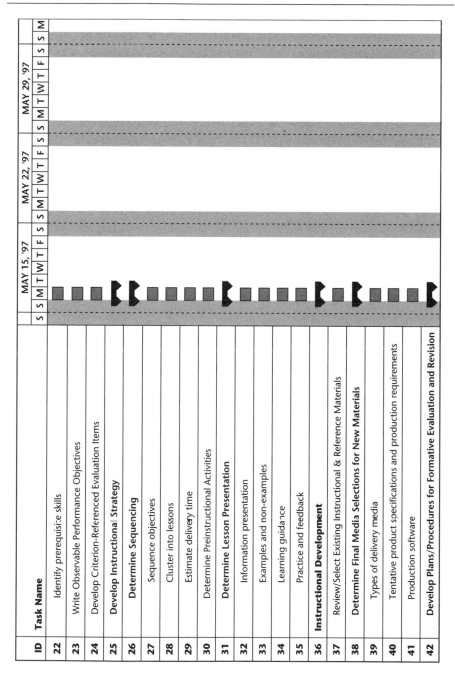

implemented, has no deliverables, and is complete when the three subtasks (which do have deliverables) are complete. When the task duration data are entered into the plan, the bars will stretch across the time scale, as will the task summary brackets indicating the total duration of the instructional analysis activities.

Lastly, notice that though 18 and 19 are at the same level in the WBS hierarchy, 18 is a task (regular text and a bar on the time scale) and 19 is a summary task (bold text and a bracket on the time scale). Why? Because task 18 is a lowest-level task. It has no subtasks and will produce a deliverable. Summary task 19 has subtasks and will not result in a deliverable. Remember, tasks do not have to break down to the same level in the WBS. Some may break down to one level, others to four levels. You will need to deal with tasks and subtasks on the same level in the hierarchy when working with scheduling software.

CHAPTER SEVEN

ESTIMATING THE SCHEDULE

After establishing the work breakdown structure, you must determine how long each task will take to complete. This facilitates looking at the total schedule to determine when each task can start and how long the overall project will take.

Bill's Story

At his desk, Bill pored over the project schedule. Something was wrong, but just what was not obvious. The performance improvement project was experiencing more schedule slips. It seemed that every project task was taking longer than the schedule allowed for. This made no sense; Bill had sat down and carefully determined how long each task should take. Why were the task owners not meeting their assigned completion times? Bill decided to find out.

He found Barb at her desk. "Say, Barb, got a minute?"

She looked up from her work. "Sure, Bill. What's up?"

Bill opened up the project schedule. "This says the video shoot should've taken three days. We're now on day seven. I was hoping you could tell me why."

Barb stiffened in her chair. She was obviously becoming defensive. "Listen, Bill. A video shoot of this complexity takes nine days minimum. I don't know where that three-day estimate came from, but it's absolutely wrong. Nobody asked me how long it would take."

Bill checked with several other project participants; if future tasks were going to take longer to complete than the schedule indicated, he wanted to know now. Bill was surprised at their answers—they didn't know; they hadn't given much thought to how long their tasks would take.

Kelly's present task was late, and other tasks were waiting for her. Perhaps she could shed some light on why things were off schedule. Bill had specifically asked her how much time would be involved; she had told him it would take two days. This was day four.

There she was, walking down the hall. "Kelly, can I talk to you for a minute? I have a question about the project."

"Only for a minute, Bill," she said. "I have some tight deadlines."

"Okay, I'll make it short. When I asked you how long it would take to test the training on the milling machines, you said two days. What happened?"

Kelly looked puzzled. "Well, of course the testing isn't done. The milling machine is used by engineering most of the time. I only get two hours a day on it. The testing only takes sixteen hours, which normally means two work days, but with limited machine availability it'll take me eight days."

"Hey, Bill!" Brian ran up the hallway. "Thought I'd better tell you as soon as possible. I just heard from the duplication department. The materials are going to take three times as long to copy. Their quote of five days was valid at the beginning of the month, but since we're three weeks late they can't do it. This is the end of the quarter and they're all tied up with duplicating financial reports for the board and the financial backers. Sorry, but I thought you'd want to know."

Schedule Estimation

Determining how long tasks take to complete, when each can be started, and when the entire project can be finished are crucial issues. The project schedule is used extensively when the project plan is set into motion (Dreger, 1992). Figure 7.1 illustrates what a project schedule looks like when the time estimates are loaded onto it.

The quality of the time estimates have a significant and substantial impact on the quality of the schedule and the management of the performance improvement project. This raises the question of what estimation actually is and how it differs from "just taking a guess."

FIGURE 7.1. SAMPLE PROJECT SCHEDULE WITH TIME ESTIMATES.

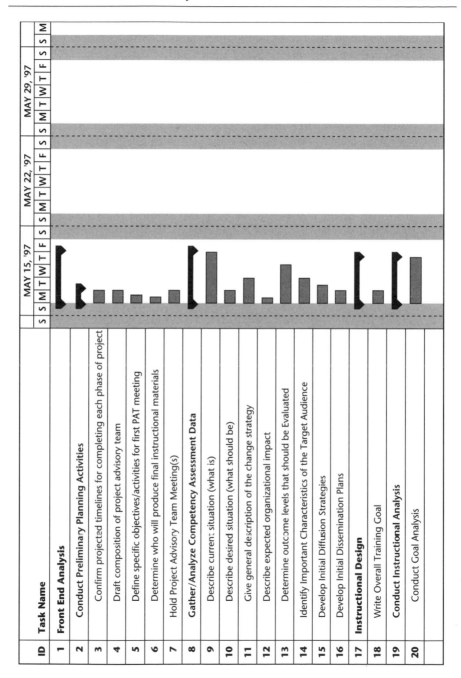

Estimation: A Definition

Estimation is a significant skill that differentiates successful project managers from those who struggle to bring their performance improvement projects to conclusion in a reliable manner (Kezsbaum, 1989).

Estimate is a word most people are familiar with. If you have substantial auto repair work done, you generally receive an estimate of the cost. If you have construction done on your home, you generally receive an estimate of the costs and time to complete the work.

People doing such estimation look carefully at the work required and use their experience and knowledge in formulating an approximation of the time or cost. They do not simply take wild, uninformed guesses. You would have little confidence in a building contractor who supplied you with an estimate without looking at the plans or material requirements. Likewise, if the estimate was based on misleading data—"the last house took a month, so this one should too"—the job requirements could easily be 50 percent greater, even though they too are house construction tasks.

The significant difference between an estimate and a guess is the method and the basis by which each is created. A guess uses no established method and creates a prediction without sufficient information. "Who do you think I saw today?" is a question that prompts a guess. There is no method of deriving an answer based on information.

In contrast, an estimate uses an established method to calculate an approximation based on known, comparative, or historical information. "How many tiles will it take to cover the kitchen floor?" can be easily estimated using an established method (calculation of area) and known information (dimensions of the room).

The Importance of Estimation

Having task estimates (rather than guesses) creates the following important benefits for the project (Lewis, 1993a):

- It leads to more realistic plans. Plans based on guesses are notoriously inaccurate. The value of the schedule is greatly diminished if there is a low probability that the tasks will happen as scheduled.
- It creates ownership. If the individuals who will be responsible for implementing the tasks participate in the estimation process, they are more likely to feel obligated to ensure that the estimates are accurate.
- It reveals uncertainties and risks in the project. If there is substantial conflict over the estimation of a task, it may indicate that the work breakdown structure is not at a sufficient level to manage the project or that additional environmental factors are having an impact on task completion.

- It balances optimism. People tend to be optimistic about their ability to complete tasks within given amounts of time. Using estimations rather than guesses significantly reduces this tendency.

Effort and Duration

A common pitfall must be avoided in schedule estimation (Grey, 1981). There are two types of time to consider in a schedule: effort and duration. The difference between them is subtle but significant. Consider the following simple example.

A football game has four fifteen-minute quarters. The actual play of the game is sixty minutes; thus only sixty minutes of effort are required to complete a football game. However, the effort time of the game is not the same as the duration. During the game there are time-outs, clock stoppages after certain plays, halftime, injuries, and other delays. Therefore, game duration (real elapsed time) is greater than the time effort required. It is not unusual for a football game to take between two and three hours to finish. If your Saturday project schedule included only sixty minutes to watch the game, the misestimation would cause any other tasks you wanted to do that day to slip.

To avoid this sort of problem in project scheduling, ensure that every participant in the task estimation process has a clear understanding of the difference between effort time and actual task duration. If effort-based estimates are used on a duration-scaled project schedule, you will have to take significant and painful adaptive action during the project to keep it on schedule. In specific cases where some effort-based times were inadvertently used rather than duration, the entire schedule had to be reestimated in the midst of the project.

Time or Period Sensitivity

Task estimation accuracy may depend on knowing when the task will occur. The duration of some tasks can vary greatly based on the prevailing environment. The environment is sometimes greatly affected by the period or time.

For instance, consider the following questions: How long do you think it takes to get on the Matterhorn ride at Disneyland? Does your estimate change if the date is July 4 (the park's busiest day)? Does it change if the date is December 24 (its slowest day)? The actual waits are two and a half hours on July 4, thirty-five seconds on December 24. Obviously, period makes a substantial difference.

Period can greatly influence the duration of your performance improvement project tasks as well. What if you need to gather data on how much your company is spending on a particular activity? The time to get it from the finance department is probably highly affected by the period. Finance folks are usually very busy at the end of the month; it might take three days to receive your information then. But if you ask in the middle of the month, you might have it in two hours.

The time of day can have an equally significant impact on task duration. Consider the following question: How long does it take to drive across Boston? Does your estimate change if it is 2 A.M.? If it is 5:15 P.M.? Again, the estimates swing wildly based on when the tasks will occur. (At 2 A.M. the drive takes about twenty-five minutes; to the best of our knowledge, nobody has ever made it across Boston at 5:15 P.M.)

At work, *when* something is done affects *how long* it will take. Mornings are usually filled with meetings, for example; in the afternoons people tend to work on their projects. The result may be that complex documents print from the network 50 percent slower in the afternoon than in the morning.

Estimation Confidence Limits

How much confidence do you want in your task estimates? Many projects strive for 90 percent accuracy. That will create a project that is no more than 10 percent late (usually less). But estimating at 90 percent accuracy can be more difficult than it first appears to be. To demonstrate, complete the following estimation exercise.

For each of the following ten items, provide a low and high guess such that you are 90 percent sure that the correct answer falls in between the two. The challenge is to be in a range that is neither too narrow (overconfident) nor too wide (underconfident). If you successfully meet the challenge, you will miss a maximum of 10 percent—one error or fewer. The answers are at the end of the chapter—no fair peeking till you're done!

	90 PERCENT CONFIDENCE RANGE	
	LOW	HIGH
1. Michelangelo's age at death	____	____
2. Length of the Nile River (km or mi)	____	____
3. Number of OPEC member countries	____	____
4. 1985 gross national product of Canada	____	____
5. Diameter of the moon (mi)	____	____
6. Weight of an empty Boeing 747 (kg or lbs)	____	____
7. Year of the Three Mile Island accident	____	____
8. Gestation period (days) of an Asian elephant	____	____
9. London to Tokyo air distance (km or mi)	____	____
10. Deepest known ocean point (m or ft)	____	____

How did you do? Did you achieve 90 percent accuracy? Compare the correct answers with your ranges. Are yours close to the actual answer, or are they broad? Having a method and information would probably have helped improve your accuracy and range.

The Estimation Process

There are many methods for estimating task and overall schedule duration. Most are highly specialized and focus on professions other than human performance technology. Bridge construction estimation, for example, is interesting but hardly applicable. At least one general estimation process, however, works well for performance improvement projects (Martin, 1976):

1. Approximate the duration of each lowest-level task. Have task owners create an initial estimate. As they will most likely implement the tasks, they will probably know how long it should take to complete them. Owners should make their best educated guesses.

2. Check documented history. Compare today's initial "guesstimates" with historical information. Look for sources of information that indicate how long similar tasks have taken under similar circumstances. Places to look for information include these:

   Historical data in participants' previous project notes

   Project notebooks from similar performance improvement projects

   Results from retrospective meetings at the conclusion of projects

3. Check historical documentation against people's actual earlier experiences. Comparing historical data with the knowledge of people who actually participated in previous projects can help increase estimate reliability. In some cases, your organization might not have done an exemplary job of capturing what it learned from earlier performance improvement projects; if so, people's recollection of their experiences may rightly replace what would otherwise be considered reliable, documented, historical data. In looking at people's experience, consider the following:

   Experience of the task owner

   Experience of other task performers

   Experience of other project managers

4. Consider existing algorithmic estimation techniques. Comparing the existing estimation with a data-driven, impartial estimation technique further improves

the accuracy of the estimate. Unfortunately, most of these sources and techniques exist in project areas outside human performance technology. There are, for example, methods of estimating highway construction based on length, number of lanes, terrain, and number of overpasses, but human performance technologists face the challenge of creating their own measurements.

One excellent source of information provides some guidelines and rules of thumb for calculating estimates for the instructional design portion of the performance improvement project: *ID Project Management: Tools and Techniques for Instructional Designers and Developers* (Greer, 1992). This book includes several good estimation calculations and generally accepted guidelines for instructional design tasks.

5. Modify estimates. Based on the comparisons, reevaluate the initial estimates and make appropriate changes. The modification should be assessed by more than one person to ensure that appropriate comparisons were made and that the modifications have sound, rational, and clear assumptions.

6. Document assumptions. All the assumptions made in the estimation process should be clearly captured in the project notebook. This ensures a learning organization environment. If highly accurate estimates are made, you will want to reproduce the performance on your next project. If the estimates are wrong, you will want to determine what assumptions were incorrect and improve the estimation next time around.

Pitfalls and Problems with Estimation

Certain problems and traps typically plague task estimation (Grey, 1981). As the project manager, you should be aware of each of them and minimize their occurrence and impact on your estimation efforts.

First, some people dislike estimating; many rank it right up there with having their teeth cleaned at the dentist and are thus hesitant to participate in the estimation process, which could adversely affect the quality of the plan. There are several causes of this aversion:

- It requires work and detailed planning. Most folks would rather avoid what they perceive as unnecessary work, and many dislike the orientation to detail.
- People are held to estimates. When people estimate how long a task will take, they are typically expected to complete the task within the estimated time. With no estimate, they cannot be held to a specific time deadline.
- Estimates are often wrong. The very nature of estimates means that many will be inaccurate at some level, and some will be flat-out wrong. People do not like being wrong, especially if they are held to the incorrect estimate.

- Estimates are criticized. Estimates are a personal conclusion based on available evidence. Personal conclusions are open to critique, and most people do not like having to defend their conclusions.

Second, people may be too optimistic. Whenever you get a group of people together, their ability to assess the time necessary for tasks is usually inaccurate on the optimistic side. Overoptimism in estimation will produce a schedule that cannot be met with the available resources. Typical causes of this behavior include the following:

- *Overconfidence.* In general, people tend to be overly confident of their abilities. This is often exacerbated when a group is estimating its capabilities.
- *Political or performance pressure.* Organizations tend to reward people perceived to be the top performers; being conservative in task estimation compared to others might not create perception of top performance. Additionally, the organization can communicate urgency to complete a project quickly, which may inadvertently (or intentionally) create pressure to be optimistic in estimation.
- *Lack of feedback.* If people have been optimistic in the past with feedback on their estimation accuracy, they are likely to continue to be optimistic.
- *Confusion about effort and duration.* As explained earlier, effort and duration are very different. When estimating, many people think in terms of effort required rather than the duration of the task.

Third, people may lack needed information. Without information, an estimate rapidly degrades to an educated guess. The following are reasons why necessary information might be unavailable:

- No historical data is available for use in estimation. This can be due to a lack of effort in retrieving and preparing the information, or perhaps to a lack of rigor by the organization in capturing data for future use.
- Insufficient or nonexistent feedback was provided about previous estimation efforts. If your estimates are typically off by 50 percent and you never receive any feedback on it, you are likely to use the same methods and information in the next estimation effort.
- Estimates are done too early. A clear understanding of the task is essential to accurate estimation. Some project managers might attempt to accelerate the project planning process by pulling up planning tasks out of sequence. If the estimates are done while project tasks are poorly defined or changing, their accuracy will be of very questionable quality.

Fourth, estimates may be done at too high a level. Often, many individual tasks are associated with a performance improvement project. Estimating how long each will take requires time and effort; thus there is a natural temptation to push estimation up one level in the work breakdown structure. This may indeed save planning time, but at the cost of schedule integrity. There are at least two reasons for this.

Generally, the ability to accurately estimate tasks is reduced as their size increases. If an estimate for a group of tasks is compared to the total of estimates for the individual tasks in the group, in almost every case the latter time will be greater than the former.

Also, when estimating large tasks, any uncertainty in a subtask is transferred to other subtasks. If one subtask has an element of risk or uncertainty, it decreases the accuracy of the estimation. By combining the high-risk task with other subtasks, the estimate inaccuracy is shared by the other subtasks and can amplify the magnitude of the risk in the schedule.

Project Task Estimation Techniques

In addition to estimating individual tasks within the project, some time should be spent estimating the project as a whole (Dreger, 1992). Comparing the estimate for the entire project to the total of estimates for the individual tasks allows for a reality check; the two estimates should not vary much. If they do, you should determine why the variance exists and adjust either the task estimates, the total project estimate, the work breakdown structure, or the dependencies. For example, if the project time generated by individual task estimation is six months and the time for the total project is estimated at eleven months, you should know something is amiss.

Methods of project estimation are similar to those of task estimation, but a few apply only to overall projects. Some of the most popular project estimation techniques follow.

Historical Basis. As with task estimation, looking at previous experience usually yields accurate information for project estimation. Although there is no guarantee that today's performance improvement project will take the same amount of time as past ones, historical comparison usually gets you in the ballpark. Places to look for historical project information include the following:

- *Retrospectives from earlier projects.* Looking over project notebooks from previous projects usually yields valuable information about estimation assumptions that were wrong or right. Likewise, you can look at previous estimated and actual schedules and see which were most accurate.

- *Personal experiences.* If you have managed previous performance improvement projects, your estimates about new ones are valuable because of your experience.
- *Vendor quotes.* If vendor bids have been submitted for similar projects, compare their estimates with yours.
- *Expert opinion.* Finding experienced performance improvement project managers is like striking gold. Ask them to estimate your project based on their experiences.
- *Analogous data.* You might find project notebooks on subjects other than performance improvement. But if their subjects were similar in scope to yours, the notebooks might still provide information that can help in estimating your project.

Partial Decomposition of the Project. If the entire project is too large and complex to estimate, break it down a level in the work breakdown structure. For example, you might be more comfortable estimating in phases (such as design, development, or implementation) or by component (such as computer-based training [CBT] or recognition system redesign).

Delphi Estimating. This approach usually takes several people one or two days to implement. Although it typically yields a very reliable estimate, the resource investment makes it a technique reserved for very large or high-risk projects. Delphi estimating is accomplished through the following process:

1. Select between four and twelve people as an estimating team. Be sure to include experts, project team members, and people from whom you need buy-in of the resulting estimate.
2. Gather the team and brief them on the project and the Delphi estimating process.
3. Discuss the project tasks and all known project, environment, and resource problems.
4. Have each team member quickly provide an estimate without collaboration from other members.
5. Collect the estimates and sort them into three groups: best, most likely, and worst.
6. As a group, discuss the average of the most-likely estimates, inviting those who supplied higher or lower estimates to provide their ideas and insights on why their estimations were so different. This will either expose incorrect assumptions or reveal aspects that others overlooked.

7. Repeat the estimation process until no difference exists in the individual estimates.

Project Probing. This method examines some details of the project to test validity. When probing indicates that the details are reliable, the phases of the project can be compared to ensure that estimation within the phases is appropriate. Begin by looking for similar tasks with very different estimates. Determine which estimates are out of line and make appropriate corrections.

Look for complex tasks with overly optimistic estimates. Look at the highest-complexity tasks and compare their estimates with historical information. Modify the estimates as necessary to bring them into line. Break the project into three phases: analysis and design, development, and testing.

Look at the work breakdown structure and determine if the project is small (one to two pages), medium (three to five pages), or large (more than five pages). Use the chart in Figure 7.2 to determine if the correct amount of time will be spent in each phase. The chart represents the typical amount of time spent on successful projects; if your analysis yields significantly different results from the chart, examine the work breakdown structure, dependencies, and estimates to determine what is causing the difference.

FIGURE 7.2. PROJECT PHASE ANALYSIS.

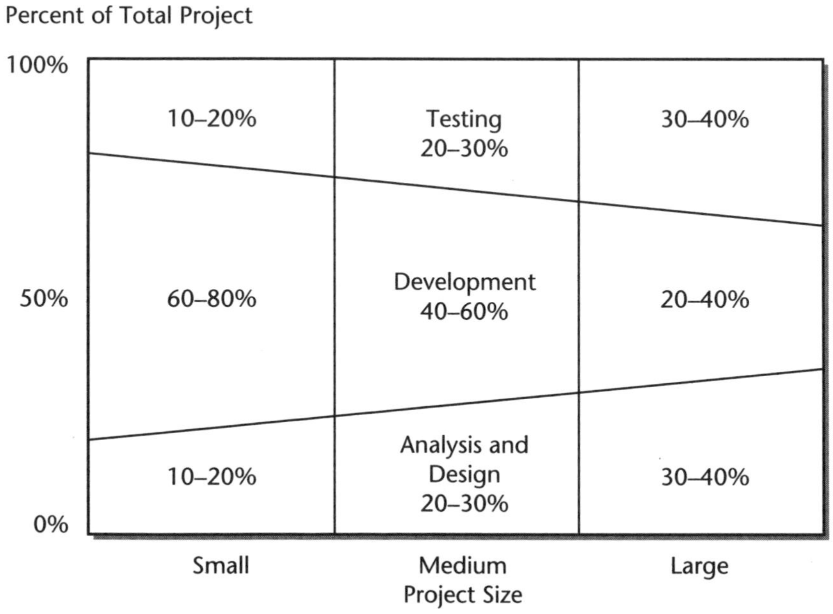

Percent of Total Project

In example one, the performance improvement project has four pages of work breakdown structure, with 25 percent of the project devoted to analysis and design, 50 percent to development, and 25 percent to testing. The project phase analysis indicates that the estimates are within the typical range for a medium-size project.

In example two, the performance improvement project has seventeen pages of work breakdown structure, with 15 percent of the time designated to analysis and design, 60 percent to development, and 25 percent to testing. The testing time percentage is a bit low, but the particulars of the project could justify that. However, the amount of time spent in analysis and design indicates a significant scheduling problem; either the schedule fails to account for substantial analysis and design tasks, or the task estimations are significantly incorrect.

Karen's Story

At her desk, Karen looked over the project schedule. Things were going pretty well, although there were a few problems. During project planning, the participants had gotten together to estimate the time required for the tasks identified in the work breakdown structure. Task owners had been made responsible for estimating their own tasks, with the assistance and review of the other participants. Several potential problems had been averted in the process.

Bob, for example, had been confused about how to estimate the time required for certain tasks. He was going to enter the amount of effort rather than the amount of actual time required to test the training. Had the others not tested his assumptions, that would have thrown the entire schedule off by six days.

Although the project participants had checked their estimates against generally accepted guidelines and the results of other documented performance improvement projects, the overall process turned out slightly optimistic. Originally the total task estimate had been *very* optimistic, but this was discovered when the team compared the resulting schedule to an estimation of the entire project. Their estimates were too aggressive; they were feeling the pressure and importance of the project. The second pass was much closer, but, as Karen was discovering, still a little optimistic.

Walking down the hallway, Karen saw Randy working away at his desk. "Say, Randy, got a minute?"

He looked up. "Sure, Karen. What's up?"

Karen opened up her project notebook. "When we all got together to work on the schedule, you indicated that the video shoot should take eight days. Your report says you're now expecting it to take nine. What can we do to pull it back on schedule? Several other tasks depend on completing that shoot."

Randy stiffened in his chair. He was obviously becoming a bit defensive. "I'm doing my best. My estimate was off, and I feel responsible to get it back on track. I'm hoping I can get some help from Kate and work a little longer today to catch up. I promise I'll do my very best."

Karen smiled. "Thanks, Randy. I know that you'll do the best you can."

"Hey, Karen!" Bob was running up the hallway. "I need to talk to you right away. The documentation team was looking at the schedule, and there seems to be some extra time in the schedule before they have to get the documentation to the duplication department. The schedule shows it's okay, but I thought we'd better check first."

Karen flipped open the project notebook to the estimation assumptions. She seemed to remember something about a potential timing conflict. There it was! "Sorry, Bob, but the team has to get the documentation to the duplication department as scheduled. If we wait, it will be the end of the quarter, and they'll be all tied up with duplicating financial reports for the board and the financial backers. It would make our documentation late."

Confidence Limits: Answers

1. Eighty-nine years (1475–1564)
2. 6,753 km or 4,187 miles
3. Thirteen countries
4. $317,326,000,000
5. 3,484 km or 2,160 miles
6. 177,000 kg or 390,000 lbs
7. 1979 (March 28)
8. 645 days (ouch!)
9. 9,610 km or 5,959 miles
10. 11,030 m or 36,186 ft

CHAPTER EIGHT

IDENTIFYING DEPENDENCY RELATIONSHIPS

Some tasks need to be completed before others can begin. Certain tasks depend on certain others. In creating a videotape, for example, tasks are done sequentially; scripting, shooting, editing, and duplication obviously cannot happen at the same time. Each activity beyond the first follows a previous task and depends on its completion.

Bill's Story

Phil stood patiently at Bill's desk, waiting to be noticed. Bill seemed pretty involved with what he was working on, but Phil's work was important too; he decided to break in. "Bill, can I interrupt you for a few minutes? I think we need to talk about your project."

Bill looked up from the schedule he was attempting to keep on track. "Uh—sure, Phil. Have a seat. What's up?"

Phil considered how to start. Never the politician, he decided to just launch in. "What's up is a good question. I guess what's up is the patience of the folks working on the project. We're all about ready to fall down from exhaustion. We all think the schedule is kind of nuts."

Bill tried really hard not to explode. Didn't they realize he had been working just as hard as they, and that he was exhausted too? He composed himself and decided to probe for more information before responding. "Why do you feel that way?" he asked.

Phil pulled out some notes. "Well, to start with, the schedule is not very efficient. It's not making the best use of our time. For instance, it says I'm supposed to do the first-pass editing on the video but not until all the shooting is done. I could actually start a couple of days after the first taping begins. Instead, I'm sitting around with nothing to do while everybody else is working like crazy. If I start earlier, I could do the work on a reasonable schedule, but waiting until all the shooting is done will force me to work thirteen hours a day for a week to stay on schedule."

Bill listened closely as Phil continued. "Then there's this critical path thing. How can a project have three critical paths? It's nuts. Some of us have two or three critical tasks on the schedule at once. We can't figure out which one is most important. Nobody minds extending themselves to make sure a critical task gets done on time, but 75 percent of the schedule tasks are listed as critical. People are getting burned out.

"And another thing," Phil went on. He was on a roll now; he turned over his page of notes. "Somehow the relationships between the tasks aren't always right. Some tasks shouldn't be started until another one is finished, but that can take weeks. So instead people are being asked to start a task without all the materials they need to proceed. It's causing slips, and people are having to work awfully hard to get back on schedule."

Phil folded up the paper and stuffed it in his pocket. "One last thing you should be aware of. I think Barb has started looking for another job. Last week she worked really long and hard to complete two simultaneously scheduled tasks on the schedule. She did an incredible job. But then she found out one of the tasks really didn't need to be completed until the end of the month. She flipped out. All that sacrifice was unnecessary and didn't help the project at all."

As Phil walked away, Bill sat staring at the project schedule. What was wrong? And more importantly, could he fix it before Linda got wind of this?

Defining Dependencies

The creation of the project schedule is a multistep process. The first step is to determine the tasks to be accomplished to achieve the goals of the performance improvement project. The second step is to determine how long each task will take to complete. After these are done, the schedule will appear to indicate that all the tasks start on the first day of the project and finish at the conclusion of the task duration. This is obviously not a workable plan.

The next step in creating the project schedule is to determine the necessary dependency relationships between the tasks identified in the WBS. This is the most complex of the steps in creating the project schedule (Thomsett, 1993). (A unique vocabulary specific to scheduling and task dependencies exists; a glossary of frequently used terms is in the last section of this chapter.)

To identify the dependency relationships between tasks in the performance improvement project, it is important to understand the different relationships that can exist.

Types of Logical Dependency

There are different relationships between various tasks in the work breakdown structure; not all tasks depend on the completion of another before they can begin. Different task relationships are needed to create a schedule that accurately characterizes how work will be accomplished (Dreger, 1992).

Finish-to-Start

The most frequently used task relationship is referred to as *finish-to-start* (Baker and Baker, 1992). In a finish-to-start relationship, the predecessor task must be fully completed before the successor can begin. This is typically the case when the successor is dependent upon the output of the predecessor.

Remember the example of the trip to Nairobi in Chapter Six? The relationship between the passport task and the visa task was finish-to-start. The traveler could not begin the visa task without the passport in hand. Being 75 percent done with the passport task is not sufficient; it must be 100 percent done.

On a Gantt chart, the finish-to-start relationship is typically indicated by an arrow that flows from the finish of the predecessor to the start of the successor. This is illustrated in Figure 8.1. Note that the successor task has moved out in time

FIGURE 8.1. FINISH-TO-START DEPENDENCY.

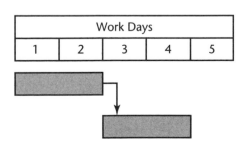

as a result of the task relationship being defined. Before the finish-to-start relationship was indicated, the second task would have begun on day one; it now begins on day three, after the completion of the first task.

The finish-to-start relationship is simple to understand and therefore tends to be overused. Be careful in using it, as it can minimize scheduling flexibility and cause a project to take longer to complete than is actually necessary. If finish-to-start dependencies were indicated for all tasks in the performance improvement project, the schedule would indicate a project duration equal to the total duration of all the individual tasks. The concept that all tasks must be implemented sequentially, with no opportunity for parallel effort, is difficult to accept as necessary (Grey, 1981).

Start-to-Start

Another type of dependency relationship is referred to as *start-to-start*. In this relationship, the start of the successor is constrained by the start of the predecessor. Remember the cheeseburger scheduling example in Chapter Six? Two of the tasks have a start-to-start dependency relationship: cooking the bun, and monitoring progress until done. This is because monitoring cannot start until the cooking begins.

Be careful with the logic associated with the start-to-start dependency. It does *not* mean that the successor *must* start when the predecessor task starts. Also, the inverse of the start-to-start dependency relationship may not be true; starting the predecessor may not require the start of the successor.

On a Gantt chart, the start-to-start relationship is typically indicated by an arrow that flows from the start of the predecessor to the start of the successor. This is illustrated in Figure 8.2. Note that the successor task has not moved out in time as a result of the task relationship being defined. Although there is a dependency relationship, the two tasks can still be done simultaneously.

FIGURE 8.2. START-TO-START DEPENDENCY.

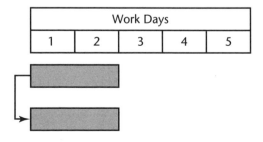

Work Days				
1	2	3	4	5

Initially, it might not be obvious why the dependency relationship needs to be identified. Both tasks originally began on day one, and are still scheduled on day one. As additional dependencies are identified within the project schedule, it is possible that the predecessor will move out in time. With the start-to-start dependency identified, both tasks will move out together, preserving the relationship between the two.

Finish-to-Finish

In the finish-to-finish dependency relationship, the finish of the successor is constrained by the completion of the predecessor. Although the two tasks may be implemented simultaneously, the completion of one task is dependent on the completion of the other.

On a Gantt chart, the finish-to-finish relationship is typically indicated by an arrow that flows from the finish of the predecessor to the finish of the successor. This is illustrated in Figure 8.3. Note that the successor task has not moved out in time as a result of the task relationship being defined. This is because the tasks are of equal duration. If the predecessor's duration changes (slips), then the start and finish of the successor will move out in time with the finish of the predecessor.

Multiple Dependencies

Dependency relationships do not have to exist between only two tasks. Multiple tasks can be involved in the same dependency relationship. Figure 8.4 illustrates a finish-to-start relationship where a successor is dependent upon the completion of two predecessors. If one predecessor is completed but the other is not, the successor cannot begin.

FIGURE 8.3. FINISH-TO-FINISH DEPENDENCY.

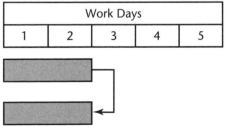

Work Days				
1	2	3	4	5

FIGURE 8.4. FINISH-TO-START DEPENDENCY WITH MULTIPLE PREDECESSORS.

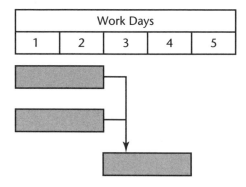

FIGURE 8.5. FINISH-TO-START DEPENDENCY WITH MULTIPLE SUCCESSORS.

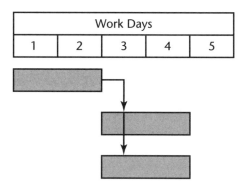

Similarly, Figure 8.5 illustrates a finish-to-start dependency in which two successors are dependent upon the finish of a predecessor. Neither successor may begin until predecessor completion.

Task Lags

In the dependencies described so far, the successor tasks started as soon as possible based on the constraints of the relationship. In the finish-to-finish dependency, the successor started as soon as the predecessor finished. In the start-to-start, the successor started as soon as the predecessor started.

However, in some dependency relationships, a time delay is desired between the dependent tasks. This is referred to as a *lag*, as one task will lag the other by a time period selected by the project manager. Lags help increase the accuracy of the schedule by accounting for inevitable delays; without allowing for these, the schedule completion end date would be overly optimistic (Randolf, 1988). A lag may be applied to any of the three dependencies.

Finish-to-Start Lags

When a lag is applied to a finish-to-start dependency, the start of the successor is delayed by the duration of the lag. This is typically applied as a risk management tool or to inject environmental reality into the schedule. If there is a high risk of the predecessor slipping, the lag creates a safety buffer in the schedule. If a single resource has multiple, back-to-back tasks, the person will need some lag time to keep up with the requirements of the working environment. Figure 8.6 illustrates a one-day lag applied to a finish-to-start relationship.

Start-to-Start Lags

When a lag is applied to a start-to-start dependency, the start of the successor is delayed by the duration of the lag. This is typically used in cases where a finish-to-start dependency would add unnecessary delay to the schedule, but a regular start-to-start cannot be achieved.

If a manual is being produced, for example, the editing does not need to wait until all the writing is done. Applying a finish-to-start dependency would thus cause unnecessary delay. But the editing cannot begin until some writing has been completed, so a start-to-start dependency would schedule editors to be ready

FIGURE 8.6. FINISH-TO-START DEPENDENCY WITH ONE-DAY LAG.

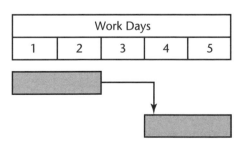

FIGURE 8.7. START-TO-START DEPENDENCY WITH ONE-DAY LAG.

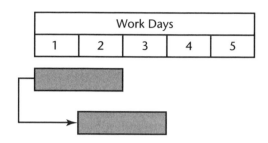

before they are really needed. A start-to-start with a lag, however, would allow some material to be written and allow the editing task to begin early. Figure 8.7 illustrates a one-day lag applied to a start-to-start relationship.

Finish-to-Finish Lags

When a lag is applied to a finish-to-finish dependency, the finish of the successor is delayed by the duration of the lag. This is typical in cases where a finish-to-start dependency would add unnecessary delay to the schedule but a regular finish-to-finish cannot be achieved.

For example, if exercises are being produced, testing of them does not need to wait until all the exercises are completed; a finish-to-start dependency would cause a delay. But testing cannot be concluded until some time after the last exercise is completed, so a finish-to-finish dependency would indicate that testing is to be done earlier than possible. A finish-to-finish with a lag, however, would allow testing to occur on completed exercises and ensure that there is time on the schedule for the testing of the exercise that is completed last. Figure 8.8 illustrates a one-day lag applied to a start-to-start relationship.

FIGURE 8.8. FINISH-TO-FINISH DEPENDENCY WITH ONE-DAY LAG.

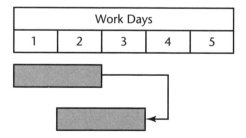

A few words of caution regarding the use of lags. Most project scheduling tools do not have a means of recording the logic behind the lags. The reason for using a lag and for selecting a specific duration can easily be lost. If your program allows notes to be associated with relationships or tasks, ensure that the lag logic is captured. If the software does not have the capacity, ensure that the logic is captured in the project notebook. As changes are made to the schedule, recheck the logic to ensure that it is still valid.

Additionally, realize that the duration of lags will be constant regardless of schedule changes. Refer to the example of the finish-to-finish lag. Suppose we discover that the testing is really going to require twice as much time as originally estimated. If we double the duration of the testing task, the duration of the lag must change too; because the testing is taking twice as long, the lag (testing after the completion of the last exercise) needs to be twice as long. If you change the duration of the task, you will need to change the duration of the lag manually. Don't forget!

Gantt and PERT

By now you are quite familiar with Gantt charts: the work breakdown structure is listed down the left column, with time-scaled bars representing the duration of the tasks and when they occur.

Another project depiction is also commonly used. Program evaluation review technique (PERT) allows a different view of the project schedule that can be helpful when determining the dependencies of tasks. In times past, a project manager had to choose whether to use PERT or Gantt, as they rarely had sufficient time to do both manually. Now, however, most project scheduling software packages allow you to switch views between Gantt and PERT without having to reenter the data.

A PERT chart shows each task as a box and each dependency as a line between the predecessor and the successor. Each box is the same size. There is no time scale such as the Gantt chart uses. Text inside the box indicates duration, start date, and finish date. Other information may be included as well. Figure 8.9 illustrates the differences between Gantt chart and PERT chart depiction of the same schedule information.

The PERT chart adds two task boxes to the schedule labeled *start* and *end*. This aids in reading the chart, which becomes quite complex as tasks are added. The PERT chart indicates that two tasks (A and C) can be started immediately. Task B can be started only after the completion of task A, as there is a finish-to-start dependency between them. When task B and task C are finished, then the schedule ends.

FIGURE 8.9. GANTT AND CRITICAL PATH METHOD CONTRASTED.

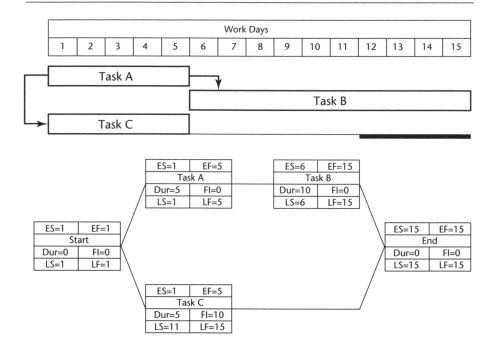

The PERT chart makes it easier to understand the dependencies between the tasks. Unfortunately, PERT makes it more difficult to appreciate task durations and when they occur. Both Gantt and PERT have their advantages in aiding the project manager in analyzing the project schedule.

Critical Path

The PERT chart for the three-task project shows that there are two dependency paths in the schedule. One flows from start to task A to task B to end. The other runs from start to task C to end. These two paths can be implemented concurrently, as they are parallel.

Inside each task box is a field labeled *Dur=*, indicating the duration of each task. The durations of start and end are 0, as they are beginning and end points, not tasks. Tasks A, B, and C have specified durations. Adding the durations of the tasks along the different paths determines how long each will take. The A to B path will take fifteen days, the C path five days.

The longest continuous path from the start of the project to the end is referred to as the *critical path*. The critical path (see Figure 8.10) determines how long the project will take to complete. If any of the tasks along the critical path (referred to as *critical tasks*) should slip and take longer than planned, the project end date will slip too.

A technique called the *critical path method* (CPM) is referred to frequently in the project management world. It is simply the process of creating a PERT chart, determining the critical path, then spending extra project management time on the critical tasks to ensure that the project stays on schedule (Martin, 1976).

Almost all project scheduling software will automatically identify the critical path. In the PERT view, the critical dependencies are usually indicated by a bold line (as in Figure 8.10) or a red line. In the Gantt view, the bars representing the critical tasks along the critical path are changed to red.

The critical path is an important tool for project management. It helps to focus attention and effort on the tasks most important to maintaining the schedule. A word of warning in regard to identifying the task dependencies: avoid creating a schedule that has multiple critical paths. Figure 8.11 shows a project schedule with two critical paths. Path A-D-I and path C-G-K take the same amount of time and thus are both critical paths.

With two critical paths, it is difficult to identify which tasks to manage closely. It becomes an ongoing issue of deciding which of the critical paths is more critical. Additionally, most performance improvement project teams comprise a few individuals rather than large groups. In such cases, one person could be responsible for two simultaneous critical tasks. If so, the risk of tasks being completed late or project participants burning out increases. If there are multiple critical

FIGURE 8.10. PERT WITH CRITICAL PATH.

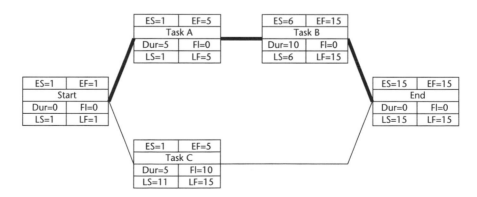

FIGURE 8.11. PERT CHART WITH MULTIPLE CRITICAL PATHS.

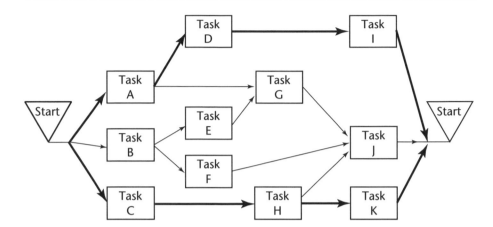

paths on the schedule, the dependencies should be reexamined to ensure that they are correct and necessary. Wherever possible, alter the dependencies to eliminate all but one critical path.

As a final risk consideration, determine what portion of the project's total tasks are critical. If more than 50 percent are so designated, there is a high probability of significant schedule slips on the critical path, as well as the end date of the project. Most groups of people simply cannot keep such a large portion of the schedule on track with the precision that the critical path demands.

Schedule Float

Look back to the three-task project example in Figure 8.10. The path defined by tasks A and B is the critical path, and any time slips on it will cause the schedule end to slip. But what will happen to the schedule end date if task C slips? Start by looking at the Gantt version of the schedule illustrated in Figure 8.12.

According to the Gantt chart, task C is scheduled to run from day one to day five. But task C is five days long and the critical path is fifteen days long. This means task C can slip and not affect the end date. This flexibility is referred to as "float" within the schedule. Some tasks can be moved around without causing the schedule end date to move.

This version of the Gantt schedule indicates float by drawing a line indicating the task's range of float. The latest possible implementation is indicated by the dark bar at the end of the line. By looking at the chart, you can determine

FIGURE 8.12. GANTT CHART.

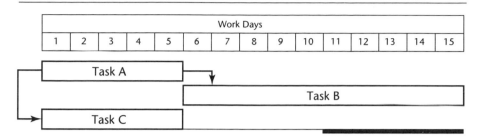

FIGURE 8.13. PERT CHART.

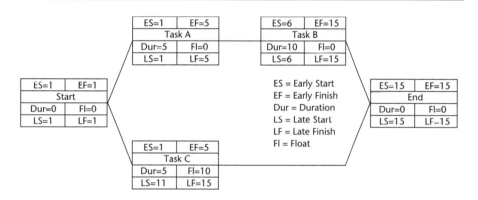

several important pieces of information about task C: the earliest start is day one, the earliest finish is day five, the latest start is day eleven, the latest finish is day fifteen, and the total float (late finish minus early finish) is ten days. That represents substantial flexibility in managing task C.

The PERT version of the schedule shows the same information, but in a very different format. Figure 8.13 illustrates this version.

The same important information about the tasks is represented in the PERT chart. The different boxes contain the same information that you were able to calculate from the Gantt chart.

You may prefer the graphic representation the Gantt chart provides, or the convenience of the precalculated dates the PERT chart provides. Consider both a tool for professional project management of performance improvement projects. The PERT calculations may seem trivial with the three-task schedule, but when you are managing a real schedule with three hundred tasks or more, the value of PERT becomes more evident.

Determining Dependencies

To begin the process of determining the dependencies in a schedule, refer back to the graphic version of the work breakdown structure shown in Figure 6.7. The graphic hierarchical structure identifies some of the existing relationships and dependencies.

Most project scheduling software allows you to establish a dependency relationship between task summaries. This is the best place to start determining dependencies. For example, if the performance improvement project includes the creation of instruction, you may choose to create finish-to-start dependencies between the analyze, design, develop, implement, and evaluate (ADDIE) phases. This will move entire blocks of tasks into dependency relationships.

Move through the entire work breakdown structure and consider the logical dependencies for each lowest-level task. Most tasks will have a dependency relationship with another task, but some might not. If you find several lower-level tasks without identified dependencies, reexamine them carefully to ensure that necessary dependency relationships have not been overlooked.

To help determine logical dependencies, consider the deliverables identified in the work breakdown structure process. When a task has a deliverable, it typically flows to another task, allowing it to start. Tracking the work flow and the deliverables will identify the majority of dependencies. Do not be surprised if the majority of identified dependencies are finish-to-start or start-to-start; this is typical of first-pass efforts (Lewis, 1993a). Later in the scheduling process, the schedule will be optimized based on the project priorities. At that time, the selected dependency relationships will be reconsidered.

When the dependencies have been identified, look at the resulting schedule in the PERT view. Determine if there are multiple critical paths or if more than 50 percent of the project tasks are defined as critical. If either is the case, reexamine the identified dependencies to determine if they are correct and necessary.

With the dependencies identified, resources can be applied to the tasks and the schedule can be optimized to ensure that it agrees with the established project priorities (see Chapter Nine for a discussion of schedule optimization and resourcing). When the task dependencies have been identified and loaded into the schedule, your schedule Gantt chart should resemble the one in Figure 8.14.

FIGURE 8.14. GANTT CHART WITH DEPENDENCIES.

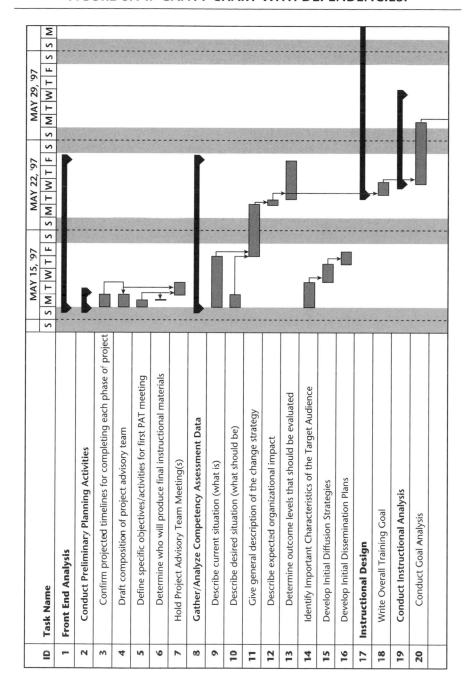

Karen's Story

As the last of the project participants sat down in the meeting room, Karen reviewed her list of discussion points.

"Thanks for coming, everybody," she said. "As I indicated in my message to you, we have more work to do on the schedule for the performance improvement project. If we leave it as is, we'll spend lots of energy and time trying to change the schedule during the project."

Karen rolled out a copy of the current schedule. "To start with, the schedule isn't very efficient. It's not making the best use of our time. For instance, it says Bob is supposed to do the first-pass editing on the video, but not until all the shooting is done. That means he'd be sitting around with nothing to do while others are busy. He could actually start a couple of days after the first taping begins, and do the work on a reasonable schedule without killing himself. I think quite a few other tasks are scheduled like that. Please review your tasks and look for opportunities to begin work before other tasks are totally completed."

Karen had the attention of her audience. She continued: "Something else needs to be fixed. Our current schedule has three critical paths, and that just won't work. Some people will end up with two or three critical tasks on the schedule at once, and who's to say which one is actually the most important to work on? Besides, having that many critical paths has caused three-fourths of the tasks on the schedule to be classified as critical. We'll burn out if we actually try to meet that many critical deadlines. I think what happened is that we started out with too many dependencies between the tasks. Let's look for ways to change them or break them up."

Karen pointed to a few specifics on the schedule. "Another thing. The relationships between the tasks aren't always right. Some tasks aren't supposed to start until another one is finished, but they really need to wait for two or three tasks to finish. When that's the case, people might start a task without all the materials they need. That'll cause slips and people will have to work hard to get back on schedule. Let's reexamine what's really needed to begin each task and make sure the schedule relationships are realistic. It could help our multiple critical-path problem as well."

Karen circled some tasks. "One last thing you should be aware of. By changing some of the dependencies, I think we can build more float into the schedule. That means more flexibility in moving tasks around to prevent heavy workloads. I assume we'd like to avoid marathon workdays if we can."

The team was already beginning to look at the tasks. "Okay, folks," said Karen. "Let's get cracking. It shouldn't take more than an hour to get the plan into shape so we can start assigning tasks and finish tuning the project."

Glossary of Scheduling and Dependency Terms

Critical path   The longest continuous path from the start of the project to the end. The critical path determines the overall length of the project.

Critical path method (CPM)   An approach to project management that identifies the critical path and focuses project management effort and activity on the critical tasks.

Critical task   Task that lies on the critical path. Critical tasks must be completed as scheduled or they will delay the completion of the entire project. Critical tasks have zero float.

Early finish   The earliest date that a task can be completed based on the tasks that precede it and on its own duration.

Early schedule   An entire project schedule that shows the earliest start and finish for every task. This is the schedule most often used for planning and tracking purposes.

Early start   The earliest date that work can begin on a specific task based upon the tasks that precede it.

End date   Completion target of the entire project determined by the duration of the tasks on the critical path.

Float   The length of time a task can be delayed without affecting the project's completion date. Float is equal to the difference between the task's late finish and early finish.

Gantt chart   A chart form that shows a list of tasks down the left side and a time scale across the top. Each task is indicated by a bar whose length corresponds to the duration of the task. The beginning and end of each bar corresponds to the start and finish date of the task.

Late finish   The latest date that a task can be completed without adversely affecting the project's completion date.

Late schedule   An entire project schedule that shows the latest start and finish for every task.

Late start   The latest date that work can begin on a task without adversely affecting the project's completion date.

Network chart   Same as a PERT chart.

Noncritical tasks   Tasks that are not on the critical path. Noncritical tasks have some float in their scheduling.

Path   A sequential series of tasks linked by logical dependencies.

Program evaluation and review technique (PERT)   A chart that shows each task as a box and each dependency relationship as a line between the predecessor and the successor. Each task box is the same size and usually includes information specific to the scheduling of the task.

Time-scaled network chart   Same as a Gantt chart, with dependencies specifically shown.

CHAPTER NINE

MANAGING RESOURCES AND OPTIMIZING THE PLAN

So far in the schedule development process, a detailed list of the tasks to be accomplished has been created, the duration of each task estimated, and the relationships between the tasks determined. The next phase is to apply resources to the schedule to determine task responsibilities and participant workloads.

Bill's Story

Bill returned to his office from a very disappointing discussion with a participant in his performance improvement project. Bill thought the schedule was pretty clear, but to others it apparently was not. How could there be scheduling conflicts? Barb's words still rang in his ears: "Bill, I didn't know I'd be asked to do it next week, and I can't. I'm going on vacation. I'll do it when I get back."

Back at his desk, Bill noticed a note on his chair. He didn't like the message: the training room was booked during the time he needed it for the project; he should have reserved it two months ahead of time, not two days. Bill crumpled the note and tossed it in the wastebasket.

This was proving to be a rough week. In addition to resolving all these scheduling problems, he had two critical path items of his own to complete. It would not look good if he was the one to cause the schedule to slip.

Originally, Bill had been confident in the schedule; none of the individual tasks alone represented an unreasonable workload. But when multiple tasks had to be worked on at the same time, as many did, some folks would have to work eighteen-hour days to keep up; few were willing to work such a long day frequently during the project.

Bill had gone to Linda and convinced her that additional resources would be needed to finish the project on schedule. She granted them, but they did not seem to be making things better. Things actually looked worse: people were spending more time in meetings as a result of the new resources.

Linda wanted to talk to Bill, and, as usual, she didn't sound cheery. Bill walked into her office and took his traditional place in the blue chair. He could hear his stomach rumble as he waited for Linda to arrive.

Linda dashed in, sat down, and opened a file folder. "Bill, I've reviewed the schedule for the performance improvement project, and it doesn't look good. It's out of alignment with what we asked for. We have a specific completion date to meet, and the schedule has slipped well past it. You asked for additional resources to catch up, but it looks like things have gotten worse, not better. The only thing left to do is start reducing the scope of the project. I want you to eliminate parts of the project until we have a schedule that finishes on time."

Bill was in shock. "Eliminate parts of the project?! But Linda, you don't understand. We did a detailed performance analysis that indicates we need all the components of the solution to achieve the desired performance improvement. If we eliminate anything, we leave performance barriers in the work environment."

Linda closed her file and looked seriously at Bill. "Listen, Bill, I don't claim to understand all this human performance technology stuff. But I do know that we're responsible for achieving results in this organization. If it comes down to completing the project on time or following your performance analysis, I choose to finish on time. Eliminate parts of the project. I'd like a revised schedule by noon tomorrow."

The Issue of Resource Planning

At the level of planning reached so far, all the tasks are scheduled to be implemented as soon as possible. The dependencies between the tasks have moved some tasks out in time on the schedule, but the current form of the schedule assumes that unlimited resources are available to work on the project. It might, for example, indicate that a total of thirty-seven people are necessary to implement the tasks in the fourth week. Also, the schedule still assumes that the resources have the capacity to implement all tasks currently scheduled to occur simultaneously.

This is typically not realistic. By adding the constraints of resource capacity, we further improve the implementation reliability of the schedule.

The process of resourcing the plan includes assigning the tasks to project participants and refining the task durations based on the new owners' additional inputs. Estimated effort is allocated to each particular task, and each participant's required commitment to the project is determined. Individual overcommitments or undercommitments can be identified, which results in moving tasks within the schedule to level the resource requirements necessary to execute the plan.

Benefits of Creating a Resource Plan

Scheduling the resources allows the project manager to avoid several conflicts and surprises. Most resource issues are difficult to foresee and avoid unless the resource requirements are incorporated into the schedule (Kezsbaum, 1989).

The involvement of people resources is one of the first issues that becomes clearer as a result of planning the resource requirements. In many performance improvement projects, many participants are not fully dedicated to the project; they may be involved in a number of other activities during the same time as your performance improvement project. Some participants may be responsible for only one task during your entire project. By creating a resource plan, you indicate to participants when they should plan to implement their assigned tasks (Lewis, 1993b).

If the project manager can inform participants early enough about when their tasks are scheduled, it reduces the likelihood of hearing comments such as these:

- "Sorry, but I'm scheduled to work on another project now. I can't start yours until . . ."
- "I can't complete my tasks on time because I have other work to do this week too."
- "Gee, I can't do that next week. I'm going to be on vacation!"

Resources other than participants are necessary to implement the project schedule. Some are scarce or in high demand, such as meeting rooms, training facilities, video production rooms, and specialized equipment. Scheduling these scarce resources provides visibility of their necessity and allows you to schedule or reserve them ahead of time to avoid conflict with others.

A number of nonproject variables also need to be compared to the resource schedule to avoid conflicts and delays in the implementation of the schedule.

Vacation. Your vacation is probably scheduled, and, as you are the project manager, probably not during the project. (Most project managers schedule their nervous breakdowns to occur after the project is complete.) Other participants are less likely to schedule their lives around the performance improvement project; when provided with expected task dates, they can work around them to ensure no conflicts. You may work for a multinational company and be expecting participants from other countries; if so, check your cultural assumptions. For example, most Europeans save up their vacation time and take off the entire month of August. Shutting down so that everybody can go "on holiday" is an inflexible cultural norm for organizations in Europe.

Holidays. This is another area where you should check your cultural and national assumptions. Independence Day is July 4 in the United States, but not in Canada (and certainly not in the United Kingdom). However, Canada Day is July 1, and it is just as inappropriate to ask a Canadian to work then as it is to ask an American to work three days later. France has Bastille Day. Thanksgiving is celebrated on separate dates in Canada and the United States. Check your religious assumptions as well. Do you have any project participants of the Jewish faith? If so, account for Rosh Hashanah, Hanukkah, and Yom Kippur. Any Christians? In addition to Christmas, remember Good Friday and Ascension. Any Islamics? Buddhists? Hindus? The easiest way to find out is to ask. Few people will be offended if you ask them which holidays they observe so that you can avoid a scheduling conflict.

Meetings. They may be considered an alternative to useful work, but meetings are a reality in most organizations. The project manager may have control over when project meetings occur, but not over other meetings that may make some participants unavailable. If the operations manager holds a mandatory quarterly meeting for all department members, the project manager certainly should not schedule a project meeting at the same time.

Maternity or Paternity Leave. Is anybody planning to have or adopt a baby in the midst of the performance improvement project? If so, schedule their participation as early as possible if you want to count on them as a resource. Estimating a baby's arrival date is not a precise science. Babies have a habit of showing up earlier than expected and surprising everybody.

Equipment Downtime. In many environments, equipment is maintained or upgraded during specific periods. In many companies, for example, electronic systems are down for maintenance and upgrades during the long Thanksgiving holiday weekend; the phone system, voice mail, computer network, and system servers are all worked on. Planning to accomplish work during such a time would cause conflict. The resources simply are not available.

The Process of Project Resourcing

Resourcing a project is usually accomplished in three steps.

Step 1: Match Project Tasks with Appropriate Owners

Reviewing the lists of tasks in the work breakdown structure, determine who are the best resources for each task. This may be simple if you are the only resource for the project and will implement all the tasks. Performance improvement projects can involve from one person to a team of sixty; most have multiple participants available to work on the project tasks. Some assignments will be simple and straightforward: the copy center will most likely do the duplication and the graphics illustrator will probably do the graphics.

However, other tasks are flexible. Who should work on the job aids or design the CBT? Consider time availability and individual capabilities in making your task assignments. You will want to staff tasks on the critical path with the best people available. Remember, any problems and slips on critical tasks result in a slip of the project end date.

Likewise, the project manager should avoid owning too many tasks, especially those on the critical path (Gilbreath, 1986). The reason is that if there are problems with the project, the project manager will need to spend time resolving issues and getting the project back on track. Problem mitigation is difficult to achieve if you are simultaneously working on a critical path task. You may fix the first problem, only to find that your own tasks are the next project areas that are in crisis and need to be fixed. The amount of project management time will relate directly to the size and complexity of the project itself.

Step 2: Refine the Duration Estimates of the Tasks

When the duration for the project tasks was estimated, it was based on a number of assumptions regarding the implementer and the implementation environment. With the assignment of the task to a specific owner, some assumptions usually change; it is then appropriate to allow for a refinement of the task duration based on input from the new task owner (Lewis, 1993b). The new owner may review the existing task duration estimates and decide that no changes are necessary. This additional validation builds confidence in the schedule and also creates a level of accountability for the task owner to meet the estimate.

However, the task owner may review the estimation assumptions and determine that an adjustment is necessary to the task duration. It is basic human nature to be overly conservative with task estimation; people want to set very safe time commitments for their tasks so as to avoid disappointment or failure. Before accepting any recommended duration adjustments, ask for justification and rationale. If they are sound, the changes should be made.

Step 3: Determine Aggregate Workload Requirements and Adjust as Necessary

With tasks assigned to owners, you can now begin to look at the workloads of the individual participants. In general, you want to avoid assigning somebody sixty-five hours of work one week and five the next. Adjustments will need to be made to level the work for participants.

Perhaps no individual task looks too demanding. However, some participants are likely to have multiple or overlapping tasks within the same time period. Looking at the total work expected of people, you may find that some periods represent unrealistic work demands.

Project scheduling software makes analyzing the aggregate workload rather simple. With the resources loaded into the schedule and the tasks owners identified, the software lets you look at the resource requirements from a number of perspectives. Depending on the software and your selection of reports, you can look at the data in tabular or graphic form.

The tabular form simply lists the project participants, the tasks that they are responsible for, and the scheduled dates for the tasks and their completion. Project participants usually appreciate receiving a tabular copy of their tasks; it serves as a reminder of what they are going to be doing. Many use the tabular listing to update their time managers so that they can plan their activities.

However, project managers typically do not use the tabular form, as it looks like a shopping list and makes it difficult to determine resource loading. More commonly, project managers use a graphical representation of loading to manage the resources. It provides a quick understanding of the resource distribution. Most project scheduling software is capable of producing a resource loading histogram, as illustrated in Figure 9.1.

The sample histogram in Figure 9.1 shows that this participant has three tasks assigned for the period selected, and that they overlap on the schedule. The histogram below the task bars indicates the cumulative work requirements

FIGURE 9.1. RESOURCE LOADING HISTOGRAM.

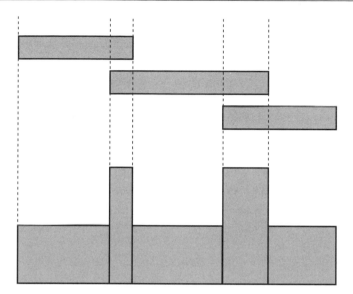

for the individual. For most of the period the workload is reasonable; however, two periods when the tasks overlap cause a sharp increase in the workload.

As the project manager, you have a decision to make about the input from the owner of the tasks. The decision to change the resource loading or not is based on several issues, such as the significance of the overloading (ten hours rather than eighteen hours per day) and the duration of the overload situation (two days rather than three months). Jointly, you should decide if something needs to be done. If it does, you could perhaps assign one of the tasks to another participant who is underutilized during the period, add resources to the project, or reschedule one of the tasks. Choosing among these is discussed in the optimization section later in this chapter.

Deciding on a Resource-Loaded Schedule

Distinct benefits and costs are associated with loading all the resources into the schedule and managing the resource loading. Some project managers insist it is crucial to the success of the project schedule; others argue that it is a waste of precious project time (Dreger, 1992; Martin, 1976). Before you decide, you should consider the advantages and disadvantages of creating a resource-loaded schedule.

Advantages

Resource loading improves schedule validity. A schedule that does not incorporate resource loading may not be achievable. Project management success is defined as achieving the intended results on time with the specified resources.

It improves ability to meet scheduled dates. If the schedule is not valid due to resource issues, there will likely be schedule slips. This can cause scheduling problems with external resources such as vendors, who are expecting to begin work on a specific date.

It helps people avoid burnout by more evenly distributing resources. If you think resource management is difficult, try it when a resource suddenly burns out and leaves the organization.

It requires project participants to think through resource commitments up front. This will help to identify issues early on, rather than when the task is under way.

It encourages people-oriented project management by ensuring that realistic workloads are created for the project participants. Most likely, you will use the same resources on the next performance improvement project; they need to survive this one.

When the schedule changes, the resource plan can rapidly be recalculated. New resource conflicts can be identified early, when corrections are easier to implement.

It facilitates the optimization of the schedule when making trade-offs between scope, schedule, and resources.

Disadvantages

A resource-loaded schedule is more complex to develop than simple task scheduling.

It requires more time for entering information and maintaining it, time that may be unavailable or better spent on task implementation.

The best resource-loaded schedule is only a rough approximation of actual resource needs, especially on complex projects or ones that the organization has little experience with.

More complex resource distributions may provide results that are only marginally better than simple resource distributions.

People work in complex, rapidly changing environments. The ability to maintain the accuracy of the resource plan may be quite limited, especially on large, complex performance improvement projects.

Optimizing the Plan

When resources are loaded into the plan, it spreads out the tasks to ensure that a workable plan has been created. However, the resourced plan as it exists at this point may not be consistent with the priorities agreed upon when defining the project. To implement the schedule as it stands may actually violate the project definition and cause the project to be deemed a failure. The schedule needs to be optimized to align it with the project priorities. This is usually done in three steps, of which the second depends on selecting one of three options.

Step 1: Review the Project Decision Priority List

The priority analysis and matrix done during the project definition should be in the project notebook. The priorities of the project may change over time. Because some time has transpired since project definition, ensure that the priorities are still accurate. Give the manager or client the opportunity to adjust the priorities while changes are still easy to make. If there are changes, ensure they are distributed to all project participants so that they are clear on the project priorities.

Refer to the sample project priority matrix in Chapter One (Figure 1.3) and recall that few projects are allowed infinite amounts of time, scope, and resources. As the project manager, you must determine trade-offs among the three. Remember also that the project priority matrix allows three levels of priority:

Constrained. This aspect must be met; it is the highest priority. The other two aspects are considered less important and will probably be fixed in the existing schedule. If scope is constrained, it is reflected in the tasks identified in the work breakdown structure. If time is constrained, it probably reflects the set completion date in the schedule. If resources are constrained, only agreed-upon resources are applied in the plan.

Optimized. This aspect is either maximized (if scope) or minimized (if time or resources) within project objectives. The project team will do its best on this aspect but will not compromise the constrained aspect to achieve it. The optimized aspect of the project is the focus of the optimization activity.

Accepted. Management is willing to accept the project team's best performance on this aspect but understands that the constrained and optimized aspects take priority.

Based on the project priorities, you must do one of the following step 2 processes. Please note that you will do only one, not all three. If the priorities of your project indicate that the schedule is to be reduced, implement step 2a.

If the priorities indicate that resources are to be reduced, implement step 2b. If scope is to be reduced, implement step 2c.

Step 2a: Reduce the Schedule

Optimizing the schedule requires making it as short as possible without violating the constraint (either resources or scope) identified in the project priorities (Kezsbaum, 1989). The schedule is both the easiest and the most difficult aspect to optimize. Software makes project scheduling easy, as it automatically creates the shortest possible schedule based on the project information entered into it. But optimizing that schedule is hard because it is difficult to improve on what the software has done. However, some tactics can be employed to shorten the schedule.

Begin by reevaluating the logical dependencies between the project tasks in the work breakdown structure, particularly those on the critical path. Question if the dependencies are absolutely necessary and if they must use the selected dependency. As appropriate, you may consider any of the following.

> Break the dependency completely. If the dependency is removed, the task can be pulled up in the schedule and implemented in parallel with its successor. This tactic will only work if resources are prioritized as accepted. Breaking the dependency is particularly effective if the task is on the critical path. However, if there is a true dependency, do not break it; instead consider using a dependency other than finish-to-start.

> Change dependencies from finish-to-start, if possible, to start-to-start or start-to-start with a lag. Figure 9.2 illustrates the effect of changing a dependency from finish-to-start to start-to-start with a two-day lag. When considering this tactic, remember that running tasks in parallel increases project risk; a lag provides less response time if there is a problem in the predecessor task.

> Break tasks into subtasks that can be done in parallel. Figure 9.3 illustrates the time savings of breaking the task down further. If resources are available to work on the subcomponents in parallel, significant schedule time can be saved.

Reevaluate task estimates to determine if durations can be realistically shortened. Task owners should be fully involved in discussions and decisions about shortening estimates, as they must achieve the shorter durations if schedule integrity is to be maintained.

Reevaluate the use of new technologies that could either reduce the number of tasks in the project or accelerate the time required to complete them. Be

FIGURE 9.2. EFFECT OF CHANGING DEPENDENCIES.

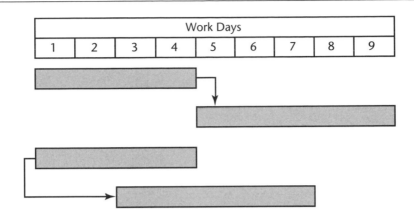

FIGURE 9.3. EFFECT OF BREAKING DOWN TASKS.

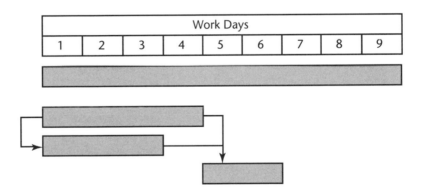

certain to consider the additional risk that new technology introduces to a project; this tactic will backfire if the technology does not work and causes the tasks to take longer.

Consider changing nonworkdays to workdays. This should be considered only under the most serious conditions and with full agreement of the project participants. Changing Saturdays to workdays can reduce a schedule by as much as 20 percent, but this arrangement usually cannot be sustained for long without a special environment or special support.

Consider adding resources to the project. More resources may allow more tasks to be done in parallel, which could significantly accelerate the schedule. However, this should be done with great care and must be planned before implementation. If there are a great number of unbreakable dependencies between tasks, adding resources may not make much improvement at all.

If the project is in motion, never add resources unless the need is extreme and doing so will make the certainty for success extremely high. A widely accepted axiom in the project management world is that adding people to an already late project makes it later. There are several reasons: existing resources are distracted from their tasks as they spend time bringing new resources up to speed; new resources tend to be unproductive until they catch up with other participants; additional communication and work hand-off issues may come into play; and, as the number of project participants grow, so do time-consuming interactions and communications. The number of potential project interactions can be calculated using the formula

$$I = (P(P-1))/2$$

where I is the number of potential interactions and P is the number of project participants.

Using the formula, we find that a project with six participants results in fifteen interactions. Eight participants result in twenty-eight interactions; twelve participants result in sixty-six interactions. This is demonstrated graphically in Figures 9.4 and 9.5, where the number of communication paths between participants is shown for projects with six and eight participants, respectively. Adding two resources to a project with six participants increases the communication paths from fifteen to twenty-eight, almost doubling the potential for necessary communication on the project.

Consider using float to reduce the schedule. Critical-path tasks may take less time if the people working on tasks with float are reassigned to help people

FIGURE 9.4. INTERACTIONS WITH SIX PARTICIPANTS.

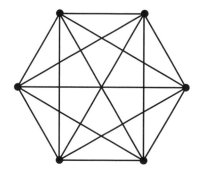

FIGURE 9.5. INTERACTIONS WITH EIGHT PARTICIPANTS.

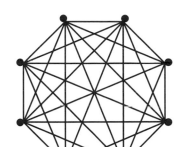

working on the critical path. Consider delaying or interrupting noncritical path tasks to achieve this. But remember that using all or most of a task's float puts it on (or near) the critical path and increases project risk.

If the scope is constrained, the schedule is optimized and resources are accepted. Refer to the Chapter Two section on rapid development for specific suggestions on accelerating the schedule.

Step 2b: Reduce the Resources

Identify areas of opportunity for reducing the resources on the project. Look for resource overcommitments that cause additional resources to be brought on to deal with them. Look for resource undercommitments, where people are not being utilized well. If you find either, assign the workers to help others or assign them other tasks to reduce overall resource requirements. Also, look for opportunities to subcontract work to vendors. The process for successfully vending out work is covered in detail in Part Three.

Level the schedule and reduce resource requirements by temporarily postponing noncritical work. This can minimize (or even eliminate) overcommitments during critical time frames. Providing a more even distribution of work for project participants typically reduces the number of participants necessary to complete the work.

Consider the technologies being used on the project to produce the performance improvement solution. Technologies may increase resource efficiency, but may also require additional training that could increase the need for resources—especially when things go wrong. Traditional technologies may provide a better balance for short-term, small-budget projects.

Step 2c: Reduce the Scope

Reducing the scope of the project is usually difficult for most human performance technologists to deal with. Typically, a careful analysis is done to discover the root causes of performance gaps. This results in the selection of performance improvement interventions needed to close the performance gaps. If a human performance technologist includes something in the performance solution, it is because it needs to be there. The goal is to close performance gaps as efficiently as possible without extraneous activities, costs, or materials. A well-designed performance improvement project has no fluff.

However, a couple of tactics can be used to reduce the scope of the work that must be done to achieve performance improvement goals. The first consideration is whether every component of the performance improvement solution must be completed at the same time. Might parts of the project be postponed and included in a separate project to be done after the current one?

Or reconsider the options of making, buying, leveraging, or reusing resources. Perhaps the amount of work that needs to be accomplished can be reduced by changing a previous decision about external or existing work.

Step 3: Gain Agreement on Changes

Chances are that during the project optimization some significant changes will be recommended. But rarely does the project manager have authority to make all the recommended changes; thus it is important to document the decisions and obtain agreement about them with the manager or client and the participants in the performance improvement project. Once the changes are agreed to, distribute them according to the infrastructure decisions made earlier. As always, ensure that all changes and their rationale are captured in the project notebook.

The schedule is nearing completion. The last phase is to carefully analyze the planned schedule for risks, and either remove the risks or put contingency plans in place to deal with anticipated problems.

Karen's Story

The participants in Karen's performance improvement project chattered away as she called the meeting to order. "Okay, folks," she said. "I took the task assignments from our last discussion and entered them into the schedule. I've printed out charts showing the workload for each of you. As you can see, we have some balancing to do if we're going to maintain a reasonable schedule."

For half an hour, the group adjusted the timing of tasks with float and exchanged a few tasks until the workload for each participant was reasonable. Karen made some notes for the project notebook and said, "Now that we've leveled the workload and made some changes to the timing of tasks, I want each of you to look carefully at the task timing and let me know about any conflicts that would prevent you from completing your tasks on time. Consider vacations, holidays, personal leave—anything."

Kathleen spoke up. "Sorry, Karen, but I have a vacation conflict. I'd change my vacation date, but my husband can't. And I don't think he'll be too thrilled with separate vacations." After some discussion, the group decided to use float in the schedule to accelerate a task that would allow Kathleen to complete the task before leaving on vacation.

Bob raised his hand. "I don't have a schedule conflict, but we'd better pay attention to a couple of the resource requirements. Otherwise we could have a resource conflict. The training room usually gets booked far in advance. If we think we can hold to the schedule, we should reserve it now. Same goes for the video equipment."

Karen nodded and made note of Bob's recommendation. "Great! Thanks, Bob. Okay, folks. I need your help with another issue. I'm concerned about the tasks I'm responsible for in week eight. The schedule modifications have put them on the critical path, but I expect to be rather busy keeping this project on track. So I'm concerned about the risk of having me on the critical path. Any ideas?"

After discussing alternatives, the group decided to double-team Karen's critical task to ensure that she could manage the project and have help in completing the task. Pleased with the results, Karen moved the meeting forward. "The last thing to do today is to optimize the schedule. I checked with the management team, and the project priorities haven't changed. Our plan is close, but if we try to implement it as it sits, we'd probably have to eliminate portions of the project midway to stay on schedule. Let's look at the schedule to make it as trim as possible. . . ."

CHAPTER TEN

ANALYZING RISK AND PLANNING FOR CONTINGENCIES

Once the project schedule is completed, the temptation to rush ahead and start the project is huge. However, to help ensure that the plan can be implemented reliably, sources of risk must be identified and removed from it (Obradovitch and Stephanou, 1990).

Bill's Story

Bill strolled into the conference room for the project review meeting. Barb, Brian, and Kelly were there, and looking none too happy. Bill sensed that tension was running high and something wasn't going well. He sat down at the table and began.

"Okay, folks, what's up? Looks like there's bad news."

Brian looked around to see if one of the others wanted to start, but apparently it was up to him. "Well, it seems we've had a little unforeseen problem. I thought the technical part of my task would be easy, but I keep running into problems, and now I'm late."

Bill looked up from the notes he was jotting down. "Just how late is late?"

Brian looked at the schedule. "My four-day task is now a week late. Unfortunately, the situation is worse than it seems. The task is on the critical path, and the entire project is slipping. To make things even worse, because of the slip

I now have two concurrent critical path tasks. I can't do both, Bill. We need to do something!"

The next two hours of the thirty-minute meeting were spent trying to fix the unexpected problem with Brian's tasks. The team finally was able to agree to a course of action, but valuable time had been lost: not just two hours in the meeting, but the huge schedule slip. Why hadn't anybody been watching for signs of technical barriers?

Bill attempted to wrap up the meeting and get the folks back to work. "Okay. Is there anything else we need to discuss?"

Barb timidly raised her hand. "Bill, I don't know how to say this, but we have another serious problem. As you know, we finished the video shooting for the first training video. We sent the tapes to Acme Studios for final editing. Well, to make a long story short, they had a fire. The only copies of the videotapes were destroyed. We're going to have to reshoot. I estimate it'll take a week and $20,000 to redo the work."

Bill was stunned. "Let me see if I have this straight. We sent the only copies of the tapes to the vendor, *they* lost them, and *we* have to spend a week and twenty grand. Is that about it?"

"Well," said Barb, "it's actually a bit worse. Because Acme's out of business, we have to find and negotiate a new vendor for the editing. It'll probably take me three additional days."

"I hate to bring it up," interrupted Kelly, "but I'd better get my situation on the table as well. Bill, do you remember that agreement you made in the hallway with Keith for him to do some of the formatting on the process documentation? The VP of marketing has asked Keith's group to take on a special project, so they can't do it after all. I checked with an outside vendor, and we can stay on schedule, but it's going to cost $8,000 to do the job."

Bill spent the remainder of the morning and his lunch hour redoing the schedule and writing out purchase orders. He had everything ready, but he knew that the meeting with Linda was going to be difficult.

He peered around the doorway of Linda's office. "Is this still a good time, or would you like me to come back later?"

Linda set down the papers she was reading. "No, this is still a good time. Come in and have a seat. This sounds pretty urgent."

There was the blue chair again. His stomach was churning before he got to the office, but now it was doing flip-flops. Bill sat down and handed her the purchase orders. "We've had a few unexpected problems with the big performance improvement project. We ran into some technical barriers, and our video editors had a fire that destroyed the video we'd shot. Also, Keith's group won't be able to help us after all, so we have to hire a vendor. We put together a plan to recover, but we slipped by two weeks, and I need your signatures on these purchase orders."

Linda stared at him. "Two weeks? Bill, we have *got* to get back on schedule. I don't care if we have to work until midnight and on weekends. How much are these purchase orders for? $28,000?! Is this in your project budget?"

Bill squirmed in the chair. "Uh, no. We weren't expecting either of these problems."

Linda signed the purchase orders and shot them back at Bill. "I hope you realize this comes out of our department's budget. We have to make up any project cost overruns. This means the organization won't be getting new PCs this year. Make sure we don't have any more surprises, will you?"

Benefits of Risk Management

Risk occurs whenever there is the potential for things not to go as well as planned. That potential can be very high, such as for a task taking longer than expected. Or the potential risk may be low but with significant ramifications, such as for a hard disk crashing without backup copies having been made.

The process of removing or planning for risks yields the following important benefits to professional and reliable performance improvement project management (Kezsbaum, 1989):

- Improves schedule accuracy and reality
- Exposes and deals with uncertainty
- Increases project team confidence
- Counteracts overoptimism
- Uncovers requirements for additional project tasks or planning

The Process of Risk Management

This chapter takes a two-pass approach to risk management, with each pass looking at a different level within the project. The first pass considers risks within the individual project tasks. The process is to identify the risks, assess their significance and probability, then manage appropriately. The second pass looks at the project as a whole. The focus is to identify, assess, and plan to reduce risk to the overall performance improvement project. The two levels of examination lessen the chance of overlooking risks.

Identifying Task Risks

The first step in removing the risk from the individual project tasks is to identify what risks may exist. Each task should be considered and potential risks to successful completion identified, regardless of likelihood. Potential risk should be assessed in the project's schedule, resources, and scope. Within each are specific risk factors to review.

Schedule Risks

Critical and near-critical tasks. By definition, tasks on the critical path are tasks at risk; if they run into difficulties, the project has difficulties. Do not overlook tasks that are related to (feed into) critical path tasks.

Long tasks. Any task that takes longer than two weeks to finish represents high risk to the schedule, as it is hard to assess progress within and during the task.

Multiple critical paths. If your project has multiple critical paths, schedule risk increases exponentially. If two critical-path tasks get into trouble simultaneously, you will probably not be able to fix both simultaneously.

Accelerated tasks. Tasks being accelerated to shorten the schedule are at risk. The acceleration plan for the task may not work.

Merge points and major milestones. Any time multiple tasks flow into a single task, there is risk. If seven of the eight tasks are on time but the final one is not, the merge point or milestone is still late. It is all or nothing as far as the schedule is concerned.

Overoptimism in task estimation. Continue to be on the lookout for task estimation that is optimistic. Optimism does not improve the ability to get the project done faster; the task time is what the task time is. Having an optimistic estimate in the schedule only makes managing the performance improvement project more difficult.

Low confidence or high uncertainty in estimates. If the people who did the estimation had little history or data to base their estimation on, those tasks are at risk.

Omitted tasks. An incomplete work breakdown structure is a low probability at this point in the planning process, but it does occur. Do not spend too much time specifically looking, but do keep an eye out for omissions.

Incorrect logic in determining dependencies. Tasks with complex dependencies and those on the critical path should have their logic checked more than once.

Having incorrect dependencies on a schedule is about as bad as it gets in managing a project.

Resource Risks

Tasks with multiple resources. If a task's completion depends on more than one resource working on it, there is risk. What if both resources are not available at the same time?

Tasks with overcommitted resources. If you are depending on a single group or person to perform a large number of the project tasks, potential risk exists. If two of their tasks overlap due to schedule changes, the project is suddenly underresourced and it will be difficult to stay on schedule.

Tasks with mismatched resources (skills). Sometimes the only resource available to complete a project task is a person who has never done it before or is not qualified to perform the task. You may have no alternative, but you had better recognize the risk.

Tasks that depend on a unique resource or individual. If only one person or one piece of equipment is capable of completing the task, the risk is obvious: they are unavailable sometimes.

Resources not fully dedicated to the project. Priorities change, and the agreement to have part of somebody's time can change too. Again, you may have no alternative, but recognize the risk.

Work environment. Do any tasks depend on being completed in a specific location? Some organizations move frequently and sometimes with little notice.

New resources. People new to the organization are a risk. They do not know their way around, they may never have implemented their specific project tasks, and they pose a potential resource drain to the project team. New equipment poses a risk as well. If you depend on a new piece of equipment not failing during the project, that is a risk too.

Technical, Scope, and Performance Risks

Changing requirements. A clear project definition should exist by this point, but some technical aspects may change (creeping elegance happens; it is a basic function of managers and often part of their job descriptions). Tasks that are likely to experience imposed technical changes are at risk.

New technology. Tasks associated with new technology for the project participants represent significant risk. They may have produced several CBT products in the past, but if this is their first attempt at incorporating full-motion video, for example, the task estimation is at high risk.

Unfamiliar development tools or methods. If the same experienced team switches to a new authoring language to work on this performance improvement project, estimation risk is high because their historical reference based on experience is no longer valid.

Extreme quality or reliability requirements. Any task that must be completed with zero defects is at risk. People make mistakes.

External sourcing for key work or information. External resources place tasks at risk because they do not experience the same consequences of failure as internal resources. Additionally, there have been cases of external suppliers going out of business in the midst of contract work.

Poorly defined acceptance criteria or testing. If the plan for ensuring that the task is completed properly is poor, it increases the probability that the criteria will not become clear until later in the project and that the task will need to be reworked.

Unfamiliar levels of complexity. If the members of the CBT team have substantial experience, but this project is more complex than any they have worked on, then tasks associated with the complexity are at risk.

Unclear aspects of the project definition. If any part of the project definition is not clear, the probability of completing the tasks successfully the first time is lower.

Assessing Task Risks

The next step in removing risk from the project tasks is to assess the identified tasks at risk. Not all task risks are the same. Some are likely to occur; others are very unlikely (Obradovitch and Stephanou, 1990). Some risks represent substantial impact, and others may just be inconvenient. Assessing the risks evaluates which ones warrant specific risk-reduction activity.

To assess the identified risks, different aspects of the risk must be evaluated. Figure 10.1 illustrates a matrix for risk assessment that keeps all the data organized. Creating a computer-based spreadsheet that replicates the matrix speeds the assessment task significantly.

Begin by listing all of the identified tasks and their risk in the column labeled *Risk*. Do not be concerned with their order in the matrix for now.

For each task listed, estimate the probability of the risk occurring as high, medium, or low (H, M, or L). Enter the rating in the column labeled *Probability*.

FIGURE 10.1. RISK ANALYSIS MATRIX.

Risk	Probability	Impact	Detection Difficulty	Priority

Then estimate the impact (such as on cost or time) of the risk as H, M, or L and enter the rating in the column labeled *Impact*.

Next, estimate the difficulty of determining if the risk is occurring; select high if you cannot detect the risk until after it is too late, medium if you can detect it while it is occurring, and low if you can see it coming. Enter the H, M, or L rating in the column labeled *Detection Difficulty*.

Finally, weigh each risk based upon the probability, impact, and detection difficulty. Prioritize each risk and reorder the list (this is where having a spreadsheet makes things easy).

Managing Task Risks

With the priority of the risks assessed, you can move on to planning how the risks will be managed. If your assessed risk list looks quite long, you will never have enough time to effectively deal with all the risks. You can spend more time preventing low-probability, low-impact risks than you would implementing the entire project.

So you will have to draw a line across the risk-assessment chart. Those items below the line will not be dealt with. Those above the line will move through the next step in the process. Where should you draw the line? It depends entirely on the size of your list, the amount of time you have to do risk reduction and planning, and the amount of risk you are able or willing to tolerate in the project plan.

Figure 10.2 illustrates the matrix to use in creating your task risk-management plan. If you are using a spreadsheet, simply add the additional column headings

FIGURE 10.2. RISK PLAN MATRIX.

Risk	Prevention	Contingency Plan	Trigger	Owner

to your existing analysis. If you are using paper and pencil, transfer the tasks and risks above the line to the risk plan matrix.

For each risk, develop and analyze ideas to reduce or eliminate it. Look to prevent, avoid, or reduce the impact of the risk. Consider the possibility of creating additional project activities that reduce the risks and that can be implemented earlier in the project than the risk tasks.

Compare costs and benefits of the ideas. Estimate the expected impact and cost of each task risk. Then, for each idea to eliminate or reduce the risk, evaluate the expected cost and effort required and the probable risk reduction. Finally, select ideas for implementation that can lower risk at justifiable cost. If the risk is high or probable, consider selecting more than one prevention plan. After selecting the best prevention solution or solutions, enter them in the column labeled *Prevention*.

Some risks cannot be avoided or are still significant even with a plan to reduce them (Thomsett, 1993). Develop contingency plans that detail what will be done to recover if the risk does occur. If the risk is high or probable, consider creating more than one contingency plan. Enter them in the *Contingency Plan* column.

You will want to establish some criteria for determining if the risk is occurring. This will help the project participants decide whether to implement the contingency plan. Enter the risk occurrence criteria in the column labeled *Trigger*.

Somebody will need to watch for the trigger events that should put contingency plans into motion. Deciding in the midst of a problem who should initiate the contingency plan is poor planning; the result is sure to be a slow response. Identify an owner for monitoring the trigger condition and implementing the contingency plan, if necessary. Enter the owner's name in the *Owner* column.

You now have a plan for managing at-risk tasks within the project plan. Be sure to update the project notebook with the results of the task risk-management plan. If you have created additional project tasks to reduce risks, be sure to add them to the project plan work breakdown structure and schedule. Also, ensure that every participant in the project receives a copy of the risk-management plan. It will serve as a reminder of the triggers each is watching for and of who has responsibility for initiating the contingency plan. If an anticipated problem occurs, you will want the owner to implement the agreed-upon plan without having to locate you and the project notebook to look up the contingency plan.

Risk Prevention

Sometimes risks can be easily identified and assessed, and the greatest difficulty is determining what can be done to manage or prevent the problems. To aid in creating alternatives in the management and prevention area, review and consider the following actions for the risk problems you are attempting to address. They are divided into schedule, resource, scope, and other issues.

Schedule Issues

Reduce the number of critical paths. If multiple critical paths experience problems simultaneously, a schedule slip is almost always imminent.

Uncouple task dependencies. Dependencies force the timing of a task and minimize scheduling flexibility. This increases the risk of timing slips. Breaking the dependency typically requires modifying the task.

Prioritize tasks and features and remove the lowest-value ones. This is typically not a favorite alternative, but it does help to maintain the schedule if problems occur.

Schedule highest-uncertainty tasks as early as possible. Do the scary tasks as soon as you can; it provides more time to recover if failure occurs.

Decompose tasks further and reschedule. By dividing the tasks, you can generally create overlapping or concurrent subtasks. This generally accelerates the schedule, but task management becomes more detailed and time-consuming.

Avoid time-related problems. Move critical project work away from known conflicts with holidays and year-end (or quarter- or month-end) requirements. The distractions almost always lower productivity and increase the probability of schedule slips.

Use rigorous task planning and tracking throughout the project. Do not wait to discover if problems are occurring. Shortening the detection cycle increases the potential for recovering from the problem.

Increase time estimates for risky tasks to allow for carrying out contingency plans. This is known as "padding your estimates." Because of the impact on the project schedule, this should be done very carefully. Having tasks completed too early can be just as disruptive to the project as having them completed late.

Never assign the same person to work on two concurrent critical-path (or near-critical-path) tasks. Avoid having the same resource responsible for successive critical tasks whenever possible. Again, this is a scheduling flexibility issue. If one person is responsible for concurrent or sequential critical-path tasks, the schedule will most probably slip.

Resource Issues

Use the best people for the most critical tasks. Doing so will increase the likelihood that the schedule and scope requirements will be achieved.

Reduce the load on fully loaded or overcommitted resources. Overloaded resources are likely to burn out in the midst of a project, and a staffing change introduces phenomenal risk into the project.

Use mentoring and education to establish redundant capabilities on the team where critical skills are scarce. This sounds like a resource investment, and it is. You need to balance the cost of building capabilities against the potential cost of losing the only person capable of performing project tasks.

Improve communications. Communication among project participants always reduces risks: potential problems are identified earlier, offering more time to take adaptive action, and many problems may be solved by the participants assisting one another once the situation is made known.

Motivate team members and build team cohesion. If the potential exists for competitiveness and team infighting, take some time at the beginning of the project to resolve the issues. Broken relationships are very difficult to repair once the project is under way and the pressure is on.

Involve customers or users in project design and testing. Adding these resources creates a double win: not only is the development and testing accelerated by the additional resources, but the quality and confidence in the results is improved.

Automate manual work. If there are resources who can be replaced by (or whose productivity can be enhanced by) technology, consider the possibility. However, be careful in your decision. Changing the work environment introduces risk. It is equally possible that the learning requirements for the new solution will negate or overwhelm the productivity gains that the solution offers.

Reduce or eliminate safety problems. If a member of the project team becomes injured, the project may suffer terribly. Employees out on temporary disability are usually not replaced; the company simply awaits their return. In the meantime, you must attempt to complete the project with one less participant. Look for trip hazards, slip hazards, and fall hazards. Look after ergonomic issues as well. You will regret not having spent $10 for a wrist pad that could have prevented a month of lost time due to a repetitive motion injury such as tendinitis.

Where people contribute to the source of a risk, involve them in dealing with it whenever possible. They will probably create effective and creative solutions to reduce the risk and also take a higher level of ownership in making the solution work.

Recruit an experienced contributor for the project team who has a reputation for effective problem solving. If the project has several areas of potential risk where real-time problem solving is a strong probability, having the resources to fix problems rapidly reduces their impact on the project.

Know and get explicit commitment for availability of all critical resources. Informal "hallway agreements" are risky; people forget about them or may not realize that the time requested conflicts with another activity. This applies to people, equipment, and facilities.

Manage and limit commitments of your project resources to other projects, maintenance or support work, or other time conflicts. Control over resources reduces risk. If a resource might be pulled away to address another matter, you have risk in your project.

Locate and gain access to experts in critical skill areas. Simply stated, when something goes wrong, you are going to need expert advice or assistance to fix the problem. Do not wait until the problem occurs to figure out who might be able to assist with its resolution.

When using outside services, whenever possible use the same ones that you or others have used successfully before. This obviously reduces risk, as their performance is more predictable than that of a new service provider. However, you should always ensure that you have a backup provider identified.

Upgrade or replace older equipment to make work more efficient, and do it at the start of the project. Old equipment has the inconvenient tendency to fail in the midst of important projects; somehow, it just seems to know. But do not replace equipment during the project. The potential for something new to not work correctly the first time is actually pretty high.

Technical and Scope Issues

On high-risk technical tasks, create prototypes, simulate, or model to uncover issues and problems as early as possible.

Avoid the attitude that anything "not invented here"—that is, created by others—is not as good. Leveraging or reusing work done before increases the probability that the technology will function as expected.

Look for ways to achieve project specifications using older, known technologies. They may not be flashy, but they reduce technical risk. They must, however, still fully meet the project specifications.

Identify appropriate goals and do not overdesign. It is all too easy to be swept away in "technolust" or creating the "grand design." Keep the design down to necessary features and capabilities.

Make sure participants are trained in advance for all necessary competencies. Attempting to learn the new CBT authoring system while working on CBT development usually results in an underfeatured product.

Use walk-throughs and scenario discussions to identify potential defects. Testing the design of interventions in design reviews, where peers are allowed to examine and critique the design, helps ensure that the design is achievable.

Avoid untried, unfamiliar, or "bleeding edge" technology whenever practical. The risk is that you will never get the technology to function according to the project design specification.

Minimize the impact of new methods or technologies by starting with simpler tasks first and moving to more complicated ones as you build expertise. If the simple tasks cannot be made to function, you will have time to revert to more stable methods.

For especially risky but essential project components, use parallel redundant development efforts. This is very costly, but if the importance of the project warrants it, consider it as an option.

Other Issues

Communicate, communicate, communicate. Risks and problems that are exposed are half resolved.

Obtain and work to sustain strong sponsorship for your project. Having support and resources assists in solving issues as they arise.

Review retrospectives of similar past projects. Be sure to review both successful and not-so-successful results to discover how risks were managed.

Overall Project Risk

Once the risks within the individual tasks have been identified, assessed, and managed, it is time to turn to the project as a whole. Risks exist for the project that would not be evident by looking only at the individual tasks (Obradovitch and Stephanou, 1990).

Areas to consider in such overall project risks can include (but are certainly not limited to) concerns as broad as the following:

- Reorganization and business changes
- Regulatory issues
- Lack of common practices (such as life cycle and planning)
- Performance change windows or other timing assumptions
- Insufficient risk management
- Inefficient project decomposition into tasks
- Unfamiliar levels of project effort
- Experience of project manager
- Weak sponsorship
- Project priority
- Motivation and morale of project participants or change targets
- Weak change management control
- Lack of interaction with target performers
- Communications issues
- Poorly defined infrastructure
- Inaccurate (or no) metrics
- Attrition (such as from illness, injury, or resignations)
- Training issues and requirements

Identifying Project Risks

As with task risks, the first step is to identify project-wide risks. Two major approaches are used. The first is to dig through retrospectives to determine what was learned in similar projects in similar environments. The other method is to use the expertise of the project participants to determine risks in one of several ways (Randolf, 1988).

Retrospectives. Without belaboring an already well-covered issue, review project retrospectives from similar past projects. Look for the following:

- Things that went wrong
- Ideas for avoiding future problems

- Applicable practices that worked well
- Assumptions, both good and bad
- Experiences of other project managers

Participant Assessment. There are several different approaches for capturing the experience and expertise of the project participants to identify project risks. You might choose to use one or two of them; they make fairly good project team-building exercises as well.

> *Nominal group technique (NGT).* This is a fancy name for getting together and figuring it out. To use NGT, get the group together and brainstorm potential project-wide risks. The group then discusses the list of risks to gain an understanding of each item, and finally prioritizes it to determine the most probable and highest potential risks.
>
> *Scenario planning.* This technique has the group address the question "What is the worst possible thing that could occur in the midst of the project?" The group then selects several probable versions to address.
>
> *Prospective hindsight.* This is similar to scenario planning but from a different perspective. Rather than looking at the cause, the group discusses specific project outcomes that they wish to avoid (such as cancellation, redefinition two weeks before implementation, and huge schedule slips). The group then assumes that these outcomes have occurred, one at a time, and works to identify events that could lead to the undesirable outcomes. These become the project-wide risks.
>
> *Aggregated task risks.* To use this approach, start with the identified task risks. Randomly put combinations of three or four task risks together and examine whether the aggregation creates any new or larger risks.

Assessing Project Risks

The number of project risks may be far greater than you want to attempt to plan for. If so, use the task risk-assessment techniques to prioritize and select the risks that you will specifically plan to reduce or eliminate. For those that cannot be reduced or eliminated, create contingency plans for the more significant risks.

If the project is large and the contingency plans are numerous, make allowance for the time and resources that may be required to implement them. If you identify four major risks and each has a 25 percent probability of resulting in a problem, what is the probability that at least one of them will result in a problem? Statistically, it is quite likely in such a situation that a problem will arise. If you do not include a contingency allowance, you run the risk of surprising your performance improvement project sponsors or management. Determine the necessary time and resource allowances as follows (Martin, 1976):

1. Assess the cost of and estimate the required effort for each contingency plan you have developed and may need to use.
2. Estimate the probability that you will use each plan.
3. Using the probabilities as weights, calculate the estimated likely cost of these plans in total for the project.
4. Again using probabilities as weights, calculate the total expected additional effort required for the project because of the use of contingency plans.

    For example, if a contingency plan will cost $1,000, require two effort-days to implement, and has a 10 percent probability of use, the contribution to the project totals will be $100 and 0.2 effort-days (1,000 x 0.1 and 2 x 0.1). By adding the weighted costs and time, you can now create a contingency plan allowance for the project, as shown in Table 10.1.

TABLE 10.1. CONTINGENCY PLAN ALLOWANCE TABLE.

Contingency	Probability	Contingency cost	Weighted cost	Contingency time	Weighted time
Replace disk	10 percent	$1,000	$100	2 days	.2 days
Subcontract	25 percent	$600	$150	1 day	.25 days
New system	15 percent	$5,000	$750	5 days	.75 days
Total			$1,000		1.2 days

5. The last step is to add the total allowance time and costs into the project plan. In the case of the example, the plan should reserve $1,000 and 1.2 days for contingency plan implementation. Table 10.1 is just an example; the number of items in your actual table depends upon the overall characterization of your project's riskiness.

Is your performance improvement project high risk, low risk, or something in between? There is a great tool for assessing and communicating the overall risk of a project. By characterizing three factors, you can determine an overall project risk. You can even use it as a tool to discuss project risk with managers and sponsors.

    Start by assessing the use of technology within the project. Rate it as high or low. Next, assess the amount of structure (definition and planning) and rate it as high or low. Finally, assess the project size as high or low.

Now, use Figure 10.3 to determine the overall risk of the project by taking your three ratings and finding their position on the grid. The boxes are scaled from A (lowest risk) to H (highest risk). The grid is also divided into three risk-level columns if you prefer.

Managing Project Risks

With the project risks identified and assessed, it is time to create the plan for managing them. The process is not markedly different from planning to manage task risks. Use the practices outlined in the task risk elimination and management section. However, a couple of points are specific to managing project-wide risks (Thomsett, 1993).

Now that all the risks and plans are out on the table, fine-tune the project plan to reduce risks. The following three aspects of the schedule will need modification:

- Using the schedule optimization techniques, change the project plan to reflect the risk reduction decisions that have been made.
- Add the selected tasks to resources to reduce risk.
- Change the task estimates of work based on the reduction decisions.

FIGURE 10.3. PROJECT RISK ASSESSMENT GRID.

Low	Medium	High
High Structure Low Technology Small Size **A**	Low Structure Low Technology Large Size **D**	Low Structure High Technology Small Size **G**
High Structure Low Technology Large Size **B**	High Structure High Technology Small Size **E**	Low Structure High Technology Large Size **H**
Low Structure Low Technology Small Size **C**	High Structure High Technology Large Size **F**	

Lastly, create an ongoing project-wide process for tracking and reassessing the project risks as the project proceeds. Assuming that the project risks will remain stable through the life of the project is itself risky.

- Identify additional risks that were not apparent at the project's start.
- Assign owners to update contingency plans when appropriate.
- Document all new risks and contingency plans.

Karen's Story

Karen charged into the conference room for the project review meeting. She was running uncharacteristically late. There sat Randy, Bob, and Kathleen, chatting away and poring over papers. Karen could sense that something wasn't going well, as they were looking over the contingency plans from their risk-management meeting. She sat down at the table and got the meeting going.

"Okay, folks, what's up? Looks like there's a problem in the works."

Randy looked up from the risk-management plan. "Well, we had a problem, but I think we're back on track. When we looked at risk in the project, we knew that the technical aspects of my tasks had some uncertainty. I was the assigned owner for monitoring the trigger. When I fell a day behind with no feasible solution, I pulled out my copy of the contingency plan and initiated it. I called Pam and had her review the problem. We were able to resolve three of the barriers, but not the fourth. So we removed the one feature as agreed to in the plan. I'm still a day behind, but I have a plan to be caught up by Thursday."

Karen was stunned. The problem was fixed as planned without her involvement. "Aren't you currently on the critical path, Randy?" she asked.

He looked at the schedule. "Yes, I am. Which means this could've been much worse. If you remember, we were concerned about technical risks and a potential slip. If we hadn't adjusted the schedule to minimize the risk, I'd be dealing with two critical path issues at the same time. I don't know how I could possibly recover from that."

Karen wanted to move to the next issue. "Anything else we need to discuss?"

Bob raised his hand. "Karen, I don't know how to say this, but lightning struck twice in the same week. As you know, we finished the video shoot for the first training video. Then we sent the tapes to the studio for final editing, and—well, to make a long story short, the FBI raided the place and caught them making illegal copies of movie videotapes. The whole place is sealed. We can't get our tapes out. Fortunately, we identified unduplicated tapes leaving the site as a risk, so I made copies per the risk reduction plan. I made another copy and sent it to the backup vendor we'd identified in the risk-reduction plan."

Karen was frantically taking notes. "What's our total loss in time and dollars?"

Bob pulled out the purchase order for the backup video vendor. "If we pay them $500 more than planned, they'll rush the job. We'll be right on schedule, plus or minus a few hours."

Karen took the purchase order. "Thanks, Bob. Anything else?"

"I hate to bring it up," said Kathleen, "but I'd better get my situation on the table too. Karen, remember that agreement you made in the hallway with John to do some of the formatting on the process documentation? The VP of finance has asked John's group to take on a special project, so now they can't do our job as promised. I checked with an outside vendor, and we can stay on schedule. But it's going to cost $8,000."

Karen finished off her notes. "Okay, gang. Let's get back to work."

Karen knocked on Jim's office door and asked, "Is this still a good time, or would you like me to come back later?"

"No, this is still a good time," Jim said. "Come in and have a seat. This sounds pretty urgent."

Karen sat down and opened her project notebook. "When we defined the project infrastructure, you said you wanted to know about any project problems the same day I found out. Here I am."

Jim leaned forward in his chair. "This doesn't sound good. What's up?"

Karen smiled. "Well, it's not *that* bad. We ran into some technical barriers with the big performance improvement project. But we identified that as a risk and had a clear trigger identified with an owner. Randy was on it right away, so we only slipped about a day and lost one minor feature. We have a plan to make up the day."

Jim sighed with relief. "You're right. That isn't bad at all. But you look like you have more on your mind."

Karen pulled out the purchase orders. "Well, now that you mention it, there are two more issues. Our video editing vendor went out of business all of a sudden, so we have to switch to a different one. But for an extra $500, we can keep on schedule. Also, John's group won't be able to help us out as planned, which means we have to go outside. That'll cost another $8,000."

Jim reviewed the purchase orders. "Is this in your project budget?"

Karen pulled a paper from her notebook. "Not specifically, but we allowed for implementing contingency plans. We weighted them by probability and figured some contingency costs would come up, so they're in the project budget. The total contingency allowance is $12,000 for this project. We're still under budget."

Originally, Jim had thought that the day they spent on risk assessment was wasted. Now he knows it was time well spent. How had Karen known?

PART THREE

IMPLEMENTING THE PLAN

Once the performance improvement project is prepared and planned, it is time to implement it and achieve the project goals. Significant planning effort has been expended to ensure a successful project, but more substantial work is ahead. Part Three covers major issues associated with plan implementation.

Most organizations have come to rely on outside resources to supplement their own capacity or capability. Contracting work out to vendors can be successful or perilous, depending upon your approach.

Managing the project to ensure that it goes according to plan is crucial. This is where planning and preparation pay off in achieving the project goal on time and with the agreed-upon resources.

We could hardly call ourselves human performance technologists if we did not apply organizational learning to the project to improve our performance as a project manager, as well as that of other project managers in the organization.

FIGURE P3.1.

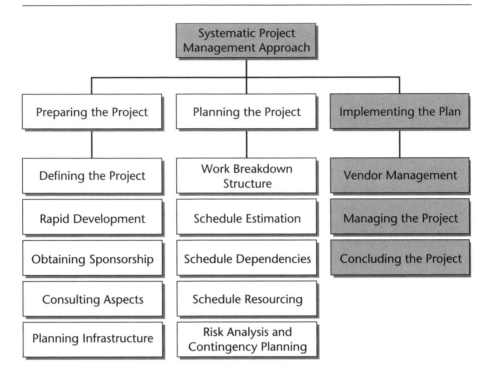

CHAPTER ELEVEN

MANAGING THE VENDOR

Very few of us have personally built or remodeled our own homes. The reason is that we lack either the capability (necessary skills and knowledge) or the capacity (necessary time, machinery, or personpower). Instead, most people hire a contractor, a vendor, to do the work for them. Similarly, vendors may play an important role in carrying out a performance improvement project—if the process of finding and using them is well managed.

Bill's Story

Bill strolled into the review meeting and found his staff and representatives of Engineering Associates, Inc., waiting for him. "Let's get started, shall we? We seem to have a few issues to resolve."

Engineering Associates had been brought into the project to help reengineer the specification process. Tim Boswik, the Engineering Associates president, was here today, as the relationship between Bill's team and Engineering Associates had become rather strained.

Tim broke the ice. "Okay, Bill, let's start with the latest requests from your team. They seem to be adding a lot of activities to the original request. We don't mind doing the extra work, but it's going to take longer and cost a lot more."

Bill was honestly confused. "What additional work? What more are we asking you to do?"

Tim flipped open his folder. "Well, your team is now asking us to do validation testing on the final process design."

"Well, of course we want a validation test," said Bill. "How else will we know if the process that you designed actually works?"

Tim pulled out his contract with NewIdea. "I don't know, Bill. But neither the original request nor the contract specify any testing. We're supposed to study your needs and deliver a redesigned process. That's what we based the time and cost estimates on. If you want additional work done, we should create an additional agreement."

Bill was in trouble and he knew it. He had rushed through the process of vending this activity out; the contract was valid, and he was out of time and money to do more. "Thanks, Tim, but we're going to accept your new process as is. What's the next topic?"

Tim looked back to his notes. "We seem to have some disagreement regarding the job aids. We delivered them on schedule, but your team won't accept them. Something about using different fonts and page format. We could've done it another way if we'd known what you wanted to begin with, but to rework it now is unreasonable. The contract makes no specification about integrating this information into another document. We lived up to our part of the agreement."

When Bill agreed to take the job aids as they were, his staff almost fell out of their chairs. The material clearly needed to be reworked, and now they would have to do it. They could not understand why he caved in. But Bill knew. He had no choice: a contract is a contract.

Bill felt the weight of the world on his shoulders as he walked from the meeting. He looked up to see his manager storming down the hallway toward him, and Linda did not look like she was having a good day either. "Bill, I just spent the last half hour with the procurement manager, and boy, is he hot. Assigning a contract without a formal open bid process opens us to a full audit by our investors. Did you hire a vendor and bind us into a contract without procurement's participation?"

The Basic Issue of Vendors

Vendors can be a mixed blessing. They might be able to achieve greater results, but they also require additional up-front work and ongoing management. Few people would give a home contractor a broad objective such as "add a bedroom" and simply let the sawdust begin to fly; most would work carefully to ensure agreement about the desired outcome, costs, schedule, and work environment.

Unfortunately, such rigorous planning and management does not always seem to transfer to the world of human performance technology. Stories are numerous of vendors being launched into projects with objectives as clear as "create a thirty-minute videotape on X" or "deliver a three-day course on Y." The results of such projects are rarely very positive and usually require extensive rework and further expense.

This chapter focuses on how to successfully use vendors within your performance improvement project and the project management tactics necessary to incorporate them into the overall plan and activities. This is a long chapter; effective and successful use of outside resources is a complex issue in project management, particularly if you are seeking services rather than products.

Why Use a Vendor?

If you are considering using vendors, you must be absolutely clear on what you are attempting to accomplish with them (Lippitt, 1986). Why are you considering an outside vendor as opposed to inside resources? Generally, use vendors when at least one of the following conditions exists:

- The organization lacks the capability to perform the task; necessary skills or knowledge do not exist internally but can be obtained externally. For example, you may need to redesign the performance feedback system and have no expertise in the area. Or you may need a computer-based training course created, and nobody in the company has created one before.
- The organization lacks the capacity to complete the task in a timely manner; the project requires more resources than are available internally. Equipment, such as a video production studio, may cause the capacity deficit. Personpower and other resources can be acquired from the outside.
- It is more expensive to carry out the task internally. In some cases (particularly in large corporations with large employee overhead) outside vendors can be more cost-effective than internal resources.

The vendor selection process will be driven by your reason for using a vendor (Martin, 1976). If you need one for capability reasons, the vendor's expertise will be the primary factor, with time and costs secondary. If you need one for capacity reasons, the vendor's depth of resources, demonstrated speed, and reliability become primary considerations. If the reason is cost, the selection might be different yet.

Within the topic of capability is the need for further differentiation. Are you looking for content expertise, development expertise, or delivery expertise? It is important not to confuse a subject matter expert with a developer. A good content person may not design an instructionally sound deliverable. Likewise, a good developer may not bring sufficient content knowledge to develop the deliverable.

Just looking at developing instructional interventions, vendors are available for either capability or capacity in any of the following instructional design phases:

- Analysis
- Design
- Development
- Delivery or implementation
- Evaluation

It is critical to be very clear on *why* you want a vendor, or you may have to spend funds in excess of the plan, go over schedule, end up with a performance improvement project that does not achieve its intended outcome, or all three.

Along with considering why you might want to use a vendor, consider why you might not. Using a vendor may introduce risk into the project plan. When you use a vendor, you are relinquishing some level of control and giving it to the vendor. Vendors will make decisions about staffing, priorities, and scheduling the work they do. If there is minimal negative consequence in being late, the vendor could decide to postpone your work to pursue other lucrative work.

There is a flip side to the control and risk issue. You may be in a large corporation where the resources you need are in another part of the business. In such a case, using a vendor could actually increase your control and reduce risk in the plan. Regardless of the situation, ensure that you consider control and plan risk when considering whether to use a vendor.

In situations where the following three concerns exist, avoid using vendors if at all possible (Obradovitch and Stephanou, 1990):

Confidentiality of content. If the content of the intervention includes highly confidential or proprietary information, stay away from vendors. Even if the vendor is under some type of nondisclosure agreement, vendors know that such agreements are almost impossible to enforce. If they have access to the information, you have a potential information leak walking around. There are many known instances of vendors using confidential information from one company to secure work at a competing firm.

Confidentiality of process. If you will be using confidential or proprietary processes on the project, avoid vendors for the same reason. If vendors experience a process, they learn it and will incorporate it into their repertoires. You may find your processes at work for another company.

Highly complex, interdependent projects and activities. Project activities that are complex in nature or interdependent with other projects may be inappropriate to give to vendors. The amount of time spent understanding the other projects and the environment is usually significant. Internal resources are usually more effective in these cases, as they better understand the implementation and work environment.

Defining the Vendor's Role

After you clearly define why a vendor is an appropriate resource to use and decide to proceed, the next step is to clearly define what you want the vendor to accomplish. The following are three major benefits that come from clearly defining the desired accomplishment (Kezsbaum, 1989):

- It provides a clear criterion for selecting the right vendor to do the job.
- The vendor can submit a more accurate proposal for required time and costs.
- You are more likely to get what you need to make the project successful.

As human performance technologists, we know that a major barrier to performance is a lack of information regarding the performance expectations (Mager, 1992). Consider the example of a performance analysis that found the root cause of a performance gap to be information about performance expectation. The intervention was simple: tell the people what is expected of them. Unfortunately, the organization had struggled for a year to meet its objectives when all it needed to do was tell the employees what they needed to do. Avoid similar costs and frustration by taking some time to clearly describe your expectations of the vendor.

If you have been using the project management approach in this book, you already have a good start; the project definition you have created will help the vendor understand the project and submit a more accurate and informed proposal.

It is unlikely that you will hand the entire performance improvement project over to a vendor. More likely, you will have the vendor complete specific tasks. This is where your work breakdown structure comes in handy. Review the structure and determine which tasks you need to have completed by vendors. Compiling the list of tasks and their relationship to the project provides additional information to the vendor.

Next, clearly specify the technical requirements associated with the task, such as the anticipated delivery method, instructional method, and intended outcomes. Some tasks are components of a larger task or need to be coordinated with another task. If so, specify the integration requirements necessary to make the completed task work seamlessly with the rest of the project. Table 11.1 shows a sample vendor task description. It is taken from a project to improve employee performance using a new communication system.

TABLE 11.1. EXAMPLE TASK DESCRIPTION.

Task	Creation of job aid for startup procedure
Technical requirements	Documents the entire startup process Employees can implement without additional assistance Achieves startup in less than five minutes Includes error-message recovery Includes troubleshooting process
Integration requirements	Same medium as other job aids (printed and laminated) Fits in job aid binder (5 x 7 inches, 7-hole punch) Includes links to detailed reference manual on machine

Determining Internal Rules of Procurement

If you are part of an organization, rules probably exist regarding the procurement (selection and purchase) of products and services. These rules may be minimal in the case of a small, privately held organization, or absolutely oppressive in the case of large, government-regulated industries. Being unaware of the rules or violating them introduces tremendous risk into the schedule. Your vendor selection may be challenged or overruled, which could cause significant delays.

What you will have to do to establish procurement procedures depends on the environment in which you work. Check on the current status of rules regarding vendor procurement. In general, consider the need to do each of the following:

- Establish a code of ethics on internal versus external work.
- Determine what kind of relationship you wish to have with your vendors.
- Document a preferred-vendor policy if you choose to have one.

Establish a Code of Ethics on Internal Versus External Work. Decide whether to consider internal resources before starting any formal vendor solicitation. An internal decision is where another division or department of your company could be selected to complete the task rather than a vendor.

It is difficult for a vendor to compete head-to-head in a selection process against an internal resource. No matter how well the requirements are written, countless items of internal procedures, experience, and relationships give internal resources a formidable advantage. Therefore, if you are considering any internal resources, evaluate and accept or reject them before soliciting proposals from vendors.

Once you decide to purchase products or services, request vendor proposals and evaluate them. It is unethical to solicit proposals from vendors, read them, and then decide to do the tasks internally based on what you read in the proposals. This is outright plagiarism. The information is submitted in good faith by the vendors in the expectation that their proposals will receive serious and fair consideration in exchange for the effort they have expended in preparing them. Few vendors will respond enthusiastically to future proposal requests if you act unethically. Word gets around quickly about companies that behave in this manner.

Determine What Kind of Relationship You Wish to Have with Your Vendors. Relationships with vendors can vary greatly. Some companies create very tight bonds with vendors and become strategic partners with them. The vendor may frequently be granted business based on the relationship and past performance. Sometimes it becomes difficult to tell employees from vendors; the latter may be allowed broad access to facilities and perhaps even have a desk on site. This tends to occur with substantial performance improvement projects in which there is long-term analysis or implementation of significant organizational interventions such as organizational construct, compensation systems, or performance evaluation and feedback systems.

On the other end of the spectrum, some companies prefer to maintain a distant relationship with the vendor. Different vendors may be used each time there is a project need. Rather than granting work, a bidding or proposal process is usually used. Vendors may never be allowed on site. Rather, they are viewed as suppliers: we specify, you supply.

It is important to determine what type of relationships your company maintains. If a close and strategic relationship exists with a vendor, you are certain to experience unwanted visibility should you put significant work out to bid. In a like manner, if your company insists on distant relationships and you grant work to a vendor based upon such a relationship, you may find your arrangements coming unraveled rather quickly. Your credibility as a professional could be called into question if you do not assess the system and work within the specified environment.

Document a Preferred-Vendor Policy If You Choose to Have One. Should you limit the number of vendors you wish to consider? It really depends upon the circumstances. The size of your company and the level of business it vends out may attract only a few local vendors who would desire the business. If this is the case, you should not limit the number of vendors who can submit proposals for consideration. If you work for a large corporation that vends major project elements (sometimes as much as $1 million), the number of proposals you receive may be oppressive; this is when to consider limiting the number of vendors you will consider (if you can).

A preferred-vendor policy states that your company will only do business with a specific list of vendors; unsolicited proposals will be neither accepted nor considered. The size of the list should be based on your specific business needs, and the list should be documented along with the criteria for being selected to the list. The selection should be reevaluated periodically, perhaps every other year. This will allow any highly qualified newcomers to eventually receive consideration and also prevent the preferred vendors from becoming complacent and noncompetitive.

Identifying Potential Vendors

After you have discovered or established the approved methods for obtaining vendor services and products, determine the process you will use for identifying the best vendor for the work (Kepner and Tregoe, 1981). Taking into account your company's procurement standards, select an approach: single source, preferred, or proposal (bid).

Although it is rare in the area of human performance technology services, some companies do have a mandated single source. This is generally because the procurement department has already evaluated the vendors and prenegotiated the prices. If this is your case, you should proceed using the selected vendor.

If your company mandates a preferred-vendor program, you will have to choose between a few potential vendors that have already been qualified. When this is the case, your next step is to send out requests for proposals. This is covered in the next section.

The most common procurement situation when working on performance improvement projects is a proposal (bid) system (Gilbreath, 1986). This generally requires gathering proposals from at least three different vendors. If your company mandates open bids, you have no choice but to consider all potential vendors; otherwise, you have the opportunity to select vendors to make proposals. But whom should you ask to submit proposals?

Develop a profile inventory of potential vendors. This becomes your invitation list for the proposal process; in a way, you are creating your own preferred-vendor system. But what information should you gather about a vendor? You probably want to know more than its hourly rates, unless you want to put risk back into your project plan. Here are some potential areas to consider as you begin to build your profile inventory on vendors:

- Capabilities
   Product or service list and description
   Production capability
   Implementation support
   Documentation and training on purchased products
- Management characteristics
   Management organization (organization charts)
   Management quality assessment
   Stability of management
   Quality controls and procedures
- Personnel
   List of top-performing personnel
   Assessment of personnel quality
   Turnover and morale
- Financial stability
   Annual report assessment of company (if available)
   Financial assessment
   List of other current clients
- Independent evaluations
   Vendor-provided references
   Competitor assessments
   Supplier assessments
   Client assessments
- Historical relationship
   Information on previous contracts or purchases
   Information on previous contacts with company and management
   Information on previous dealings with company management

From a risk-management perspective, creating an inventory of assessed vendors is a good thing to do even if you are not planning to use vendors on the performance improvement project in question (Hertz and Howard, 1983). The reason is that if a need suddenly arises (for example, if somebody on the project leaves or gets sick) you can backfill the project quickly. This is substantially preferable to beginning the vendor qualification process while the project clock is running.

Creating a Request for Proposal

With your list of potential vendors narrowed down, you will need some information from them on which to base your selection. But before they can provide a proposal of how they would do the work, they need information about the project and the information that you seek. This is a crucial point in the vendor relationship. Most vendor failures are caused by sloppy work at this stage (Gilbreath, 1986).

Send out a document describing the service or product you need and the information you need to make your vendor selection. This document is typically referred to as a request for proposal (RFP). The first section in the RFP should clearly outline the work you want done. This is where your previous efforts are applied. You should have a clear description of the project as well as the technical and integration requirements of the tasks you want a vendor to accomplish. A method to help you organize and communicate this information is referred to as "entry, task, validation, and exit," or ETVX. Each of the four steps provides important information to the vendor who is assessing the work to be done. Entry information tells vendors what conditions will exist before they are expected to begin the task. Task information tells them what they are expected to do. Validation creates an agreement for determining the finished quality of the task. Exit information tells the vendor the conditions for completion of the task. As you can imagine, having clarity and agreement on these issues before the work begins saves substantial misunderstanding and resulting delays.

ETVX is usually expressed in a chart, with one chart per page in the RFP. Table 11.2 shows the ETVX format and the information typically found in each area.

Table 11.3 shows the task description example from Table 11.1 in the ETVX format and additional information that the vendor will want to know (and that you will want them to agree to).

TABLE 11.2. ETVX LAYOUT AND CONTENTS.

Entry	Identifies predecessors Establishes quality criteria for predecessors
Task	Describes task Identifies necessary resources
Validation	Establishes testing or validation procedures Declares expected outcome
Exit Criteria	Identifies dependent activities Establishes criteria for formal completion
Assumptions	Identifies any assumptions regarding task or its completion

TABLE 11.3. TYPICAL ETVX FROM AN RFP.

Entry	Start-up process complete and stable Detailed reference manual complete and stable Error messages completed

Task	Creation of job aid for start-up procedure
	    Technical requirements
	        Documents entire start-up process
	        Employees can implement without additional assistance
	        Achieves start-up in less than five minutes
	        Includes error-message recovery
	        Includes troubleshooting process
	    Integration requirements
	        Same medium as other job aids (printed and laminated)
	        Fits in job aid binder (5 x 7 inches, 7-hole punch)
	        Includes links to detailed reference manual on machine
	    Resources
	        Vendor will complete this task on vendor's site with vendor's resources
	        Company personnel will not participate in this activity
	        Must be completed five working days after Entry conditions met

Validation	Job aid tested with five different employees to validate time Job aid tested with three different fail modes to test recovery
Exit Criteria	All technical and integration requirements met Validation criteria met
Assumptions	Validation scenarios selected by company Validation conducted by vendor

You will receive proposals from different vendors; to be able to compare their proposals, you need them to submit similar kinds of information. The second part of the RFP specifies what information you want from the vendors and which format it should take. Consistency and richness of detail are the most important aspects, as they allow you to choose the best vendor quickly.

Generally, an RFP format specification asks for information in the following three proposal areas (Kezsbaum, 1989):

- *Statement of work.* This is where the vendor details the work it will do. The statement is important, as it represents the vendor's interpretation of what you have asked for; unless a piece of work is documented specifically in the statement of work, the vendor does not have to do it. Specify that the statement of work be broken down according to the work breakdown structure, not just stated as an overall activity. This allows examination and evaluation of process, approach, and reliability in meeting the schedule.
- *Management proposal.* This is where the vendor details how the work will be managed and by whom. It states who will oversee the work, evaluate progress, take any corrective action necessary, and other responsibilities. Do not assume the vendor is performing these tasks. Ensure that the vendor is committed to doing them and has recovery plans if work falls behind or does not meet the validation criteria.
- *Costs proposal.* This is where the vendor tells you how much the work will cost. Be sure to specify that the costs be broken down according to the work breakdown structure. This allows better valuation assessment and the ability to select which services you want the vendor to provide.

By the way, do not let the word *bid* bother you; it usually does not mean that you have to take the lowest cost proposal. Cost is only one of several potential criteria. Depending on the situation, the vendors might be evaluated on speed or quality rather than costs.

Vendor Selection and Negotiation

Once you have received proposals from the vendors, it is time to begin evaluating them to determine which one will best meet your project's needs. The evaluation process can be as elaborate or as simple as you wish to make it, but the key is to remove as much subjectivity from it as possible.

Create evaluation criteria and a judging method to assess each evaluation against the criteria, and give each a score. You can then compare the scores that the proposals receive and select the appropriate vendor. This method can be used equally well with single evaluators or a panel of evaluators. Its data-driven nature makes the selection decision defensible and reduces potential claims of favoritism.

The first step is to determine the evaluation criteria (Kepner and Tregoe, 1981). This is driven primarily by the detail of the RFP and the specific needs of your performance improvement project and the work environment. Generally, you should have criteria for all three of the RFP areas. Following are some sample criteria to consider.

Criteria for Evaluating the Statement of Work Proposal

- Does the vendor demonstrate an accurate understanding of the work that is requested?
- Is the statement of work accurately divided according to the tasks' place on the work breakdown structure?
- Does the vendor specify the resources needed to complete the tasks?
- Has the vendor agreed with the validation criteria?
- Does the vendor's plan reasonably allow work completion within the specified time?
- Does the vendor include and meet all the work requirements as specified in the RFP?
- Does the vendor include and meet the integration requirements specified in the RFP?

Criteria for Evaluating the Management Proposal

- Are the senior managers in the vendor's organization committed to the success of this project? Will they actively participate in the project?
- Have contingency plans been developed to support this project with additional quality or quantity of human resources should problems occur?
- Does the vendor have sufficient resources to complete the project if turnover occurs on the project team?
- Does the vendor have a clearly defined and appropriate process for problem identification and resolution?
- Have the assigned resources performed an identical or similar task before?
- Are adequate quality controls established for the duration and completion of the tasks?

Criteria for Evaluating the Cost Proposal

- Does the cost of the work correlate with your assessment of the effort and resources necessary to complete the task within the time allotted?

- If the technical merit of the proposal is excellent or exceptional, is the cost reasonable? Should a lesser capability be sought at a reduced cost?

- If the management merit of the proposal is excellent or exceptional, is it because there is an unnecessary premium for management overhead?

- Is the vendor delivering high quality at reasonable prices because it has demonstrated how to be highly cost-effective, or is it bidding low to get the job?

- If the technical or management proposal for this work requires improvement to make it satisfactory, will substantially higher costs be required?

- If the work were to be done internally at fully loaded costs, adding 20 percent administrative expense and 10 percent profit, would the internal cost be reasonably close to that of the vendor's proposal?

- Is there anything in the proposal that would require increasing internal costs in lieu of paying the vendor?

- Is the quality of the resources proposed in the management plan consistent with the labor rate in the cost proposal? Is there any indication of a potential "bait and switch" situation?

- Is the vendor making use of previously developed solutions but charging for the full development costs?

After you have specified the criteria, select an assessment method for assigning a score to each criterion when evaluating a proposal. Many assessment methods are available; select or create one that works best for you. Be certain that the one you choose includes a clear definition of how scores are determined to ensure consistent assessment between proposals, and also multiple evaluators if you use them. Table 11.4 shows a simple three-point scale, and Table 11.5 shows a more detailed gradation assessment scale.

TABLE 11.4. THREE-POINT ASSESSMENT SCALE.

Evaluator's assessment	Definition	Score
Clearly exceeds requirements	The vendor's response to the requirement provides a capability that exceeds the need.	2
Fully meets requirements	The vendor's response fully meets or barely exceeds the minimum requirement.	1
Clearly less than required	The vendor's response is noticeably deficient in a number of characteristics compared to the requirements.	0

TABLE 11.5. GRADATION ASSESSMENT SCALE.

Evaluator's assessment	Definition	Score
Exceptional	The vendor's response is far beyond the requirements and sets the vendor apart from others.	10
Excellent	The vendor's response significantly exceeds several of the requirements.	8
Advantage	The vendor's response meets all the requirements and noticeably exceeds some of them.	6
Fully satisfactory	The vendor's response fully meets all the requirements.	5
Adequate	The vendor's response does not meet all the requirements, but minimal work would be necessary to correct.	4
Inadequate	The vendor's response is not satisfactory and would require substantial effort to create an acceptable solution.	2
Unacceptable	The vendor's response was totally unacceptable, or the vendor did not respond.	0

The next stage is to implement the assessment, collect the data, and determine the outcome. Developing a spreadsheet is a natural process for managing the data and calculating the results. Once the decision is made, formalize the agreement using the vendor's proposal.

If contracting is not one of your skills, get assistance. Ensure that you have a valid agreement that specifies the working relationship. Will the vendor be paid as the work is completed or not until all the work is delivered? Do you have the right to terminate the agreement if you are not satisfied with the results? Is there a penalty to the vendor for not meeting schedule commitments? All these considerations must be built into the terms and conditions of the contract.

Managing the Vendor

With the agreement signed, you are ready to go to work—or, rather, the vendor is. You have provided the vendor with detailed information on its role in the project and the specifics of the work to be done; the working relationship has been detailed in the contract. The majority of the work is completed, but a job still must be done: you must manage the vendor relationship. The work you have done so far makes this simple.

Only a few tasks remain. If you asked the vendor to design a performance improvement deliverable, conduct a formal design review to ensure the integrity and quality of the design (Kezsbaum, 1989). This will eliminate rework and schedule slips by allowing modifications to design aspects (easy to do) as opposed to reworking the final deliverable (difficult to do).

A design review is simply a review and evaluation of the completed performance improvement design. There are essentially three major objectives to be accomplished in the review:

- Verify that all requirements have been incorporated in the design.
- Measure the vendor's progress against the schedule for this milestone.
- Validate that the evaluation plan is consistent with the acceptance criteria.

Without clear specifications in the RFP, the design review could be an opinion-based shouting match between vendor and client; new design criteria could be created and disagreement over interpretation of what was requested could rage on. The net result: damaged relationships, schedule delays, and cost overruns.

If the work to be completed will take long (more than two weeks), have the vendor provide you with status reports on progress (Obradovitch and Stephanou, 1990). This will help you assess whether the work is proceeding appropriately and allow you to take corrective action early if necessary. What should you look for in a status review? Here are a few issues to consider:

Status Report Review Criteria

- Is the reported accomplishment or progress credible?
- Is the status report substantiated by partial completion of deliverables?
- Are the accomplishments consistent with the requirements and the statement of work?
- Are the resource and time requirements for this task still appropriate?
- Is the linkage to other project tasks still functioning properly?
- Is the entire project schedule still credible given the results of this report?

The final task in vendor management is to ensure that the completed work meets the established criteria as detailed in the statement of work. Having the validation and exit criteria agreed upon before beginning the work makes this easy: if the work meets the criteria, it is accepted and the task is completed; if not, the vendor must make the necessary corrections.

Vendor management is much like instructional design. If you do the design work well, the rest of the work flows easily. If you skimp on the early phases, you usually pay a large premium in attempting to make corrections to the work later on.

Karen's Story

Karen strolled into the review meeting, where her staff and some representatives of Process Innovations, Inc., sat waiting for her. "Let's get started, shall we?" she said. "I'm eager to see the results to date."

Process Innovations had been brought into the project to help reengineer the specification process. The company had not been Karen's initial choice, but the open bid process that NewIdea's procurement department had helped her design showed that it was the best vendor for the job.

Tom and Susan were the lead engineers at Process Innovations; the contract specified that they were to do the work, conduct the validation, and make this presentation. Susan turned on the overhead projector. "As you can see, the initial validation test showed that the new specification process meets the design requirements, except for phase five. We made two minor adjustments, and the second test indicates that all the requirements have been met."

Tom stood up and handed out copies of the job aid he and his staff had developed. "We've completed this on schedule. Here are your copies."

Karen reviewed the job aid quickly. "Tom, this looks good, but it doesn't meet the integration requirements specified in our agreement. We'll be happy to accept this work and release payment when the job aid meets specification. The work is really looking good. Thanks for the review. We'll see you next week for the final acceptance and sign-off meeting as specified in the agreement. Thanks again!"

CHAPTER TWELVE

MANAGING THE PROJECT

Now that the project is completely planned and the appropriate work carefully contracted out to vendors, is it time to just sit back and watch the plan roll out? Well, not exactly. No performance improvement project goes exactly as planned; unexpected events always occur during implementation. If you took the chapter on risk management to heart, you should have contingency plans in place for most of these. However, the project still needs to be managed.

Bill's Story

Bill waited for the last project team member to shuffle through the conference room door, and then started the meeting. "I'm glad you could all make it. Thanks. I'd like to spend some time discussing where we are on the project. I'll need to update the management team soon, and I thought we'd better update the schedule. Normally I run around and ask you folks individually, but I'm finding it difficult to find enough time. Phil, let's start with you. What's the status on the video editing task?"

Phil looked down at the table. "Well, I'm about 90 percent done."

Bill looked up with amazement. "What?! You were 90 percent done three weeks ago when I asked. What have you been doing since then?"

Phil flushed with anger. "Listen, Bill. If you had bothered to check more than once every three weeks on this project, you would know I'm having some difficulty with the special effects that were added."

Bill quickly turned to Kelly. "What's the status on your next task, Kelly?"

"Um—sorry, Bill," she said, "but I didn't know we'd be discussing task completion today. I'd guess I'm about halfway done. But I do have a question. How are we doing on meeting our deadline?"

Bill brought out his project schedule. "Well, it's difficult to say. With all the changes we've made I can't really tell how we're doing compared to the original schedule. I'll have to figure that out sometime. I do know we're running late because of Phil's task. What do you think we should do?"

Phil jumped right in. "We need to put more effort into the task. I need help. I think Barb should postpone her task and help me."

Barb looked puzzled. "How do we know more effort will help resolve the technical difficulties? What if we're trying to do something that can't be done?"

Bill, eager to close the meeting, said hastily, "We can figure that out as we go. I'd like you to help Phil with the editing."

Later that afternoon, Bill strolled into Linda's office. "I hear you want to see me."

"Yeah, Bill. Have a seat." Linda did not look at all pleased. As Bill sat in the blue chair, he felt his stomach assume its usual position in his throat. "Bill, we seem to be having a problem managing the performance improvement project. I heard from the operations manager this morning. He's really getting annoyed with the huge reports you continue to land on his desk. He feels that a task-by-task analysis of the project is entirely too much detail. I, on the other hand, don't seem to be getting enough detail. When the operations manager asked me some questions about the project, I was at a complete loss. I looked like an idiot. Please get me some reasonable detail so I can manage this organization."

Project Management

In project management, the activities that consume time are identifying schedule variances from the plan, determining their impact, and developing and taking adaptive actions (Randolf, 1988). By effectively managing the project, you fulfill your responsibility as the project manager by helping ensure that it is completed on schedule, using the least possible resources, and with results that meet specifications.

But sponsors and managers are rarely willing to wait until the conclusion of a major performance improvement project to find out how it went. As the project manager, you must track its progress and report on it to management and the project team.

An Approach to Managing the Project

Randomly running around and attempting to manage a project rarely works well; a systematic approach is needed to ensure that plan implementation problems are not overlooked (Martin, 1976). Additionally, you must ensure that the various parties interested in the project receive information specific to their needs.

A systematic four-phase process allows your project management efforts to be both effective and efficient. The four phases are collecting project status, analyzing variances, taking adaptive action, and reporting project status.

Collecting Project Status

Before you can take adaptive action or report status, you need to know what the status of the project actually is. During the status collection phase, the project manager ensures that progress data is collected according to the processes established when the project's infrastructure was planned (see Chapter Five), and that the project schedule is updated to reflect the new status (Lewis, 1993a).

Status of the project changes hourly. Somewhere between collecting status every hour and waiting until the end of the project to do it lies a reasonable approach: collecting project status based on the unique characteristics of the project. It is still a lot of work, but the following are some benefits of systematically tracking the progress of your performance improvement project:

- Reduces project uncertainty and team stress
- Reduces excessive optimism or pessimism
- Is essential to being proactive in managing the project
- Helps anticipate potential problems
- Reduces reliance on the hope that things will simply "work themselves out"
- Helps to center discussions on project issues
- Reduces the ability to suppress problems and bad news
- Facilitates discussions by providing substantiated data
- Facilitates the communication of dependencies across organizations
- Makes it difficult to ignore early danger signals

The process of collecting project status has three steps.

Step 1: Set the Baseline of the Schedule and Resource Plans. The baseline is the plan against which all project progress will be measured. Once set, it should not be easily changed (Kezsbaum, 1989). The problem is that if the schedule is changed every time the status of the project changes, the schedule becomes a record of what has happened rather than a plan for what should happen. By the time you reach the end of the project, the schedule will indicate that you are right on time because of all the changes that have been made. But compared to the original plan, you may be three months late.

By freezing the schedule at the beginning of the project, you ensure that the original plan is always clearly understood and visible. But though it should be done cautiously and only under specific circumstances, there nevertheless are times when you will want to change the baseline schedule: if a project change has a massive and unrecoverable impact on the schedule, recalculate the baseline. Such occasions include times when the project is required to be finished earlier, when the resources available for the project must be substantially increased or decreased, or when the scope of the project is forced to change (remember, you cannot increase the scope without increasing the schedule or the resources).

If you do need to change the baseline schedule at some point, ensure that the events that are causing the change have been made visible, and that the impact of the change has been approved by the sponsors and managers of the performance improvement project.

Also, communicate the resetting of the baseline to other groups affected by it. Distribute approved plans and supporting assumptions according to the project infrastructure decisions, and archive a copy of the schedule and resource plan along with the assumptions.

Many software project management systems allow you to manage concurrent schedules. That is, they allow you to freeze the baseline version and update a version that reflects current status. This allows the project manager to quickly compare the baseline with the current status. Later in the process, you should update the schedule. The actual version, not the baseline version, should be updated with status information.

Step 2: Collect Progress Data and Estimate Time and Resources for Remaining Activities.

With the baseline set, you can now begin the project and monitor its status as progress is made. But some questions need to be answered before the project status is collected. For starters, what information are you going to collect? How are you going to collect it? What form should it be in? How often are you going to collect it?

One of the first issues is deciding on a data-collection method. All the performance improvement project participants need to be involved in deciding this part of the strategy, as they will be involved in collections. Do not attempt to select the method for them; allow them to own the collection process. Some of the alternatives include the following:

Project team members update their status reports and submit them to the project manager for consolidation. This works well on large performance improvement projects but is unnecessary for small projects.

The project team meets periodically to report status. This works well for small- to medium-size projects if the team can meet frequently. But this becomes a time sink if the number of project participants is large.

The project manager holds one-on-one meetings with project team members. This conserves their time but uses lots of the manager's. Agree to this only if there are three or fewer project participants.

Team members report to the project manager via electronic mail. This works well if the capability is available to you, and it can be particularly effective if the participants are not physically local to one another.

The project manager collects data by walking around. Although this might seem rather serendipitous, it is possible to discover information this way that participants overlook in their project reporting. It is probably not best to rely on this method exclusively.

Any combination of these may work. Who says you have to stay with a single method?

After determining how you will gather status, another question must be resolved: What data are you going to collect? There are many ways to measure progress on project tasks. If you are going to collect data from several project participants, you will want some commonality in data that allows you to accurately assess project progress. The available data falls into two categories: hard and soft.

Hard data are defined as information based on measurement with tangible evidence. Hard data typically collected to update project status include the following:

- Tasks complete or not complete
- Milestones complete or not complete
- Actual duration and remaining activity (recommended)
- Actual start and finish dates
- Percentage complete (not recommended)

The percentage data are difficult to measure because they are subjective guesses. How often is a task 90 percent complete the day before it misses its deadline, or 90 percent complete for more than half of the task duration? This measure can only be of use if the deliverable of the task (not work on the task) can be measured and the task duration is short relative to the total duration of the project. Even then, percentage complete should be used only as a last recourse.

Consider the following story that addresses the issue: a rancher wanted to put up a fence along his property line. He hired a college student to dig the holes and set the posts. After three weeks, the student told the rancher that he was not yet done but had to return to school. He said that he had installed ninety of the one hundred posts required to complete the job, and that paying him 90 percent of the agreed-upon $1,000 would be fair. The rancher agreed, paid the student, and sent him on his way.

Later, the rancher discovered that solid rock underlay the soil where the last ten posts had to be placed. It took another three weeks and an additional $2,000 to have the posts drilled and set. The lesson: from a "post count" perspective the student was indeed 90 percent finished, but from an effort perspective he was barely half done.

Soft data are defined as information that is subjective, based on interpretation or opinion. Although these data are not based on measurement or evidence, you should not discount their value in managing the project. Soft data can help keep a project out of trouble. When managing a project, use soft data, but rely on hard data. Examples of soft data frequently collected during performance improvement projects include the following:

- Problems encountered and anticipated
- Resources being threatened (people being pulled off projects)
- Individual productivity
- Inhibitors to productivity
- Persistent problems and proposed actions to correct
- Planning ahead for things such as key deliverables and documentation

Frequency of the project status data collection is the final decision to be made in this step of the process. Unfortunately, it is not an easy one. Not even the experts in the field of professional project management can agree on a method for determining how often to collect project status.

However, some general guidelines should be considered when determining frequency. At a minimum, status should be collected every two weeks. This is the maximum duration of any task in a well-planned project. Collecting the status every two weeks should then mean that there are several completed tasks to report. In general, hard data should be collected periodically and systematically, and soft data should be collected continually. Frequency does not need to be set; increasing the frequency during high-risk periods of the project is not only acceptable but good risk management as well.

Frequency of your data collection will vary based on geographic distribution of project participants, the number of interfaces or relationships with external work groups or vendors, the size of the project team, management-imposed requirements, and client-imposed requirements.

Another consideration is that the quality and detail of the progress data is related to the duration of the update cycle. The longer the cycle, the less detail and quality can be reported. Conversely, collecting progress data too frequently will add a heavy workload for the project participants, who are supposed to be making progress on a performance improvement project, not writing reports.

Step 3: Update Schedule and Resources Using Hard Data; Document Soft Data. Now that you have data in hand, do something with it. Use the hard data to update the project schedule (the "actual" schedule, not the baseline). This data will be used in the next phase where the project variance is analyzed. Also, update your records on other hard data such as completion commitments ("it will be done by Tuesday"), future estimates ("it took two days to read Chapter One, so Chapter Two should also take two days"), and any changes to project assumptions based on collected status. Note everything in the project notebook.

Also note soft data that have adversely affected (or might later adversely affect) the project outcome in the project notebook, with a couple of exceptions (Stallworthy, 1983): as the notebook is open to examination by any member of the project at any time, do not record confidential information specific to individuals (Jill is having difficulty meeting her completion dates due to her medical problems) or hearsay (Jill mentioned that Bob is thinking about leaving the company).

Analyzing the Variance

After the project status has been collected, the actual status can be compared to the planned status to measure how the project is proceeding. Variance from the plan is the basis for deciding if any adaptive action needs to be taken to keep the project on track (Grey, 1981).

The common approach to variance analysis has three steps. First, the actual progress and estimates of remaining work are compared to the baseline plan. Next, the comparison is used to determine actual and potential variances (both positive and negative). Finally, the impact of the variances to the schedule are analyzed.

Step 1: Compare Actual Data and Remaining Work Estimates to the Baseline Plan. Comparing the baseline and actual schedules is quite easy. Simply compare the current point on the schedule with the planned point. If they are the same, the plan is on schedule. In addition, examine the schedule, resource, and milestone data. Even if there is no variance in the current position in the schedule (meaning you are right where you planned to be), a change in other data may indicate a future variance that you should deal with now. Here are some of the data changes to look for:

- Schedule data
  - New activities moving onto the critical path
  - Changes in milestone dates or the end date of the project
  - Reductions or increase in float for upcoming activities
  - Slips in the schedule of particular groups of activities
- Resource data
  - Investments of more time than planned
  - Not investing enough time to get the task done on schedule
- Deliverable and milestone data
  - Completed or not
  - Whether tasks met quality or ETVX requirements
  - Number of major changes being made to the project definition or plan

Step 2: Determine the Cause of Each Variance. If you found changes during the comparison, you must determine their causes; doing so will allow the adaptive action to put the project back on track to be more effective. Determining the cause of a variance requires some investigation. As in human performance technology, the obvious aspects of a problem may be only symptoms, and finding the root may require digging.

If you have done an effective job of collecting the project status data, you should have some useful information available for determining root cause. The first analysis should be to combine soft data and hard data to identify potential causes of the variances. Many times soft data will explain hard-data variances.

In looking for the causes of the variance, remember that schedule, resources, and scope are all interrelated. Each affects the other two. If there is a change in scope, there will be an impact on schedule and resources; but the change to scope may not be obvious, while the changes to the schedule or resources stand out. It is important to determine what changed first.

Consider using a trend-analysis approach. Is this variance occurring more than once during the project? The variance cause might be a single occurrence or a consistent and repetitive pattern. If all the systems are slowing down on Fridays due to heavy workload, you can expect the variance to occur every Friday during the project. This information is essential for the next phase: taking adaptive action.

Step 3: Analyze and Document the Impact of Each Variance on the Schedule and Resources. The next phase in managing the project is to take adaptive action to correct the variance and prevent further variances in the project. Correcting variances requires time, effort, and sometimes dollars. Does every identified variance require adaptive action? If a one-time occurrence causes a one-day slip in a one-year project, are you going to react? Not likely.

Before taking adaptive action, assess the variances and their causes and analyze their impact on the project. Consider both the long-term and short-term impact on schedule, scope, and resources:

Schedule

- Short-term impacts
  What is the schedule impact on key milestones and project finish date?
  Should we notify other team members that their tasks must be delayed or notify other team members that they can start early?
- Long-term impacts
  If this trend continues, what impact (good and bad) will it have on the project schedule?
  Based on this variance, what is the reliability of other estimates provided by the same person?
  How does this variance affect the contingency plans? Should the contingency plans be implemented? Do they need to be revised based on the variance?
  How does this variance affect the overall project risk?

Scope (Deliverables)

- Short-term impacts
  What is the impact on the end product, deliverables?
  If the variance exceeds quality and ETVX objectives, is that improvement desired?
  If the variance compromises the quality or scope of the deliverables, can we recover that quality or mitigate the damage?
  What is the impact on other activities and tasks?
  Will the variance require additional work for successor tasks because of a change in the predecessor deliverable?
  Will we need improvements to any processes involved throughout the project?
- Long-term impacts
  Is this variance an indication of continuing quality problems?
  Does this variance represent a potential additional risk point in the project?
  Should we continue to monitor it closely?
  Should we consider development of new (additional) contingency plans?

Resources (Internal and External)

- Short-term impacts

    Identify drastic peaks or valleys in resource requirements.

    Can they be corrected by working overtime?

    Can we utilize slack time for training or work on other more critical tasks?

    Can we pull resources off less critical tasks?

    What are the results of resource shortages (longer durations, delays)?

    How much additional time will be required by activities due to resource shortages?

    Will the shortages cause the task to become more critical?

    Will they create a shift in the critical path?

- Long-term impacts

    How will the schedule be affected by lengthened task durations?

    Will this be a continuing problem (is it likely to occur again)?

    If a resource is continually overutilized, plan for relief in the future.

    If a resource is continually underutilized, plan to use it for additional future work.

Taking Adaptive Action

Adaptive action is the phase where actions are planned, recommended, and taken to eliminate problems or enhance advantages identified in the variance analysis. The adaptive actions can be minor changes within the original schedule, resource, and scope parameters; implementation of previously created contingency plans; or major changes to the project plan (Baker and Baker, 1992).

Step 1: Plan Adaptive Action. Before taking adaptive action, careful planning is in order. Remember that adaptive action does not show up on the project schedule; any action you take will require unplanned time and effort. Be certain to involve project team members in the planning process. They will most likely have to live with the decisions that are made, and they are closer to the project tasks and will probably have additional information or insights.

Before agreeing on any adaptive action, review the project infrastructure to ensure that all planned actions are consistent with project decisions and processes. Remember, the project infrastructure is an agreement on how decisions, changes, and information are handled in managing the project. Be certain to review the project change control process to see who needs to be involved in decisions regarding changes in scope, schedule, or resources.

Be sure to review the contingency plans that were developed during the risk-analysis process. The use of existing contingency plans could be the adaptive action needed to correct the variance. Consider implementing those that make sense for the current situation. In reviewing the contingency plans, be sure to keep them accurate and useful by revising or discarding those that no longer fit the situation.

Ensure that you are attempting to solve the problem, not just treating the symptoms. It is easy to get pulled away from the root cause and focus on seemingly urgent symptoms. Remember, fixing the symptom may work in the short term but can make the problem much worse in the long run.

Remember to be creative! It does not take much project management skill to slip the schedule every time there is a variance. Consider different methods of dealing with the variance. Because the environment is dynamic, the contingency plans cannot anticipate all potential actions. You will need creative solutions.

Be certain to revisit your assumptions when you are in the planning stage. Are they still valid given new information and changing conditions? Creating a plan based on incorrect assumptions could actually create more damage rather than correct the intended variance.

Spend a reasonable amount of time planning the adaptive action. Do not be in a hurry and jump at the first alternative presented. There may be other alternatives that are more effective or more efficient. On the other hand, do not contract a terminal case of "analysis paralysis" either. The goal of the project is to achieve performance improvement, not to take adaptive action.

A number of adaptive actions can be taken, and perhaps the project participants have created a number of alternatives. Which one should be selected for implementation? Here are some possible adaptive actions (Thomsett, 1993):

Guidelines for Adaptive Action

1. Check status data for accuracy.
2. Implement the contingency plans.
3. Hold key milestones while rearranging task schedules and resource commitments.
4. Plan to escalate problems and alternatives within the organization.
5. Do nothing and wait for more trend data (this action, although appropriate for certain situations, should be used with great caution).
6. Replan and reestimate the schedule or resource plans while overwriting the original schedule (use this action only when absolutely necessary).
7. Consider other suggested actions—do not be limited by this list!

The adaptive action of last recourse is changing the baseline. It is an admission or realization that there are no means to correct the variance and that the formal schedule must be modified to reflect this reality. If this sounds dismal, it is.

A couple of points to remember in changing the baseline schedule: if the baseline is constantly revised there will be no point of comparison either during or after the project, regardless of the scheduling tool being used. If you do change the baseline schedule, ensure that the process by which it is changed is consistent with appropriate change control processes identified in the project infrastructure.

Step 2: Take Adaptive Action as Appropriate. With the adaptive action carefully considered, it is time to implement the plan. Be certain to communicate any changes to every participant in the project. Few people like operating under old assumptions or being surprised by the adaptive action. Ensure that the appropriate managers, clients, and sponsors are aware of any substantial adaptive actions.

Document, document, document. This is especially critical when changes are made to the project. The changes and their rationale are quickly forgotten in the heat of the project. Do not make assumptions without writing them down. If the plan fails, determine why so as to avoid a similar failure in the future.

Step 3: Follow Up to See That Actions Obtain Expected Results. Projects are undertaken in very complex environments. Even the most carefully planned actions do not always have the desired effect, and changes in one aspect of the project (scope, schedule, or resource usage) will usually affect the others to some extent. Carefully monitor any changes that are made to ensure that the adaptive action is working properly. If not, take additional action as needed, including cycling through the entire adaptive action process again.

Reporting Project Status

If your performance improvement project is of any size or consequence, others outside the project will want to know how it is going. Most interested parties are not willing to wait until the end of the project to receive information on the development of the performance improvement project. If the project is large, the project team members themselves may want status information to determine if the start of their tasks is still on schedule. As the project manager, you will be expected to be the source of the status information. Taking a systematic approach to the dissemination of project information will improve communication effectiveness and preserve your sanity.

Step 1: Review Project Reporting That Relates to Infrastructure. The project infrastructure will provide information significant in determining the strategy for reporting status of the performance improvement project. Begin with a review of the pertinent information. Ensure that the infrastructure decisions are still relevant. Organizations and environments can change rapidly; be sure all the reviewers and approvers of the project are still the same, and ensure that they still want to see the agreed-upon data, in the agreed-upon format, at the agreed-upon frequency. Do not forget to ensure that you understand your manager's expectations regarding project reporting.

In addition to the reviewers and approvers, others may benefit from receiving status information. You should consider these:

- Project participants (they might like to know what is going on)
- Management in addition to your own
- Members of the client organization (targets of the performance improvement project)

Step 2: Communicate Project Status Information Upward, Downward, and Sideways.
Using the decisions in the project infrastructure, you can determine how you want to communicate the project status and to what level of detail. Typically, the project status is communicated through written reports or project meetings and presentations.

Written Reports. These are the most frequently used method to communicate project status (Lewis, 1993a). They can be created rapidly and can be read by the audience members at their convenience. The key to creating successful written status reports is the application of your human performance technology abilities. You should always begin with understanding the different audiences for the reports and what their specific information needs are.

Operations managers rarely want a task-by-task analysis of the project. Typically they want to know if the project is still on schedule and if there are any issues that they need to be aware of or help to solve. Sending them a ten-page analysis is a great way to ensure that the project receives little executive attention.

Your direct manager, however, would probably not be satisfied with an executive report. More likely, a direct manager wants the ten-page report to contain selected information that is of import at the moment. But do not guess; find out what information the manager needs and design reports accordingly.

Many types of status reports may be used when managing a project (Grey, 1981). Using a software project-management tool allows you to easily and quickly generate different views of the project at different levels of detail. Project status reports typically fit one of the following descriptions:

Typical Status Reports

- Executive summary
  Format is a one-page-maximum high-level overview
  Consists of three to seven bulleted key points the reader needs to be aware of
  Contains only highlights and changes since the last report
- Management report
  Incorporates executive summary and adds management issues
  Describes accomplishments during the previous period
  Gives a discussion of major milestones and any changes in the project
  Lists planned work for the coming period and necessary management support
  Lists near-term tasks on the critical path
  Lists near-term tasks with high risks
  Lists tasks that have slipped their late or early start or finish dates
- Project analysis
  Gives detailed information on the status of individual tasks in progress
  Incorporates executive summary and management report
  Explains variances
  Discusses problems encountered and action taken to correct them
  Discusses advantages presented and actions taken to incorporate them into project
  Discusses risk issues
  Lists unresolved issues, their owners, and due dates for their resolution
  Generally discusses how things are going
  Answers any questions the reader might have regarding the status of the project
  Contains at most three pages more than the management report (perhaps less for small projects)
- Additional detail as required by audience
  Detailed schedule bar chart
  Resource histograms
  Key milestone progress report
  Other useful reports

Project Review Meetings. This is the other method commonly used to communicate project status (Randolf, 1988). These should be used sparingly for mid- to large-size projects; the amount of time spent in meetings reviewing the information on a large project can rapidly eat into the project's time resource. Remember, the goal of the performance improvement project is not status meetings.

Prepare an agenda and send it to all participants in advance. This will allow them to determine if they need to be present and if they need to prepare information to present or discuss. A typical status meeting agenda should include the following:

- Purpose of meeting and review of agenda
- Major accomplishments since last review
- Schedule status (plan versus actual or estimate)
- Discussion of where project currently is and where it is going
- Explanation of variances, any corrective action taken, and results of the actions (if any)
- Resource status (plan versus actual or estimate)
- Other topics (usually not technical issues)
- Agenda for next meeting

To increase the effectiveness of the meeting, plan to cover the most important topics early, so that if meeting members need to leave early you will still have communicated the most important messages. Use the meeting as an opportunity for project participants to ask questions and get clarification from you, the management team, or the clients.

Be sure to make a record of the meeting and the actions taken. Record unresolved issues along with their owners and due dates for their resolution, and ensure that a copy is placed into the project notebook. Be sure to keep individual discussions outside the meeting so as to not waste others' time; many project issues are best handled in informal team or individual meetings.

Informal Team Communication. Another form of project status reporting is the informal meeting (Lewis, 1993b). For years, management schools and books have extolled the value of management by wandering around (MBWA). Just wandering around to the participants in the project and seeing what they are up to provides a natural and safe environment to discuss issues or raise doubts about the project. This provides you with the opportunity to share status and information on issues that might never be raised in a formal project review meeting.

Encourage project participants to approach you promptly whenever potential problems arise; you can manage a project more effectively with timely information. But if you value early information, reinforce the behavior that allows you to receive it. If you kill one messenger, others will wait until the last possible moment to give you bad news. Be appreciative of their willingness to share the issues candidly and proactively; asking for their inputs or participation in resolving the problem may also reinforce the activity.

Take the opportunity to celebrate milestone completions. Not only does it encourage the project participants but it provides an opportunity to share information on the status of the project. The celebration does not have to be a big deal; it is surprising how much information can be exchanged over popcorn and sodas.

Step 3: File Project Status Information in the Project Notebook. Ensure that copies of all the project status reports make their way to the project notebook. Besides needing the important history, you will probably need to go back and find out who took responsibility for resolving a specific problem, and by when.

Karen's Story

At her desk, Karen sorted through the weekly status reports each project participant had sent her about their progress. She was in the midst of updating the actual schedule so she could compare actual progress against the original schedule the management team had agreed to.

Bob's report concerned her; she gave him a call. "Hi, Bob. This is Karen. Listen, I was just going through the reports, and I noticed you said you're 90 percent done with the editing tasks. I'm hoping you can give me more information. What exactly do you have left to do, and how long will it take?"

There was a short silence as Bob gathered his thoughts. "Well, all that's left is the special effects. It shouldn't take too long."

Karen looked up his task on the schedule. "According to the original schedule, we should be done with the editing now. I'm not so concerned about the number of edits left. The percentage might be small, but if they're the most difficult ones, can we still meet the schedule?"

Bob understood. "No, I suppose not. You better have Brian drop what he's doing and help me get caught up."

Karen thought for a moment. "Bob, I'm not sure the amount of work is the root cause of the problem. It sounds like the technical feasibility of the special effects is the biggest difficulty. I'd like you to list the edits remaining and what is preventing their completion. Then we can determine how to proceed. We may decide to drop some of the more difficult effects."

The phone rang as soon as Karen hung up. "Hello, this is Karen."

"Hi, Karen, this is Jim. I have a meeting with the operations manager this afternoon, and my latest project update report didn't indicate the next few critical path tasks. I'd like to update her on who's in the hot seat and how she can lend support and encouragement."

Karen examined the actual schedule and was able to quickly tell Jim what he needed to know. She said, "Jim, upcoming critical path tasks weren't on the original list of items you want me to report on. Should I update the list to include it?"

He thought for a moment. "No, I don't think so. The operations manager and I think the reports we're getting now give us the right information. You helped us determine what we need to know and when, so I doubt we'll need the critical path information again before the end of the project."

CHAPTER THIRTEEN

COMPLETING THE PROJECT

After the last milestone has been accomplished and the performance improvement project has been fully implemented, the natural inclination is to take an extended vacation or move on to the next project. However, a vitally important activity still remains to be done: evaluating the project.

Bill's Story

Bill headed to Linda's office to discuss the results of the performance improvement project. The desired performance had been achieved, but later and more expensively than had been anticipated. He had mixed emotions about this meeting; the results were as expected but he did not feel good about the process he had used to achieve them.

He brought a copy of the schedule and some notes he had jotted down about the project that morning. Linda motioned him into the office as she was hanging up the phone. Bill took his traditional seat in the blue chair.

"Bill, I'd like to take some time today to discuss the project and your management of it. I've taken a look at the performance results, and it looks like your analysis of what was needed to achieve our desired performance was right on. The interventions were quite effective too. So I'm pleased with your human performance technology skills."

Bill beamed. "Thanks, Linda. We really worked hard to complete this project."

"Well," said Linda, "that's the other thing I want to discuss. While the end product was great, the process of getting there was painful. Besides the hard work to pull the pieces together, implementation was late and we went over budget. Why? And what can we do to prevent it in future projects?"

Bill shifted in his seat. "I've been giving that a lot of thought. I've really racked my brain trying to figure out where all the extra activities came from and why the schedule kept slipping. I think the project was just bigger than we thought. There was no way of knowing until we got into it. Next time, all I can figure is to allow more time and ask for more people, money, equipment. . . ."

"Hmm," said Linda. "How would you describe the process you used to manage the project?"

Bill thought for a moment. "Well, I made a list of everything that had to be done, figured out what had to be done first, and guessed how long it would take. But that wasn't the hard part. The real problem was answering all the questions, resolving the disagreements, and keeping people on track."

Bill's comment caused Linda to think back to the past week. Three participants in Bill's project had come to see her privately. They had some insightful observations about the project problems, and even made some reasonable recommendations about how to avoid them in the future.

She had asked them why they were not giving this information to Bill; they responded that Bill did not seem very receptive to recommendations on how to improve the management of the project. They also said they felt their contributions to the project were not appreciated.

As Bill left her office, Linda started to wonder if she could trust him with the next big performance improvement project. For a guy who takes a systematic approach to improving others' performance, he didn't seem to take a very systematic approach to improving his own. Would the next project go any better?

Concluding and Evaluating a Project

In managing a project, not everything goes according to plan. Perhaps some assumptions were incorrect, or your task estimates might have been in error. Some things worked really well, others did not. Intentionally or unintentionally you discover and learn things while managing a project.

As human performance technologists, we are concerned with improving the performance of individuals and organizations. This includes your organization and you as an individual. If you made an error in managing the project, do you want to repeat it on a future project? Do you want others in the organization to repeat your mistakes? Mager (1992) lists information as a tool for improving performance. The focus in concluding the performance improvement project is to ensure that what has been learned can be used by you and others in the future.

Creating a Learning Project Environment

The learning organization is a topic on which many books have been published. The ability of an organization to use the knowledge that exists within it provides substantial potential for improving performance (Kepner and Tregoe, 1981). Yet with all the books available, many groups suffer from "organizational Alzheimer's"—they rapidly forget what they learn and typically repeat the same errors.

As the project manager for the performance improvement project, you will want to manage a project environment that fosters a learning approach. At the beginning of the project when you defined the project and the project infrastructure, you looked for existing information within the organization that might indicate a course of action. That was the start of creating the learning project environment. At the end of the project, you need to be concerned with capturing what you have learned so it can be put to use on future performance improvement projects.

To create a learning project environment, focus on the following three major activities:

- Determining the learning ability of the organization in which the project team exists
- Creating a project environment where it is safe to learn
- Determining the system of project management

Determining the Learning Ability of the Organization. The project team exists and operates within an organization, either as employees or contractors. The organization's approach to organizational learning will have an impact on your project's approach to learning. Knowing the organization's learning ability and approach will help you understand any potential barriers to learning and what you will need to do to overcome them (Kline and Saunders, 1993). It will also allow you to align your learning approach with the organization's accepted methods.

At the end of this chapter is a tool to assess the learning ability of an organization. Like the other tools in this book, it can be used by the project manager alone, or by other members of the organization, to assess ability. The assessment will give you an indication of overall learning ability but also identify potential learning issues.

Creating a Project Environment Where It Is Safe to Learn. Learning requires doing some new activities. Not all will go perfectly; some failures may need to be corrected. As the project manager, your response to failure will be part of an environment that accepts (or rejects) learning and its occasional setbacks. If you punish project participants for failing while attempting a new activity or approach, it will be clear that learning is not worth the risk on your project (Kline and Saunders, 1993).

Likewise, the providers of learning information may need to be made safe to share it. If project participants are punished for identifying areas where management needs to improve, it will likely be the last such information shared.

Determining the System of Project Management. Any project management approach is really a system. It has inputs, activities, and outputs. Understanding what your project management system is gives you the ability to improve it over time (Kepner and Tregoe, 1981).

As you begin to think about streamlining the project management system in your environment, you will confront issues that systems in general must address. Without trying to cover all the ins and outs of systems theory, here are some key points about effective systems that are particularly relevant to a learning environment:

Memory. Good systems keep track of themselves. If your project management system is designed to record the important things that happen in your organization, you are off to a good start.

Most likely, your organization is good at recording the type of data it needs to survive an audit. But many organizations regard collecting data as a necessary evil instead of an opportunity to establish and maintain information gathering and remembering systems. In many cases, data from one part of the system could prove useful to other parts. You might want to improve ways to provide immediate access to the organizational memory for anyone with a need to know.

Purpose. The purpose of a system must be clearly defined. By knowing quite clearly what the system is supposed to accomplish, you can make its operations more efficient, for you can eliminate from it everything that fails to contribute to the fulfillment of its goal. Activities, reports, and meetings that do not contribute to the purpose of the project management system are particularly suspect.

Rules. Articulate the rules by which a system operates. The rules determine what is done and why. If there is a failure in the system, there is a failure in the current rules; fixing the rules prevents the failure from occurring in the future. To devise these rules, you have to comprehend the full scope of the system. This includes knowledge of the total web of relationships within the system. It means having a capacity to predict consequences of various changes. It means knowing which points should be informed with feedback.

Continual Improvement. Keep revising the rules of the system to continually improve operations. By defining and then restructuring your system's operating rules, you can continue improving the system itself even if there is no failure. Sometimes a bit of trial and error is necessary to accommodate all the dimensions and relationships within a system. Rules and processes should accommodate change as long as the changes better fulfill the goal of the system.

Feedback. Systems need monitoring and regulating. Think about designing sources of feedback into each system so you will know how well it is meeting its goals. As more and more is learned about how the system works and how it can be changed, the power of each individual to effect such a change is increased.

Human Behavior. People are part of the system. Good systems encourage people to act in the most positive and effective ways; systems that fail to do so are squandering their greatest and most vital resource. The principles of human learning and human behavior have been shown in innumerable cases to bring out the best in people. When the members of your system are accountable, interact positively, think on the job, take risks, work cooperatively, seek personal mastery, align themselves with the group's vision, and think systematically, they will function as vital participants in the system (Kouzes and Posner, 1988).

The Project Notebook

A classic videotape used in interventions to improve group effectiveness includes a scene set in a courtroom. The accused has been found guilty, but before the judge passes sentence he asks the bailiff to read the accused's criminal record. The bailiff, defense attorney, and prosecuting attorney get into a large argument over what his last offense was and whether he was found guilty. The judge finally breaks in and asks, "Didn't anybody write it down?"

The bailiff replies, "No, your honor, it all seemed pretty clear at the time."

The same is true of projects. As events occur and decisions are made, it seems pretty clear at the time; but when it comes time to conclude the project and determine what did and did not work, it may be quite difficult to remember just what occurred. Hence the importance of maintaining the project notebook all during the project. Attempting to accurately document all the practices and decisions after the fact rarely works well (Randolf, 1988).

The project notebook should be the information repository for the project. If you are hit by a bus in the morning, somebody should be able to manage the project in the afternoon based on the contents of the project notebook (cheery thought, eh?). All activities and decisions should be well documented in the notebook.

Project successes should be captured as they occur during the project. What happened, environmental factors, and why it worked should be captured. The next time a similar opportunity presents itself, the success can be repeated.

Each project error should be documented as well. What happened, environmental conditions, why it did not work, and recommendations for avoiding the error next time should be captured and documented as they occur. This will help avoid falling into the same error in the future.

At the end of the project, create specific reports for archival use and for sending to other project managers who would benefit from the information. You, as well as the organization, should maintain an archival copy of the information; you will want to use it on your next performance improvement project.

If the project is large and sweeping, consider creating an ad hoc video on the learnings from the project. Others will be interested in what the major factors were behind your success.

Retrospective Meetings

Project notebooks are typically maintained by project managers for capturing their observations. But a project manager's view of the project may be incomplete or even incorrect. Thus there should be an opportunity for the project participants to capture and summarize their observations as well (Kouzes and Posner, 1988).

Often this is done through a retrospective meeting specifically designed to capture and document information and observations from the participants as well as you, the project manager. The following issues should be examined:

- Aspects of the project that went well and should be repeated on the next project

- Why the aspects went well
- Errors made on the project that should be avoided on the next project
- Why the errors occurred
- Environmental factors that created errors
- Needed changes in the project environment
- Comparison of the documented assumptions in the plan with reality
- Accuracy of the work breakdown structure (overlooked activities)
- Task estimation accuracy (the time it really takes for activities in this environment)
- Specific recommendations for future projects

A variable that will be very difficult to replicate on the next performance improvement project is the participants; some will most likely be different the next time around. But the results of the current project—which skills were used and how they contributed to success—can be assessed and reproduced (or avoided) in future projects (Lewis, 1993b).

One simple process to assess results is actually initiated at the beginning of the project and provides information that can be used during the project as well. The first four steps are completed at project start, the last is completed in the retrospective meeting:

1. Have each member list every talent, ability, or other skill or resource he or she might contribute to a project, no matter how unrelated it may at first seem to any activity currently in the works. The goal is to list at least twenty of these, even if they do not seem particularly significant.

2. Next, have each person list an equal number of resources, talents, abilities, or other skills the team might conceivably need under circumstances not yet foreseen. Obviously the two lists should be different—possibly very different.

3. Place each item on the second list at the head of a separate sheet of paper. Have every member of the team sign up on as many of these sheets as appropriate. In most cases several names will be listed under each resource needed.

4. If one or more sheets remain blank, the team can then spend some time deciding whether this particular resource is important or not. If it is, the team can take whatever steps are necessary to acquire the needed resource.

5. At the end of the project, review the project activities and determine which skills and resources were critical to the success of the performance improvement project. Document the results so they can be considered when planning the next project.

Create Vendor Performance Reports

If you used vendors in your project, capture information specific to their performance. Other members of the organization who later consider using these vendors will benefit from your experiences. If a centralized procurement function is in place, ensure that it has copies for use in advising other or future project managers. Potential areas that you will want to consider assessing and reporting are these:

- Ability to produce work in compliance with the requirements
- Ability to maintain schedule and commitments
- Ability to effectively manage costs
- Quality of management approach and practices
- Quality of final product or services
- Recommendations on future use by the organization

Document People-Management Issues

As the project manager, you had the opportunity to work with other people and coordinate their participation in a complex performance improvement project. In addition to the mechanical aspects of the project, assess and capture your performance in dealing with the people aspects of the project (Stallworthy, 1983). (The assumption is that you would like to continue to improve in this area.)

This is an exercise for your personal benefit. The results should probably not be incorporated into the project notebook for all to see. Depending on the relationship with your manager, you may want to review the results with him or her. Your manager may have some recommendations or incorporate aspects into your personal development plan.

Like the mechanical aspects of the project, capture and assess what worked, what did not, and why. Create a list of specific changes to adopt next time.

Evaluate the Project Manager

On the topic of personal growth, consider soliciting feedback on your performance as the project manager. The participants in the project are uniquely positioned to provide you with an evaluation of your performance (Kouzes and Posner, 1988). Some of the most valuable feedback to receive comes from the people that you work with rather than from your manager.

To receive useful feedback, make it safe for the participants to provide the information. If you have demonstrated that you receive feedback well, you might be able to ask the participants to provide you with an assessment personally. Other methods include gathering information anonymously (survey or typed comments) or commissioning a few participants to collect and consolidate feedback into an overall performance evaluation.

Again, this is information that you will probably not place into the project notebook but keep for your own personal reference and development.

Create Participant Performance Reports

In many cases, project participants report to managers throughout the organization. As the project manager, consider creating performance reports to send to participants' managers for use in performance evaluations and development plans.

As these people have taken the time to participate in your project, it is only reasonable that you take the time to capture and report their contribution to its success (Lewis, 1993b). In general, consider covering the following areas:

- Specific responsibilities or activities within the project
- Specific accomplishments and contributions
- Feedback on positive performance aspects (such as initiative, dependability, and quality)
- Recommendations for performance improvement

Do not present this report to the participants directly. Remember, you are not their manager; your objective is to provide their managers with information to facilitate the performance management and development process.

Celebrate and Bring to Formal Conclusion

To feel accomplishment, people need to sense closure on major projects and activities that have required time to complete (Kouzes and Posner, 1988). Otherwise, they are left with a sense that the work is still hanging out there with more to be done. This is precisely the reason graduation ceremonies are conducted when educational milestones are reached: they bring recognition of completion and accomplishment.

If you want to entice people to participate in your next performance improvement project, ensure that the participants of the current project feel a sense of accomplishment and recognition. Consider holding a completion ceremony or celebration at which the project is pronounced complete and recognition for participants is liberally doled out. Having high-level managers attend or preside over the recognition process adds impact. The inexpensive certificates and trophies presented after project completions still hang proudly on cubicle walls years after a project.

Karen's Story

Karen headed to Jim's office to discuss the results of the performance improvement project. The desired performance had been achieved and the project was ready to be wrapped up.

She had invested some time concluding the project and systematically learning all she could from the experience to help improve the next one. The retrospective was a tough meeting. Some things she had not done as well as she would have liked; a few clear errors were brought to light and analyzed. A rather uncomfortable process, but Karen was pleased with the results.

Jim hung up the phone and waved Karen into the office to have a seat. "That was the procurement manager. She was raving over the vendor performance reports you sent her—says they'll really help others if they want to use Process Innovation, Inc., in the future.

"Karen, I'd like to discuss the project and your management of it. I've already taken a look at the performance results, and it seems like your analysis of what was needed to achieve our desired performance was right on. The interventions that were created were quite effective.

"As far as your management of the project is concerned, I'm impressed you were able to complete a project this complex on time and within budget. I'm even more impressed with your analysis of the project—I've been going over all the materials you sent me. Your assessment of the organization's learning ability was interesting, and I'll want to set up some time later to discuss the recommendations for improvement in detail."

Jim picked up a large binder. "I think your work in creating a detailed project notebook for others to refer to in the future is great. And your documentation of the project management process with recommendations for systemwide improvement is equally valuable."

He settled back into his chair. "There were obviously a few mistakes made on the project, but your analysis of what went wrong and why makes me fairly confident they won't happen again. I was interested to see your analysis on your people management skills. Dealing with a participant who has a dependability issue is never easy, but I think I can provide you with some advice for the next time around."

As Karen got ready to leave, she thought to remind Jim about the project completion event. "Don't forget, you and the operation manager are scheduled to present the project recognition awards tomorrow. The whole team is looking forward to the event."

"I wouldn't dare miss it," he said. "Thanks for the reminder."

EXHIBIT 13.1. A TOOL FOR ASSESSING ORGANIZATIONAL LEARNING ABILITY.

1. People feel free to speak their minds about what they have learned. There are no threats or consequences for disagreeing or dissenting and no fear of them.

1	2	3	4	5	6	7	8	9	10

Rarely the case   Usually the case

2. Mistakes made by individuals or organizations are turned into constructive learning experiences.

1	2	3	4	5	6	7	8	9	10

Rarely the case   Usually the case

3. Multiple viewpoints and open, productive debates are encouraged and cultivated.

1	2	3	4	5	6	7	8	9	10

Rarely the case   Usually the case

4. Experimentation is endorsed and championed and is a way of doing business.

1	2	3	4	5	6	7	8	9	10

Rarely the case   Usually the case

5. Management practices are innovative, creative, and periodically risk taking.

1	2	3	4	5	6	7	8	9	10

Rarely the case   Usually the case

6. The quality of work life in our organization is improving.

1	2	3	4	5	6	7	8	9	10

Rarely the case   Usually the case

7. There are formal and informal structures designed to encourage people to share what they learn with their peers and the rest of the organization.

1	2	3	4	5	6	7	8	9	10

Rarely the case   Usually the case

8. The organization is perceived as designed for problem solving and learning.

1	2	3	4	5	6	7	8	9	10

Rarely the case   Usually the case

9. Learning is expected and encouraged across all levels of the organization.

1	2	3	4	5	6	7	8	9	10

Rarely the case   Usually the case

10. People have an overview of the organization beyond their specialty and function and adapt their working patterns to it.

1	2	3	4	5	6	7	8	9	10

Rarely the case   Usually the case

11. "Lessons learned" sessions are conducted so as to produce clear and specific organizational learning.

1	2	3	4	5	6	7	8	9	10

Rarely the case   Usually the case

12. Management practices, operations, policies, and procedures are being improved or replaced with workable systems and structures.

1	2	3	4	5	6	7	8	9	10

Rarely the case   Usually the case

13. Continuous improvement is expected and treated receptively.

1	2	3	4	5	6	7	8	9	10

Rarely the case   Usually the case

14. Middle managers are seen as having the primary role in keeping the learning process running smoothly throughout the organization.

1	2	3	4	5	6	7	8	9	10

Rarely the case   Usually the case

15. The unexpected is viewed as an opportunity for learning.

1	2	3	4	5	6	7	8	9	10

Rarely the case   Usually the case

16. People look forward to improving their own competencies as well as those of the whole organization.

1	2	3	4	5	6	7	8	9	10

Rarely the case   Usually the case

17. The systems and procedures of the organization are designed to be adaptive and flexible to incorporate new learning.

1	2	3	4	5	6	7	8	9	10

Rarely the case   Usually the case

18. There is a burning urgency to learn and improve within the organization.

1	2	3	4	5	6	7	8	9	10

Rarely the case   Usually the case

19. Teams are recognized and rewarded for their innovative and paradigm-breaking solutions to problems.

1	2	3	4	5	6	7	8	9	10

Rarely the case   Usually the case

20. People are encouraged and provided the resources to become self-directed learners.

1	2	3	4	5	6	7	8	9	10

Rarely the case   Usually the case

Scoring the Organizational Learning Assessment
Step 1:   Total the responses to all 20 items.
Step 2:   Divide the total by 20 to determine the average score.
Step 3:   Review the lowest item scores and list the four that you believe will contribute most significantly to organization learning problems.
   Issue 1:
   Issue 2:
   Issue 3:
   Issue 4:

Interpreting the Results of the Organization Learning Assessment

High-Risk Situation: Be Aware of Danger (1.0–3.4)
A score between 1.0 and 3.4 indicates that there have been significant problems in the area of organizational learning in the past. Information about mistakes is typically left in the past, and, as a result, is frequently repeated within the organization. Efforts to pass significant lessons on to other or future project managers are typically not embraced. Major investments of time and effort will be needed to ensure that the organization learns from what it already knows and improves its ability to implement projects and achieve the intended performance improvement goals.

Moderate-Risk Situation: Exercise Caution (3.5–6.5)

A score between 3.5 and 6.5 is sufficiently high that it should be considered a significant issue in attempting to create learning that will help future performance improvement projects. Be aware of the areas that pose the most significant issues, and create work-arounds that allow as much learning from your performance improvement project as possible.

Low-Risk Situation: High-Opportunity Organization (6.6 and above)

A score over 6.6 is sufficiently high that it should not be considered a substantial issue when planning how to transfer learning from your performance improvement project. However, be alert to any changing conditions within the organization during the project. Additionally, any item with a score of 7 or greater should not be ignored. These items require some special attention to ensure that they do not *become* a problem during the transfer of learning.

CONCLUSION

I hope you have enjoyed our trip through the world of project management as it applies to the profession of human performance technology. The ability to effectively manage performance improvement projects and achieve reliable results is important if acceptance of our profession is to continue to grow. If you have been able to improve your personal performance in managing the complex projects associated with systematically improving the performance of people, then this book has served its purpose.

What's that? You want to know how the story ends? What happens to Bill and Karen? Let's drop into Linda's office and find out.

The Rest of the Story

Bill was in desperate need of a vacation. This project had been the worst nightmare he had ever lived through. It seemed that almost everything that could go wrong did. The stress on the organization had been fairly substantial as well; everybody had worked overtime trying to keep the project on schedule. Bill felt like he had spent months in meetings attempting to keep up with all the problems as they occurred, but there just were not enough hours in a day.

Linda had called and asked that he come to her office. She said she needed to discuss something of significance with him.

"Hi, Bill," she said as he arrived. "Thanks for coming on such short notice. We have to talk about some big changes coming up in the organization." She motioned him into her blue office chair. Bill's stomach churned.

"Bill, I wanted to let you know that my career plans have taken a significant change. This last product really helped me come to some decisions, and I've decided to retire early. As a matter of fact, today will be my last day."

Bill's heart jumped. This was it: his big break had come. He was the most senior member of the department and considered the heir apparent. All his hard work on the project was about to pay off.

"Bill, the management team sat down and discussed who should fill my position. The discussion went on for quite some time and it wasn't an easy decision. The group finally decided to offer the position to a woman from the West Coast operation. Her name is Karen, and I think you'll enjoy working for her. She has some extraordinary project management skills, and I think you can learn a lot from her."

Linda stood and extended her hand. "I've never been one for long or mushy goodbyes, so I'll just say thanks for your hard work and best of luck." She walked out of the office to finish her exiting paperwork with personnel.

Bill stayed behind, dumbfounded. He had worked hard but was unable to manage the project effectively; now his goal of becoming the next department manager seemed just as elusive. What was he to do? It suddenly became clear.

He stood up, grabbed the blue chair, and threw it out Linda's fourteenth-story office window.

REFERENCES

Baker, S., and Baker, K. *On Time/On Budget.* Englewood Cliffs, N.J.: Prentice Hall, 1992.

Barkley, B., and Saylor, J. *Customer Driven Project Management.* New York: McGraw-Hill, 1994.

Conner, D. R. *Managing at the Speed of Change.* New York: Villard Books, 1992.

Dreger, B. *Project Management: Effective Scheduling.* New York: Van Nostrand Reinhold, 1992.

Gilbert, T. F. *Human Competence: Engineering Worthy Performance.* New York: McGraw-Hill, 1978.

Gilbreath, R. *Winning at Project Management.* New York: Wiley, 1986.

Greer, M. *ID Project Management: Tools and Techniques for Instructional Designers and Developers.* Englewood Cliffs, N.J.: Educational Technology Publications, 1992.

Grey, C. *Essentials of Project Management.* Princeton, N.J.: Petrocelli, 1981.

Hertz, D., and Thomas, H. *Risk Analysis and Its Applications.* New York: Wiley, 1983.

Jackson, S., and Addison, R. "Planning and Managing Projects." In H. Stolovitch and E. Keeps (eds.), *Handbook of Human Performance Technology: A Comprehensive Guide for Analyzing and Solving Performance Problems in Organizations.* San Francisco: Jossey-Bass, 1992.

Kepner, C. H., and Tregoe, B. B. *The New Rational Manager.* Princeton, N.J.: Princeton Research Press, 1981.

Kerzner, H. *Project Management: A Systems Approach to Planning, Scheduling, and Controlling.* (3rd ed.) New York: Van Nostrand Reinhold, 1989.

Kezsbaum, D. *Dynamic Project Management.* New York: Wiley, 1989.

Kissler, G. *The Change Riders.* Reading, Mass.: Addison-Wesley, 1991.

Kline, P., and Saunders, B. *Ten Steps to a Learning Organization.* Arlington, Va.: Great Ocean, 1993.

Kouzes, J. M., and Posner, B. Z. *The Leadership Challenge: How to Get Extraordinary Things Done in Organizations.* San Francisco: Jossey-Bass, 1988.

Lewis, J. *The Project Manager's Desk Reference.* Chicago: Probus, 1993a.

Lewis, J. *How to Build and Manage a Winning Project Team.* New York: AMACOM, 1993b.

Lippitt, G. *The Consulting Process in Action.* San Diego, Calif.: University Associates, 1986.

Magcr, R. F. *What Every Manager Should Know About Training.* Belmont, Calif.: Lake, 1992.

Martin, C. *Project Management.* New York: AMACOM, 1976.

Obradovitch, M. M., and Stephanou, S. E. *Project Management: Risks & Productivity.* Bend, Oreg.: Daniel Spencer, 1990.

Randolf, W. A. *Effective Project Planning and Management.* Englewood Cliffs, N.J.: Prentice Hall, 1988.

Smith, P. G., and Reinertson, D. G. *Developing Products in Half the Time.* New York: Van Nostrand Reinhold, 1991.

Stalk, G. *Competing Against Time.* New York: Free Press, 1990.

Stallworthy, E. A. *Total Project Management.* Aldershot, Hants, England: Gower, 1983.

Stewart, J. *Managing Change Through Training and Development.* London: Kogan Page, 1991.

Stolovitch, H., and Keeps, E. (eds.) *Handbook of Human Performance Technology: A Comprehensive Guide for Analyzing and Solving Performance Problems in Organizations.* San Francisco: Jossey-Bass, 1992.

Thomsett, R. *Third Wave Project Management.* Englewood Cliffs, N.J.: Prentice Hall, 1993.

Weiss, A. *Million Dollar Consulting.* New York: McGraw-Hill, 1992.

INDEX